96

THE RETURN OF THRIFT

ALSO BY PHILLIP LONGMAN

Born to Pay: The New Politics of Aging in America

THE RETURN OF THRIFT

*How the Coming Collapse of the
Middle-Class Welfare State
Will Reawaken Values in America*

PHILLIP LONGMAN

THE FREE PRESS

New York   London   Toronto   Sydney   Tokyo   Singapore

THE FREE PRESS
A Division of Simon & Schuster Inc.
1230 Avenue of the Americas
New York, NY 10020

Designed by Carla Bolte

Manufactured in the United States of America

10   9   8   7   6   5   4   3   2   1

Library of Congress Cataloging-in-Publication Data
Longman, Phillip.
    The return of thrift: how the coming collapse of the middle-class
welfare state will reawaken values in America / Phillip Longman.
        p.   cm.
    Includes bibliographical references and index.
    ISBN 0–684–82300–4
    1. Entitlement spending—United States.   2. Saving and investment—
United States.   3. Middle class—United States—Economic
conditions.   I. Title.
HJ7543.L66   1996
330.973—dc20   95–53812
                                                                      CIP

TO ROBIN

Contents

1. Turning Point   1

PART I: HISTORY

2. Origins   29
3. Hubris   41
4. Denial   51
5. The Big Crack-Up   60

PART I: CASE STUDIES

6. Manufacturing Social Security   73
7. Hair of the Dog   87
8. The Private Pension Bailout   107
9. Subsidizing Suburbia   120
10. Everyman a Hero   127
11. Yesterday's Generals   140
12. Yesterday's Bureaucrats   157

PART III: SOLUTIONS

13. What the Country Must Do   171
14. What You Should Do   184

Notes   207
Index   231

1

Turning Point

It was the kind of story that sets conservative radio talk show hosts to howling. Uncle Sam, a congressional report revealed, was regularly mailing benefit checks to forty indigent alcoholics, in care of their local Denver liquor store. The tab came to $13,000 a month, most of which, no doubt, went straight for Colt 45 and Thunderbird.

How could this be? Well, the Denver drunks were entitled, it turned out. The Social Security Administration had deemed all forty alcoholics to be "disabled" by virtue of their "illness." And because they professed to have little or no income, they were thus eligible for Supplemental Security Income (SSI), an entitlement program that pays benefits to the poor and the disabled. And since these particular poor disabled persons either lived on the street or preferred that the government not know their whereabouts, they had simply designated their convenient local liquor store as their "representative payee"— which is all quite legal and indeed normal, the public soon learned. Congressional investigators discovered that in 1993, SSI, together with the Disability Insurance program run by Social Security, paid out $1.4 billion to 250,000 addicts—including abusers of heroin, PCP, pot, cocaine, and crack.

The Social Security Administration had required less than a third of the addicts on its rolls to attend any kind of treatment while picking up benefits. Most were active street users. A few were dealers with a criminal record. Of course, everyone acquainted with the program thought it was a horrible idea, for both the nation and the beneficiaries. This sort of government benevolence, remarked the director of a Denver homeless shelter, amounted to nothing less than "suicide on the installment plan."

That such a story gave huge offense to the public hardly needs explaining. Nothing could more insult the American ideal of rugged individualism than the image of tipsy street people lining up for government checks at a liquor store. Predictably, members of Congress scrambled to announce a crackdown, while op-ed writers fulminated about government subsidizing addiction and dependency. But was there perhaps something else about this spectacle that caused wholesome, upright, middle-class Americans to feel angry and uneasy?

Middle-class Americans know and think a lot these days about addiction. The bookstore shelves groan with self-help titles about overcoming dependency, whether to alcohol, drugs, cigarettes, sweets, speed, sex, and even romantic love. The concepts and clichés of recovery programs ("denial," "co-dependency," "twelve steps," "stinking thinking") now pervade the popular culture—even our humor. "Denial ain't no river in Egypt," Stuart Smalley jokes on "Saturday Night Live." Never before in our history has the stigma associated with addiction and dependency been stronger.

With one huge exception: dependency on government benefits.

During the Great Depression and even as recently as the 1960s, the biggest problem met by social workers in the United States was convincing down-and-out Americans to overcome the "humiliation" of accepting a helping hand from government. Today every American—rich, poor, and middle class—knows he or she is entitled to a plethora of social benefits as a matter of "earned right."

Indeed, our sense of entitlement has become so strong that in the past fifteen years we've had to invent a new word, *entitlements,* to describe the social benefits we now feel our government owes us. What exactly are entitlements? The Office of Management and Budget, the Congressional Budget Office, and other federal bureaucracies cannot agree on an official definition. But roughly speaking, *entitlements* has come to refer to social benefits that the government automatically distributes to citizens on the basis of their membership in some group or class.

Today just over 50 percent of all U.S. households contain at least one member who is receiving a direct entitlement benefit from the government, such as a veterans or Social Security pension, unemployment compensation check, or disability payment. Such families on average collect more than $10,300 a year in benefits, which adds up to a total of $750 billion, or more than half of the total federal budget.[1]

At any given time, 30 percent of the U.S. population is receiving another form of entitlement: indirect benefits, expressly designed to subsidize some favored group such as home owners, farmers, or senior citizens, that government delivers through loopholes in the tax code. A prime example is the home mortgage deduction. The government could subsidize home ownership by mailing a check to everyone who borrows to buy a home. Instead it has decided that it is easier to let home buyers write off their mortgage interest costs on their income tax returns. The result is an entitlement that pays 27 million home owners an average of $1,900 a year, and that dwarfs all other federal housing programs in its cost.[2] Altogether, the mortgage interest deduction and other tax subsidies to individuals cost more than $354 billion in 1993. (By comparison, tax subsidies to corporations, including all depreciation allowances, came to "only" $47 billion, according to the U.S. General Accounting Office.[3])

Not all tax expenditures provide benefits to individuals, but all are essentially like direct entitlements in certain key respects. As Howard E. Shuman has noted:

> Tax expenditures and spending entitlements are a common breed. They are like the animals in Noah's Ark which marched aboard side by side. Both are automatic and paid out by law and formula. Neither is regularly reviewed. Both are uncontrollable without a change in the law. Once legislated, they create powerful interest groups that are dependent

on their benefits, deeply entrenched and difficult, if not impossible, to oppose. Tax expenditures and spending entitlements are entered on opposite sides of the budget ledger. While they may not be of the same gender they are of the same species.[4]

The tax expenditure concept still strikes many Americans as wrongheaded, so it's worth pausing here for the benefit of readers who have objections. A common complaint is that the concept somehow assumes that government "owns" all your income before doing you the favor of letting you keep part of it. Certainly politicians often behave as if that is true, but such a notion really has nothing to do with the concept of tax entitlements. Instead, the presumption behind the concept is simply that, as a people, we have decided on a general rate of taxation. When certain groups secure exemptions to that general rate, everyone else has to pay more. And when that happens, it's no different, fiscally or morally, than when government just sends benefit checks to certain favored groups.

Most tax expenditures, as it happens, go disproportionately to affluent Americans, yet these affluent Americans rarely feel grateful. As with Social Security and Medicare, the common refrain is, "I'm only getting my own money back." Certainly the feeling is understandable, but ultimately it is based on an illusion. As one's tax dollars are consumed by more and more groups claiming direct and indirect entitlements, receiving any tax subsidy may seem simply like recovering stolen property. But one is still receiving a benefit that must somehow be paid for, and to that extent, one is contributing to the problem just as much as everyone else at the trough.

Counting tax expenditures flowing to individuals, the total bill for entitlements comes to well over *$1.1 trillion* each year. Staggering though that sum may be, however, it is hardly the full measure of what has gone wrong with our system of entitlements. The subject of this book is not a pleasant or an easy one, because entitlements, like other sources of dependency, breed their own sustaining myths and deep-seated denials. The businessman calls four martinis at lunch "social drinking" but thinks every pot-smoking professor is a craven druggie. The prosperous retiree calls her windfall Social Security benefits "social insurance" but thinks food stamps for poor children are just corrupting dole. Entitlements, like drugs or alcohol, breed "stinking thinking" and also a willingness to act as if the future simply did not exist. This book will confront middle-class America's $2 billion-a-day addiction to entitlements. It will explain why the cost of entitlements has grown out of control, and it will explain what middle-class Americans must do, starting now, to prepare for the inevitable collapse of the middle-class welfare state.

MIDDLE-CLASS WELFARE

Of the trillion-plus dollars the United States spends each year on direct and indirect entitlements, only a small fraction actually goes to the poor. If Congress were suddenly to zero out the entire U.S. welfare state, including all entitlements conveyed through the tax code, the poverty rate among children (currently running at over 20 percent) would increase by less than two percentage points.[5] That should give a strong indication of who the real beneficiaries of our system of entitlement are.

Reform of the U.S. entitlement system means reform of the middle class and the well-to-do. It doesn't matter how exactly you care to define those terms; if you're an American citizen living above the government's official poverty line, you are eligible under current law to receive far more in lifetime government benefits than any welfare mother. And especially if you belong to the generation currently in retirement, the value of those benefits will be far in excess of your lifetime contribution in taxes.

Middle-class Americans have plenty of reason to be alarmed and angry about the degree of welfare dependency in today's poorer neighborhoods. But don't scapegoat "those people" on the other side of the tracks for running up your taxes or the national debt. Certainly they are part of the problem, but the rest of us are a far bigger part. In 1990, fully 75 percent of all direct outlays for federal entitlements went to families earning $20,000 or more annually.[6] Even families earning $50,000 or more, it turns out, are major consumers of the welfare state. According to recent estimates by the Congressional Budget Office (CBO), in 1990, such families received:

- Nearly 30 percent of all veterans' benefits.[7]
- Nearly 24 percent of all unemployment benefits.[8]
- About 33 percent of all federal civilian pensions and more than 50 percent of all military pensions.[9]

Entitlements conveyed through the tax code are even more heavily skewed in favor of the middle class and the well-to-do. Consider, for example, the child care credit, which cost the Treasury more than $3 billion in 1991. Households with incomes below $10,000 received virtually no benefit from this tax subsidy. Those with incomes above $50,000 however, received $1.2 billion to help pay for nannies and other child care expenses.[10]

It is a similar story with other major tax subsidies flowing to individuals. By and large, it's not the poor who are responsible for the runaway cost of social benefits. For example, 99 percent of the $49 billion the United States spent subsidizing home mortgages in 1992 went to families earning more than $20,000 a year.[11] According to the congressional Joint Committee on Taxation, the average value of the mortgage interest deduction for taxpayers with incomes over $100,000 was $3,469 in 1991. In contrast, the same deduction was worth an average of only $516 for taxpayers in the $20,000 to $30,000 bracket who qualified to take the benefit—and, of course, many, including renters and those who opted for the standard deduction, did not.[12]

Once middle-class Americans reach age sixty-two (now the most common age to begin collecting Social Security), they really start to cash in. In the retirement villages of Florida and Arizona, few residents could afford to have retired as early as they did, or to shop and travel as much as they do, without being able to rely on Social Security, Medicare, and other entitlements as a financial base. Under current law, a typical middle-class couple retiring at age sixty-five in 1995 can expect to receive Social Security and Medicare benefits with an annuity value approaching $500,000. This includes (in constant 1993 dollars) $185,000 worth of future Medicare benefits and $223,400 in future Social Security benefits. Most of this money is pure windfall. A typical retired couple today has paid little more than $57,000 in Medicare taxes over their lifetimes and only about $109,000 in Social Security taxes (even after adjusting for inflation and the time value of money).[13]

The magnitude of these federal transfer payments has transformed vast regions of the country. It's no coincidence that during the 1970s and 1980s, as federal entitlement spending exploded, Florida and the rest of the Sun Belt boomed. Every thirty days, Treasury plants around the country transfer $1.78 billion of Social Security checks and direct deposits into Florida, for example. This is besides $1.3 billion in Medicare and military health insurance reimbursements, $229 million in military retirement pensions, and $220 million in civil service retirement benefits.[14]

Largely because of such benefits, a typical eighty-year-old now consumes $1.16 cents for every dollar consumed by a typical thirty-year-old, according to one recent study. In the early 1960s, by contrast, the average eighty-year-old was spending just 65 cents for every $1.00 a thirty-year-old spent. Not surprisingly, the savings rate among persons approaching retirement age has plummeted in recent years (why save when you can live off entitlements?) while it has remained unchanged among younger Americans.[15]

Who pays for this windfall? Younger workers, by and large. But the fact that most recipients are receiving back far more in benefits than they ever paid in taxes (even after adjusting for inflation and imputed interest) continues to make entitlements the most popular form of government spending. When speaking among themselves, politicians often refer to Social Security, for example, as the third rail of American politics: "Touch it," they say, "and you die." Tampering with the home mortgage deduction is equally, if not more, politically incorrect.

Behind all the political sloganeering in support of entitlements lurks a darker reality—one that most Americans privately suspect but still often want to deny. It's that middle-class America's binge on entitlements is as unsustainable as a welfare mother's crack habit. While Newt Gingrich has been busy trying to reinvent the orphanage, another Victorian idea is in even greater need of rehabilitation: middle-class thrift and self-reliance.

READ THE WARNING LABELS

The government hasn't yet taken to airing public service announcements about the impending collapse of Social Security, Medicare, and other entitlements. But in budgetary and other technical documents, it has issued plenty of official warnings about its inability to keep the checks flowing indefinitely—for example:

• *Medicare.* As of this writing, the latest actuarial projections show Medicare's main Hospital Insurance program going broke between 2000 and 2006.[16] The Clinton Administration and Congress are currently debating cuts in Medicare's future rate of growth, but none of the proposals on the table are anywhere near adequate to the problem. Balancing the Medicare Hospital Insurance trust fund over seventy-five years would require cuts in future spending *ten times* larger than those proposed by the Clinton administration and *over five times* larger than those proposed by Congressional Republicans.[17] Meanwhile, Medicare's Supplementary Medical Insurance program (which pays for doctors' visits) is growing 19 percent faster than the economy as a whole and is also unsustainable.[18]

• *Disability Insurance.* Thanks in large measure to a definition of disability that has now grown so loose that it includes stress disorders and alcoholism, the Social Security Administration's Disability Insurance program is also careening out of control. To prevent the trust fund from growing broke in 1994, Congress diverted revenues from Social Security's main pension trust fund. Nonetheless, the outlook for the program is gloomy. The latest trustee report projects that the Disability Insurance trust fund, despite the most recent bailout, could be "exhausted" by 2005.[19]

• *Civil service retirement system.* The total present value of benefits promised under the system now exceeds $1.1 *trillion.* No real reserves exist to defray this cost. Today this encumbrance is roughly equal to $4,600 for every man, woman, and child in the United States.[20]

• *Military retirement system.* The retirement age for military pensions is so young and the benefits so rich that the average officer leaving the service this year at age forty-two with twenty years of experience can expect to receive over $1.1 million in pension checks before reaching age sixty-five and another $1 million by age seventy-five. As a result, the present value of benefits already promised by the system comes to more than $713.4 billion, or nearly $3,000 for every American man, woman, and child.[21] No real reserves exist to defray this cost. If the federal government accounted for its unfunded pension liabilities in the same way it requires private employers to do, it would have to admit to deficits about $90 billion larger than the current admitted deficits.[22]

• *Veterans' benefits.* Due to the rapid aging of the veterans' population and to the ever-looser connection between veterans' benefits and actual war experience, the cost of veterans' benefits continues to hit new records. The Department of Veterans Affairs estimates that the present value of its liability for entitlements promised to ex-servicemen and women comes to more than $189.85 billion. No money has been put aside to pay for this debt from the past, which is as large as a Reagan-era deficit.[23]

• *Housing subsidies.* As of September 30, 1992, the Federal Housing Administration held $329.5 billion in mortgages on single and multifamily homes, of which about $13.8 billion was in default.[24] But this was trivial compared to middle-class housing subsidies delivered through the tax code, including the deductibility of local real estate taxes, the deferral of capital gains on home sales, and the forgiving of up to $125,000 of capital gains on houses sold by those over fifty-five years of age. Together with the mortgage interest deduction, these entitlement-like subsidies cost the Treasury $76.8 billion in 1993.[25]

• *Social Security pension fund.* The system's actuaries show the pension fund running huge deficits as early as the year 2000.[26] Even after making optimistic assumptions about future rates of economic growth and other trends, the actuaries still cannot see any way the Social Security system as a whole can maintain positive cash flow after 2002.[27] Using realistic demographic and economic assumptions, the actuaries project that the main Old Age, Survivors, and Disability Insurance trust fund will go broke within twenty-five years.[28] To sustain just the pension and disability programs would require revenues equivalent to between 17 and 20 percent of all wages earned by low- and middle-income workers in 2030.[29] Add in the cost of Medicare, and the tax burden on the next generation rises to between 25 and 34 percent of payroll in 2030—and to more than 48 percent by 2070.[30]

Like the surgeon general's findings on cigarettes and cancer, the government's official warnings about entitlements are beyond serious debate at this point. Certainly a few well-funded special interest lobbies quibble with some of the data and with conclusions concerning their favorite spending programs. Some special interests even sponsor their own research, purporting to show that we don't really know how harmful the effects are—or that their own brand of benefit is somehow actually good for you and the country. But those in the know take such self-serving pleading no more seriously than they do the scientific contributions of the Tobacco Institute. As Senator Daniel Patrick Moynihan once retorted to a lobbyist for the American Association of Retired Persons who rose to object to one of his speeches on entitlements: "Lady, you are paid to object."

The future of entitlement programs as a whole is even bleaker than the projections for individual programs might suggest. In 1995, President Clinton's Entitlements Commission found, for example, that unless appropriate policy changes are made in the interim, *outlays for entitlements and interest on the national debt will consume all tax revenues collected by the federal government within seventeen years.*

Imagine such a world. You would pay even higher taxes than you do today, but the federal government would still have no money for policing borders or collecting customs, for FBI agents, for courts, for medical research, or even for an army the size of Luxembourg's. The federal government's sole role would be to collect taxes, distribute entitlements to certain favored groups, and pay interest on the exploding national debt.

And it gets worse. By 2030, the commission projects, spending for Medicare, Medicaid, Social Security, and federal employee retirement programs alone will consume all federal tax revenues. This would leave the federal government with no role except subsidizing old people, providing health care for the poor, and paying interest to bondholders.[31]

These projections are echoed by warnings from the Congressional Budget Office, which in November 1995 calculated the effect of prevailing policy on the taxes paid by members of different generations. Whereas Americans born between 1900 and 1920 will end their days having paid an average of 24 percent of their lifetime income in federal, state and local taxes, Americans born after 1990 will face a net tax rate of 82 percent if current spending programs are extended indefinitely. (This 82 percent net rate is in *excess* of all future benefits they are currently promised to receive.)[32]

In sum, the official position of the U.S. government is that current policy, extended indefinitely, will result in the near-total confiscation of the income of today's younger Americans and future generations. If the government tried to push costs still further into the future, it would have to run *annual* deficits exceeding $1.4 trillion by 2020 and $4.1 trillion (or 10.4 percent of gross domestic product) by 2030, according to estimates by the Office of Management and Budget.[33] If you cannot imagine that happening, that's because it won't. Long before we get anywhere near that point, your entitlements will be cut.

NEW MATH FOR THE MIDDLE CLASS

So what is all this going to cost you? No less than a way of life. While recent attempts to lower the deficits may cause anguished howls from affected special interests (and much self-congratulation from congressmen who tell themselves they are making "tough choices"), Americans haven't even begun to face up to the consequences of what's coming. The table summarizes some of the official projections for entitlement programs for Americans of different age groups. What does all this actually mean for people's lives? Here is an example that hints at the dimensions of the cultural and economic changes in store.

Let's suppose you are forty years old. If you can't count on Social Security and Medicare to subsidize your retirement, how much will you have to save to pay your own way? Let's assume you've already accumulated $50,000 in IRA (Individual Retirement Account) savings, which is a lot more than most Americans that age have man-

What Uncle Sam Has Really Promised You
(Latest official projections available as of January 1996)

If you were born in	Medicare's main Hospital Insurance trust fund is projected to go broke by the time you reach age . . .	Social Security's pension and disability fund is projected to go broke by the time you reach age . . .	Without further cuts, entitlements and interest on the national debt will consume all federal revenue by the time you reach age . . .	To provide you with the Social Security and Medicare benefits you are promised at age 65, the government would have to raise payroll taxes to . . .
1935	65	80	77	17.8%
1945	55	70	67	20.0
1955	45	60	57	26.3
1965	35	50	47	34.1
1975	25	40	37	38.4
1985	15	30	27	41.7
1995	5	20	17	44.6

Sources: Board of Trustees of the Federal Hospital Insurance Trust Fund, *Annual Report* (Washington, D.C.: U.S. Government Printing Office, April 1995); Bipartisan Commission on Entitlement and Tax Reform, *Final Report to the President* (Washington, D.C.: U.S. Government Printing Office, 1995); Board of Trustees of the Federal Old-Age and Survivors Insurance and Disability Insurance Trust Funds, *Annual Report* (Washington, D.C.: U.S. Government Printing Office, April 1995).

aged to save. Assume further that by investing in the stock market, you'll be able to enjoy an average annual return on your savings before you retire of 6.5 percent above inflation, which was the average real return on common stocks (not counting the cost of commissions) between 1871 and 1992.

Because they must live off their savings, retirees usually invest more conservatively than younger workers do. Accordingly, assume that after you retire, you'll invest in a prudent portfolio that pays you the same real return as the historical real return for long-term bonds, which averaged 2.3 percent between 1871 and 1992.[34]

Assume, finally, that you would like to retire at age sixty-two (the current average age of retirement for private sector workers) and that you want to consume the equivalent of $35,000 a year in today's dollars without exhausting your savings before age ninety. How much should you be saving for retirement now?

To have spending power equivalent to $35,000 annually in today's dollars (before taxes), you would need to save $11,460 a year for the next twenty-two years. And even after such a regime of thrift, if you live one day past ninety you'll die a pauper.

What if you don't already have $50,000 socked away for retirement? What if, after paying for the car loan, the mortgage, the credit cards, and your taxes, you've only managed to save, say, $10,000 in your IRA or 401(k)? And what if, God forbid, you wind up getting laid off before you turn sixty like so many of today's blue-collar and middle-management workers? If you're already forty, here's what you are up against. To have spending power equivalent to $35,000 a year for ages sixty through ninety, you must save $18,962 annually starting immediately. And again, if you live a day past ninety, you'll exhaust your savings and be flat broke.

The unfunded liabilities of Social Security, Medicare, and other entitlement programs are so large that they are incomprehensible to the average American. But these examples suggest a better way to look at these debts from the past. Their true measure is how much you will have to pay.

You already know what you are paying in taxes today and that this amount will continue to rise inexorably so long as middle-class entitlements are not severely reduced. So what will it cost you in addition once *your* entitlements are cut? To replace just the amount that Social Security and Medicare currently pays to a typical middle-class couple in retirement, you would have to save more than $400,000 (in today's dollars) by age sixty-five, and probably much more.[35]

Since chances are you're not saving anywhere near enough to accumulate that sum, you have your own personal, unfunded liability to worry about. It's not quite the same as your other debts. No one is going to come and take your house or your car if you don't keep up with your payments from month to month, at least not right away. But this debt is nonetheless very real. If you don't keep paying it off on time, it will eventually reduce you to poverty.

Few Americans are prepared to face that reality. Princeton economist B. Douglas Bernheim estimates that the typical baby boom household is saving at only one-third the rate required to finance a standard of living during retirement comparable to the one it enjoys before retirement—and this is assuming Social Security and Medicare won't be cut.[36]

Don't count on your house to bail you out either. True, many of today's retirees managed to accumulate large nest eggs just by owning their own homes. During the 1960s, 1970s, and much of the 1980s, the combination of relatively high inflation, federal regulations capping mortgage interest rates, and tax subsidies for home buyers meant that the real after-tax cost of home ownership was less than zero. In other words, Uncle Sam would pay you to buy a house, and then you could count on its rising in value by about 20 percent in real terms by the time you were ready to retire.[37] Those days are long gone.

The comparatively small (and downwardly mobile) generation coming along behind the baby boomers, combined with continued cutbacks in government subsidies to home ownership, makes rapid home price appreciation unlikely in the coming years. Indeed, one widely cited paper published in 1989 predicts that the lack of demographic pressures on the housing market will lead to a 47 percent real decline in the price of houses over the lifetime of the baby boom generation.[38]

Don't count on the private pensions system to save the day either. Private, defined-benefit pension plans, which promise workers specific benefits upon retirement regardless of the actual performance of the plan's investments, have provided enormous windfalls to many participants during the postwar period. As new plans were formed, older workers were routinely granted benefits, or "past service credits," despite their having paid in little or nothing in previous contributions, thus putting most plans in debt from day one. Subsequently, companies constantly expanded benefit levels without putting additional assets aside to cover the future cost, thereby compounding the original debt. Moreover, the availability of under-priced federal pension insurance encouraged both management and labor to conspire in lax funding practices, much as the availability of federal deposit insurance led to reckless lending by savings and loans.

Today the result of such fiscally irresponsible practices is a private, defined-benefit pension system that, despite receiving over $8 billion a year in federal tax subsidies and another $10 billion worth of insurance subsidies, is deeply encumbered by debts from the past.[39] Already more than fifty major American companies have pension funds that are out of balance by more than $100 million.[40] After adjusting for inflation, underfunding in single-employer plans nearly tripled from $27 billion in 1987 to $53 billion in 1992 and $71 billion in 1993, the latest year for which data are available.[41] "Unless Congress and the Administration act now, these problems will worsen," Congressman J. J. Pickle (D-TX) warned in 1993, "and this country's pension-guarantee program will become the next savings and loan bailout."[42] Congress and the administration have not enacted significant reform, and the threat to future taxpayers continues to build.

Meanwhile, the percentage of workers covered by private pension plans is declining. By 1990, only one out of five workers was still covered by a defined-benefit plan, and even among this lucky minority, many will never collect full benefits due to loss of their jobs or plan terminations. As we will explore in greater detail in Chapter 8, there is little hope that, in the absence of major reforms, the traditional private pension system will be capable of playing a significant role in financing the retirements of most baby boomers. Quite the contrary, the cost of bailing out the system will likely impose just one more significant obstacle to the baby boomers' ability to save on their own for retirement.

Some observers have optimistically predicted that baby boomers and younger Americans will make up for any lost or reduced retirement benefits by simply retiring later than today's senior citizens did. But as we will explore in greater depth in Chapter 7, this suggestion rests on some rather shaky assumptions. Sure, the average age of retirement will go up in the next century, but it is not clear at all how many of today's thirty- and forty-year-olds will have either the job skills or the health status needed to hold a job in the high-tech economy of 2020 or 2030.

Rapid technological change and perpetual restructuring in American business have already rendered the job skills of many middle-aged Americans obsolete. Massive layoffs among middle-aged middle managers at high-tech companies like IBM demonstrate that the economy has less and less demand for knowledge workers unless they are truly at the cutting edge of their professions. From 1989 to 1992, the number of those over fifty who were unemployed jumped 68.1 percent, compared with a 40.6 percent increase for people under fifty.[43] By the mid-1990s, unemployment among Ph.D. scientists and engineers had become pandemic. Information age work may not be as physically demanding as industrial age work, but it is no less punishing on the middle-aged and the old.

At the same time, baby boomers and younger Americans cannot count on their health's allowing them to put off retirement indefinitely. Over the past twenty-five years, life expectancy rates have increased dramatically, but so have rates of disability and morbidity among middle-aged and elderly people. By many measures, today's seventy- and eighty-year-olds are actually frailer than were their counterparts a century ago. They are less likely to die from infectious diseases or heart attacks, but having survived such insults to the body, they are more likely to suffer from arthritis, incontinence, Alzheimer's disease, and other crippling but nonlethal conditions.[44]

So there is no use pretending that a Buck Rogers future will solve the financial crisis facing today's workers. This will be especially true if America puts off entitlement reform well into the next century. If that happens, even though productivity will undoubtedly continue to rise, the cost of entitlements is bound to rise even faster, leading to stagnant or even declining after-tax income for most workers. In the absence of serious entitlement cuts, a continuation of current economic and demographic trends will lead to a devastating 59 percent decrease in real after-tax income per U.S. worker between 1995 and 2040, according to projections by economist Neil Howe.[45]

For a lucky few, large inheritances will save the day. But despite the unprecedented wealth controlled by today's retirees, most younger Americans will receive only modest bequests, if any at all. After taking into account factors such as the increasing cost and need for prolonged nursing home care, studies suggest that among baby boomers who receive any inheritance at all, the median amount will be something less than $23,000.[46]

Collectively, then, today's workers face a long-term financial challenge that is unprecedented in U.S. history. Through Social Security, Medicare, and even to some extent the underfunded private pension system, they must subsidize the consumption of today's retirees, rich and poor alike—a burden that, due to early retirement, advancing life expectancy, and comparatively generous benefit levels, has never before been higher. But because they are in effect caught at the end of a chain letter, today's working-aged Americans won't be able to collect in turn. Meanwhile, they must save to cover the cost of replacing other government benefits that are likely to be cut or severely reduced, from student aid for their children, to the home mortgage deduction, to disability and unemployment compensation, or else pay ever higher taxes to support these programs. Something must give.

COLD TURKEY

The politics of entitlement reform are exceedingly tough, but the politics of no reform are just as bad and getting much worse. Public support for entitlements programs, particularly among Americans under forty-five, has begun to erode dramatically. A 1994 poll found, for example, that:

- Fully 78 percent of all Americans agree that major reform of Social Security and Medicare should be undertaken now.
- Seventy percent of Americans believe that reform should include some form of means testing.
- Even more disconcerting to the conventional political wisdom, 74 percent of Americans now say they would think better of their elected representatives if they would discuss the need for entitlement reform.[47]

Politicians can still procrastinate, but they cannot put off entitlement reform much longer—not just for economic but for political reasons as well. By 1998, people born in the 1960s and 1970s will represent the largest potential voting bloc in the country. And among this group, more people believe in UFOs than in the viability of Social Security. In 1994, 83 percent of persons eighteen to thirty-four said they did not believe Social Security will exist by the time they retire.[48]

The eroding legitimacy of America's entitlement system is evident across the political spectrum. As the Clinton health care plan went down in flames, for example, the traditionally liberal *New Republic* magazine drew this hard lesson from liberalism's worst debacle in a generation:

> Clinton appears to have absorbed . . . the paleoliberal notion that the political payoff for health care reform depends on creating a new entitlement. That was the case for FDR and Social Security in the 1940s, but it hasn't proved true for Democrats since the 1960s, when they created Medicare, Medicaid and extended welfare benefits. Those programs all created open-ended, unsustainable obligations on the part of the federal government, and did far less to help the unfortunate than originally anticipated.[49]

It is possible, of course, that all the projections will prove to be wrong and that today's growing pessimism about entitlements is unwarranted. It is also possible that the historical forces that are eroding welfare states around the world, such as population aging and the effects of global economic competition, will for some reason reverse themselves. But the more we know about the assumptions behind the projections, the less likely it seems that the American welfare state will escape the death spiral seen among other contemporary welfare states, from Europe to New Zealand.

Writing from New Zealand, Professor David Thomson of Massey University notes that political resistance to welfare states has been growing around the globe for a common reason: younger workers are coming to understand that the essential function of the welfare state has been to redistribute resources not between rich and poor but between generations. Thomson notes that throughout the industrialized world:

> The generation now middle-aged and entering old age is the "welfare generation," the cohort who have been the prime beneficiaries of the welfare state throughout their adult lives. Their lifetime financial contributions to the program of pooled resources which is the essence of the welfare state have been small, and their claims much more considerable. Those who preceded them into old age found the welfare state of more limited worth—and those who follow are being asked as a generation to invest a great deal more than they will ever receive in return.[50]

That's a reality that today's younger Americans are unlikely to escape. As the World Bank recently reported, "Today, as the world's population ages, old age security systems are in trouble worldwide."[51]

EATING THE SEED CORN

Some optimists fondly hope for the only painless way out: a spectacular growth in future living standards—enough to endow tomorrow's workers with such affluence that they could easily bear all (or at least most) of the burden being thrust upon them. Yet a fond hope is rarely a sane expectation. In fact, the relentless growth of entitlements directly undermines the very national investments that might make a productivity miracle possible. As such, entitlements constitute a double-whammy against the young.

The growth of entitlements is one large reason that the American economy no longer shows the dramatic productivity gains and mass upward mobility it did during the 1950s and 1960s. As of the end of 1991, America's social insurance programs had racked up $15 trillion in unfunded liabilities. Were this money at work in the economy today, our rates of productivity would be much higher, and the burden on workers supporting an aging population would be much lower. Instead, the growing cost of entitlements continues to erode America's ability to invest in its future. The supply of savings available for private investment, or net national savings, has dropped from more than 8 percent of the economy in the 1960s to 2 percent today.[52]

Part of the problem is that the availability of programs like Social Security, Medicare, unemployment compensation, and other entitlements causes many people to put away less for a rainy day than they otherwise would. A recent national poll commissioned by the Congressional Institute on the Future and the National Taxpayers Union Foundation found, for example, that two-thirds of all those surveyed said they would respond to a cut in Social Security benefits by increasing their savings.[53]

Another part of the problem is that as the cost of underfunded pension programs and other entitlements rises, working-aged Americans find they are increasingly unable to save. As recently as 1972, the maximum Social Security tax anyone could pay was a mere $936. Today the maximum tax is more than ten times that amount, with the system consuming more than one out of every seven dollars earned by most American workers. Economist Laurence Kotlikoff writes, "For over four decades, government, at the federal, state and local levels, has been shifting fiscal burdens from current to future generations. . . . This process of 'pass the generational buck' has left today's young and middle-aged Americans paying such a high fraction of their labor earnings in net taxes that many have little wherewithal from which to save for their old age."[54]

The mounting cost of entitlements makes it increasingly difficult for the public sector to save and invest as well. The rising cost of entitlements forces legislators to slash all nonbenefits spending such as public investment in infrastructure, education, research and development, and other initiatives that might benefit the future, including possible tax cuts. Making matters worse, since legislators cannot slash enough to balance the budget so long as entitlements remain off-limits, deficits result. And to finance the deficits, the government borrows from the dwindling pool of private savings, making still less money available for productive investment. As such, our system of entitlements might be construed as an enormously large and complicated machine that, for all its moving parts, performs one essential function: converting investment in the future into current consumption.

What does all this mean for the average American today? Unless you are already in your seventies or eighties, it means you are going to take a big hit—one that will not only transform your own life but the very culture and economy you live in. Just as welfare has fostered dependency among the poor, programs like Social Security and Medicare have fostered dependency among the middle class (young and old alike), and learning to live without them won't be any easier for most Americans than withdrawal from a powerful narcotic.

A GENERATION UNDER WATER

What size house can you afford? How often should you buy a new car and what kind? How much of each month's income should you be saving? Most of us answer these kinds of questions without ever really thinking about them. In deciding how much to consume and how much to save, we take our cues from the way our parents lived, from the consumption patterns of our colleagues or neighbors, or from the lifestyles that advertisers present to us as just deserts for our travails.

Until recently, most middle-class Americans could afford to let such cultural conditioning determine their personal finances. "Keeping up with the Joneses" didn't lead to massive debt and an impoverished old age. But remember that what Americans casually came to view as a "decent middle-class lifestyle" during the decades after World War II was in fact a lifestyle largely financed by massive and (as it has turned out) *unsustainable* government subsidies to the middle class. Now those debts are coming due. Accordingly, if today you continue to cling to the consumer values that emerged in that postwar era, you will learn soon enough that you have lived far beyond your means and the government won't bail you out.

Because of the imminent collapse of the middle-class welfare state, most working-aged, middle-class Americans are headed toward insolvency if they do not radically change their lifestyles. They face predictable accruing liabilities—primarily for their children's education, their health care, and their retirement, for which the government won't pay, and which will cost far more than the assets they have accumulated, or are ever likely to accumulate at their present rates of saving and home price appreciation. Call it slow-motion bankruptcy.

It is possible for such Americans to go along for years, paying all their monthly bills and even putting a little aside in the bank without their realizing that they have long since passed the point of insolvency. After all, they are living much as their parents did twenty years ago, and in two-paycheck households, they may even be taking home slightly more total real income. It's not easy for them to see that because the rules of middle-class membership have changed, they are risking impoverishment. That insight will come only later, usually at major life transition points, such as when it comes time to sell a house that has barely appreciated in value, or to send a child to college, or when they discover that they cannot afford the golden years their parents enjoyed in retirement.

Today 70 percent of all white households headed by a person age fifty-one to sixty-one have financial savings of less than $53,000. Fully half have savings of less than $17,300 saved up for their retirement or any other purpose.[55] Yet to finance a twenty-year retirement with purchasing power of just $20,000 a year in today's dollars requires accumulating a nest egg of around $317,000.[56] Clearly most members of even the comparatively affluent generation now approaching retirement will either remain or become deeply dependent on government transfer payments as they age. But if baby boomers and younger Americans continue with the same thriftless habits as they pass through midlife, they won't find much, if any, safety net to catch them.

Government may try to bail out the middle class by creating new entitlements or making old ones more generous from time to time. But without rapid economic and population growth to swell the tax base, the cost of these entitlements will be borne by the middle class itself, leaving its financial crisis unchanged. Even if baby boomers organize into senior boomers and demand special new benefits, any windfall they secure will have to be spread thinly over a huge population, and the burden to their children will be immediate and unbearable. In a sense, the coming end of the middle-class welfare state will transfer huge unfunded liabilities off the government's books and transform them into personal liabilities of individual Americans, who will have to pay them off as best they can. Especially for members of the baby boom generation and their children, there is no escaping these debts from the past.

THE NEW BOURGEOISIE

Who then will prosper in the next century? Americans who realize that they can no longer count on middle-class subsidies and adjust their values and expectations accordingly. For most of the postwar period, membership in the middle class was, for most Americans, an entitlement. In the next century, sustained membership in the middle class will in fact be an accomplishment, achieved for the most part only through self-denial and self-help. The most dramatic cultural changes among the American middle class in the next century will be the restoration of the following bourgeois values:

Thrift. In the 1870s, that most eminent Victorian and popular moralist Samuel Smiles became famous for his lively defense of what was then the orthodoxy of the striving middle-classes in both Europe and America. "It is the savings of the individual which compose the wealth—in other words, the well-being of every nation," Smiles asserted in his relentless volume, simply entitled *Thrift*. "On the other hand, it is the wastefulness of individuals that occasions the impoverishment of states. So it is that every thrifty person may be regarded as a public benefactor, and every thriftless person as a public enemy." For Smiles, as for most other Americans of his era, individual thrift was not only a virtue in itself. Its widespread practice was considered a requisite of civilization and nation building. Americans who hope to attain or maintain middle-class status in the next century will have to adopt a similar thrift ethic.

Family. The collapse of the middle-class welfare state will cause Americans to become more reliant on family ties. Entitlement programs were originally designed to take the place not just of individual savings but of many of the transfers of wealth that once took place within extended families. With the demise of the middle-class welfare state in the next century, families will again assume not just sentimental but economic importance. The elderly will need the support of their adult children much more than they do today, and will find themselves in much greater need of maintaining proximity and usefulness to their adult children, including the usefulness that can come only from having saved up a large bequest. Already rare, but unthinkable in the next century, will be those bumper stickers on the back of RVs stating, "We're spending our children's inheritance." Adult children will also find themselves increasingly dependent on their parents as subsidies for home ownership, education, and other needs of the nonelderly continue to disappear.

Work. The collapse of the middle-class welfare state will force new attitudes toward work. Though the work ethos is perhaps the least eroded of the traditional bourgeois values, it too has weakened in the middle class during the past half century. Even as life spans have increased, the average age of retirement has decreased, leaving American workers free from labor for up to 30 percent to 40 percent of their adult life spans. Meanwhile, for more and more younger Americans, work appears to be merely an unpleasant but necessary means of acquiring coveted consumer items or leisure time rather than an end in itself. Again, these attitudes are inconsistent with the cultural values needed to attain or maintain middle-class status in the next century in the absence of major middle-class subsidy programs.

Citizenship. As the middle class is forced to become more self-reliant, its members will likely change their view of the proper relationship between government and the individual. Historically, support for middle-class entitlement programs has largely derived from group claims of victimization. Beginning in the last century, farmers saw themselves as victims of an industrial economy in which farm prices lagged behind rises in the cost of living, and so argued that they were entitled to crop subsidies. Senior citizens, particularly in the 1970s, saw themselves as victims of inflation and of a youth culture that denied their generational achievements, and so believed they were entitled to generous Social Security pensions. Today beneficiaries of the home mortgage deduction claim they are owed this tax subsidy because they bought their homes on the assumption that it would always be available. And so it goes.

Such claims of victimization have propelled the growth of the middle-class welfare state in the twentieth century. But as the welfare state becomes delegitimized by its exploding cost and unsustainability, its deference to group claims will become delegitimized as well, at least in the eyes of those Americans who, through individual thrift, hard work, and devotion to traditional family values, escape descent into the lower classes. In addition, liberal guilt, already on the wane, will become practically nonexistent among the new bourgeoisie. The next century will not be an easy time to be poor, making it all the more important for average Americans to save themselves from downward mobility by rediscovering bourgeois virtue.

How did the ethos of entitlement insert itself into the heart of the American middle class? As we shall see in Part I of this book, traces of the attitude can be found as far back as the days of Valley Forge, when General Washington's officers threatened to desert him if he didn't grant them half-pay pensions for life. The difference today is that ordinary citizens have developed a righteous sense of entitlement without ever having marched barefoot through the snow for their country. The process of corruption was so subtle and gradual that hardly anyone noticed it was occurring. Today understanding how and why the middle class became addicted to entitlements is essential to understanding our present predicament and what it will take to survive its consequences in the future.

PART I

HISTORY

2

Origins

"The American idea of war," complained Thomas Brackett Reed, Speaker of the House in 1897, "is to take the farmer from his plow, and return him to his plow—with a pension."[1]

Military pensions are the *locus classicus* of the modern middle-class welfare state. Veterans were the first (and, for a century and a half, the only) broad-based group in American history to demand and receive social benefits based on some criteria other than abject need. The military's demand for social benefits began in the midst of the Revolutionary War, when a disgruntled officers' corps leaned on General George Washington to provide a retirement plan that would offer half-pay for life. Washington at first resisted, arguing that such a plan was too expensive and that it would "give a great disgust to the people." But later, during the hard winter at Valley Forge, he capitulated, because, as he later noted, "no day nor scarce an hour passed without the offer of a resigned commission."[2] To this day, half-pay pensions remain an entitlement of the professional military.

After the Civil War, rank-and-file Union soldiers also did well for themselves. Between 1880 and 1910, the U.S. federal government devoted over a quarter of its expenditures to providing pensions for aging veterans of the Grand Army of the Republic. Only veterans permanently disabled by combat-related injuries were supposed to qualify, but the program was marred by wholesale fraud. "I hold it to be a hideous wrong inflicted upon the republic that the pension system instituted for the benefit of soldiers and sailors of the United States has been prostituted and degraded," complained Charles Eliot, president of Harvard University, in 1889. "As things are, Gentlemen, one cannot tell whether a pensioner of the United States received an honorable wound in battle or contracted a chronic catarrh twenty years after the war."[3]

Today, of course, you don't have to have been honorably wounded in battle to collect from the Department of Veterans Affairs. In fact, you don't even have to be a veteran in the nineteenth-century sense of the word. Of the 27 million Americans currently eligible for veterans' benefits, barely half have ever even served in a war zone, much less seen combat.

This difference is the great divide between the modern era of entitlements and its archaic period. To be sure, many early veterans' groups used all the same pressure tactics as today's senior citizens' lobby and other modern entitlement tribes. But Eliot spoke for most respectable, middle-class people of his time when he condemned the very idea of government's paying benefits to ordinary civilian Americans—even those who might be suffering from, say, a chronic disease of old age.

It was a harsh code, but the bourgeoisie of the nineteenth and early twentieth centuries were convinced (correctly, it turned out, in the long run) that American greatness depended at the very least on middle- and working-class Americans' not accepting benefits they had not earned. As late as 1932, total government expenditures for social welfare benefits at all levels of government came to only $208 million, or $1.67 per inhabitant, with middle-class Americans denying themselves virtually all benefits except workman's compensation.[4] Ironically, it was this very credo of self-help and self-reliance that a few years later led to the passage of Social Security, the program that, more than any other, broke down middle-class resistance to accepting subsidies and eventually fostered a new middle-class ethos of entitlement.

AGE FOR LEISURE

In 1936, the economist Eveline Burns wrote a book to explain and celebrate the significance of the recently passed Social Security Act. "Perhaps its most important achievement," Burns enthused, "is the introduction of a new kind of security. For the first time, workers will be *entitled* [italics in the original] to income when their wages cease."[5]

The Social Security Act was indeed unlike any other program that had ever come before. In the act's fine print, sure enough, Congress carefully reserved the legal right to reduce or cut benefits at any time. But from the beginning, politicians and program officials described Social Security as establishing an unprecedented political contract between government and ordinary citizens. In exchange for paying certain taxes during their working years, Americans would become entitled to certain specified benefits in old age. Unlike the case with the dole or relief programs, you wouldn't have to convince some bureaucrat or social worker that you were deserving. If you paid your taxes, you got your benefits, whether you needed them or not. It was the quintessential modern entitlement, the cornerstone of America's new middle-class welfare state.

Why did Social Security come about when it did? The pat answer is that the depression impoverished millions of Americans and shook the confidence of tens of millions more, to the point that long-standing inhibitions about receiving government benefits began to give way. But the real answer is actually more nuanced and interesting. In the context of the 1930s, the original Social Security Act was a profoundly conservative document, or at least so it seemed to many conservatives at the time. Perversely, many conservatives, as well as moderates, hoped that its passage would tame the growing political power of the elderly and save the taxpayers billions in subsidies. And in fact the passage of the Social Security Act did have this beneficial effect—for about one generation.

The explanation for this great historical irony begins with one

man, Francis Townsend, an unemployed doctor and real estate salesman who had ended up in Long Beach, California, after a long and
difficult life. Southern California had already become a haven for senior citizens. Attracted by its temperate climate, tens of thousands of
pioneering older Americans from across the country had moved
there in hope of establishing a new lifestyle: a comfortable, independent retirement, free from snow and family ties. But after the crash
on Wall Street, most lost their meager savings, and with the unemployment rate soaring, even those fit enough to work could not find
jobs, including Townsend.

It was in this setting that Townsend came to see his own misfor-
tune as that of his generation. His moment of epiphany, he would
later claim, came to him one morning when he spotted three elderly
women outside his window rummaging for edibles in a trash can. "A
torrent of invectives tore out of me," Townsend recalled, "the big
blast of all the bitterness that had been building in me for years. I
swore and I ranted, and I let my voice bellow with wild hatred I had
for things as they were."

At that moment, he would later claim, Townsend conceived the
radical idea that would soon make him one of the most controversial
figures of the 1930s. Simply put, he proposed a plan under which
the federal government would give any American over age sixty the
then-princely sum of $200 per month, provided only that beneficia-
ries spend the money within thirty days.

"Elderly people, trained and experienced by life's activities, can
be made the greatest asset humanity possesses if they are liberated
from the slavery of poverty and are permitted to exercise their tal-
ents as circulators of money," Townsend explained in 1935. By that
time, the Townsend movement had attracted an estimated 10 million members, united under the banner "Age for Leisure, Youth for
Work."[6]

Soon Congress and Roosevelt himself would be struggling against
the sudden potency of the Townsend movement, as local chapters
sprang up in congressional districts across the nation. The movement alarmed mainstream politicians, liberals and conservatives
alike, because there seemed to be no end to benefits the elderly

might demand once the precedent of subsidizing old age was established. As historian Jerry Cates has pointed out, "The danger, it was argued, was clear: the aged would drain away all available social welfare funds for themselves, leaving orphans, the blind, and other needy citizens to starve."[7]

Townsend and his followers intimidated politicians even more than the American Association of Retired Persons and the Gray Panthers do today—and at the same time threatened to bankrupt already overstrained governments. After Colorado adopted a constitutional amendment promising all the aged a minimum income of $45 a month, one observer noted, "The state capital is in a turmoil . . . funds are running short for nearly every State activity . . . hundreds of State employees are being dismissed . . . children are fainting in the schools from hunger . . . homes are being broken up . . . relief in Denver averages less than half of the minimum for subsistence."[8]

The solution to Townsendism, many influential Americans soon concluded, was to adopt a rival program under which only people who "contributed" specially earmarked taxes during their working years would qualify for pensions. "If we do not get a contributory system started," warned Social Security advocate Edwin E. Witte, "we are in for free pensions for everybody with constant pressure for higher pensions, far exceeding anything that the veterans have ever been able to exert."[9]

This was the original genius of the Social Security Act. By presenting Social Security as a program in which beneficiaries in some sense paid for their own benefits, the program's advocates wound up creating a pretext for denying benefits to the desperate poor elderly of the day. Members of the current older generation had paid their share of taxes over their lifetimes, to be sure. But since none of those taxes had ever been earmarked as Social Security taxes, these seniors wouldn't be entitled to any Social Security benefits—or to any other old age benefits, for that matter, except the dole and the poorhouse.

The strategy worked. Lest you doubt that denying benefits to the depression-ravaged elderly was a major factor in the creation of Social Security, consider the results. In 1940, just 222,000 seniors, or less than 1 percent of the elderly population, received Social Security benefits.[10] Even as late as the 1950s, the majority of Americans over age sixty-five did not receive Social Security, either because they had retired before the program started or because they had never had a chance to work a sufficient number of years under covered employment to qualify for benefits.

Because Social Security did so little for the elderly of the time, many seniors continued to press for so-called flat plans similar to the one Townsend proposed, which would be financed out of general revenue. Meanwhile, organizations representing active workers, most notably the AFL-CIO, and the labor movement generally, threw their weight behind Social Security. A sense of the generational politics of the era was captured by a speaker at the 1949 American Public Welfare Association convention, who warned: "The organized pressure of the aged is already becoming ominous in California and Colorado. If the same old peoples' lobbies spring up in our eastern and idle-western States, the old folks will become a ghoulish nightmare that saps the vitality of the younger generation."[11]

But over time, that younger generation became the older generation, and for its members, Social Security, far from serving as a brake on social spending, would instead fuel it. By promoting the illusion that recipients were only getting their own money back when they collected benefits, Social Security fostered a new ethos of entitlement that thrust America into a new age of middle-class dependency and fiscal recklessness.

THE MYTH OF SOCIAL INSURANCE

Franklin Roosevelt seems to have understood far better than most other Americans of his day what the long-term effects of his Social Security plan would be. When a visitor complained that the payroll taxes Roosevelt was planning to use for funding Social Security would impose an unfair burden on low-income workers, FDR responded with stunning prescience: "I guess you're right on the economics, but those taxes were never a problem of economics. They are politics all the way through. . . . With those taxes in there no damn politician can ever scrap my Social Security program."[12]

ORIGINS

Nothing in law, or in the actual financial operation of Social Security, justified the belief that its benefits were truly an "earned right." As we will explore in greater detail in Chapter 5, the government, far from saving or investing anyone's "contributions," actually spent the revenues it collected in payroll taxes as fast as the money came in the door. But Roosevelt predicted correctly that by earmarking a particular tax as an individual's Social Security "contribution," Americans would eventually come to view their Social Security benefits as, in effect, their own personal property and to see any reduction in benefits as akin to theft.

The growth of this mythology was also greatly fostered by the Social Security Administration's long-standing practice of describing the program as a form of insurance. Originally Social Security advocates carefully avoided the term, fearing that the Supreme Court would find the program unconstitutional if it appeared to bind future Congresses with a contractual obligation to pay future benefits. For this reason, the original Social Security Act at no place contained the word *insurance*. And the first Social Security cards referred only to the "federal old-age retirement benefits" program. In defending the act before the Supreme Court, the Roosevelt administration even went so far as to state in its brief that "the act cannot be said to constitute a plan for compulsory insurance within the accepted meaning of the term 'insurance.'"[13]

But once the Supreme Court affirmed the constitutionality of Social Security in May 1937, program officials immediately lost their inhibitions about describing it as insurance. Indeed, on the very day the Court handed down its decision, the chairman of the Social Security Board signed off on a suggestion by a young staffer named Wilbur Cohen that the board from then on refer to the old age benefits program in official communications as "old age insurance." Cohen would later explain, "The American public was and still is insurance-minded and opposed to welfare, 'the dole,' and 'hand outs.'"[14]

By 1939, the reverse side of the Social Security cards carried by individuals referred to the program as "federal old age insurance." In a press conference that same year, the commissioner of social security attempted to explain the intricacies of the program this way:

"Think of it! It is just as if you had written a group insurance policy, covering 45 million people, and it is because it is like trying to read the fine print in that insurance policy that it is hard to understand."[15]

In 1940, the same misleading rhetoric appeared in a pamphlet the Social Security Board issued to the public, entitled *Old-Age and Survivors Insurance for Workers and Their Families.* "If you work on a job covered by this law," the pamphlet explained, "you pay a tax to the Federal Government and so does your employer. These taxes go into the fund, out of which your benefits will be paid later on. The tax is a sort of premium on what might be called an insurance policy which will begin to pay payments when you qualify at age 65 or over, or in case of death."[16]

Gradually Social Security administrators abandoned any qualifications whatsoever in their descriptions of the program as insurance. A 1948 publication announced: "Old-age and survivors insurance and unemployment insurance are insurance." A 1951 pamphlet read: "Treat this card like an insurance policy." And again in 1952 an official pamphlet stated: "Your card is the symbol of your insurance policy under the Federal social-security law."[17]

Social Security advocates knew what they were doing. The program still remained unpopular with much of the population over sixty-five, mostly because it did so little for them. Even as late as 1953, more than 55 percent of the aged population (mostly persons too old to have "contributed" to the program) were still not eligible for Social Security pensions.[18] But by this period, despite the generally conservative drift of American politics, the program was beginning to win broad support among middle-aged and younger Americans, thanks in no small measure to its carefully cultivated image as a well-run insurance program, with all the associations of probity, equity, and conservatism that that word implied.

THE BIG LIE TRIUMPHS

There were very few Americans at the time who could see through the double game Social Security was playing, but there were exceptions. One of the most noteworthy was Carl T. Curtis, a straight-shooting county attorney from Minden, Nebraska, who, shortly after the Social Security Act was passed in 1935, renounced his membership in the Democratic party and successfully ran for Congress as a Republican.

Though little remembered today, Curtis was so far ahead of his time in his thinking about the welfare state that many of his contemporaries, including conservatives, regarded him as hopelessly backward. But history has shown Curtis's analysis of Social Security was dead on the mark. Beginning in the late 1940s, he perceived correctly that the misleading use of insurance terminology by social security advocates was not only providing a convenient rationalization for ignoring the needs of the current elderly but was also fostering an enormous, and unearned, sense of entitlement on the part of people who would be retiring in the 1960s, 1970s, and beyond.

In 1953, Curtis got his chance to lead what turned out to be the last serious attempt by conservatives in Congress to debunk the myths surrounding Social Security and to propose more fiscally responsible alternatives. After Republicans gained control of the House that year, Curtis secured permission from the new chairman of the Ways and Means Committee to hold hearings on Social Security's first eighteen years of operation. He used this opportunity to summon current and former Social Security bureaucrats, often against their will, and to grill them about whether Social Security was indeed a form of insurance or just another government benefits program that transferred money from one group to another.

The hearings were often tempestuous. Arthur J. Altmeyer, a former Social Security commissioner, resisted testifying until Curtis served him with a subpoena. Once under oath, Altmeyer grandstanded, literally for hours, about Curtis's lack of appreciation for the subtleties of "social insurance." Meanwhile, sympathetic Democrats did their best to make Altmeyer's very presence into an issue. "Bringing a man like you in here under subpoena! Mr. Chairman, you ought to be ashamed of yourself," exclaimed one. A long, angry exchange of words then ensued, the Democratic member demanding that the chairman cease pointing "that damned gavel." In the transcript, Altmeyer noted many years later in his memoirs, the word *damned* was discreetly omitted.[19]

But after intense cross-examination, Altmeyer was finally forced to admit the plain truth. Curtis asked him if it was his position that a person paying into the Social Security system had no contractual right to benefits.

"That is right," Altmeyer replied, reluctantly.

"And he has no insurance contract?" Curtis pressed.

"That is right," Altmeyer conceded.

But his concession that Americans had no contractual right to Social Security hardly mattered, Altmeyer hastened to add, because 90 million Americans already believed that they did have such rights. "You have at the present time about 90 million people who have accumulated wage credits," Altmeyer reminded the chairman. "Now it is inconceivable to me that the Congress of the United States would ever think of taking action to prejudice their rights that have developed under existing legislation. On the contrary, the Congress of the United States has continually improved, increased their rights."[20]

This was precisely the political dynamic Curtis feared. Since Social Security wasn't a real insurance program, with its own fully funded reserves and surplus, and since most of the current elderly were excluded from the program, Congress could continually liberalize benefits without having to raise revenues up front. Instead, the full cost would be borne by future generations when these benefit promises came due. Yet because Social Security was continually described to the American people as a form of insurance to which they had an "earned right," cutting future benefits would be well-nigh impossible, no matter how egregious or unjust the encumbrance on future generations might turn out to be.

Curtis believed this dynamic could be checked only by extending Social Security coverage immediately to the current elderly. "The only way to diminish future costs and to prevent the unwise expansion of Social Security into such new fields as disability, education, and Medicare," Curtis would reflect in his memoirs, "was to mature the system immediately by paying benefits to all retired aged. . . . Collecting taxes from the many and paying benefits to a few gave the public a false picture of the financial picture."[21]

Covering all the current elderly would have cost far more in the short term. But in the long term it would have saved money, Curtis believed, because it would have made the public aware of both the true cost of Social Security and its essential nature as just another government transfer program. And once they saw Social Security for what it really was, Curtis reasoned, they would not stand for the other inequitable and inefficient features of the program, such as its pattern of delivering its largest benefits to those least in need.

"Who is now eligible to receive the maximum benefits under our social security law?" Curtis once asked in a speech to the National Conference of Social Work. "They are those people with dollar incomes in their productive years substantially greater than the income of those around them. Included are the corporate executives, the successful business proprietors, the higher paid employees—and even a large number of wage earners—who might be described as being in the middle and upper income brackets."[22] Meanwhile, Curtis asked, "Why is it that the man or woman, who, because of lack of education or opportunity or because of physical handicaps or other shortcomings is unable to earn but a pittance through his best years receives the smallest amount of benefit in his old age?"

These were hard questions to answer, especially once one saw through the rhetoric of insurance. But unfortunately, in trying to clarify this picture, Curtis may have inadvertently made matters worse. In the course of trying to debunk the insurance myth, Curtis widely publicized the fact that the first cohorts of Social Security recipients would wind up collecting up to twenty times the values of their previous Social Security tax payments. As Martha Derthick, one of the leading historians of Social Security, wryly notes, "The public did not in fact get much aroused by the news that it would get far more in benefits than it had paid for, nor did Republican politicians in Congress."[23] Nor, in fact, did President Eisenhower. With Republicans controlling both houses and the presidency, many observers had expected that Social Security might at least be in for wholesale reforms. But on January 14, 1954, Ike announced his position on the issue in a much-anticipated message to Congress. Social Security's so-called Old Age, Survivors, and Disability Insurance system, Eisenhower declared, was the "cornerstone of the Government's programs to promote the economic security of the individual."

Despite Curtis's best efforts, Republican opposition to Social Security and other middle-class entitlements had collapsed and would never reemerge in any serious form. Indeed, throughout the postwar period, the fastest annual growth rates in total (inflation-adjusted) federal benefits would wind up occurring during two Republican presidencies: those of Eisenhower (fiscal years 1953 to 1961) and Nixon–Ford (fiscal years 1969 to 1977).

By the time Eisenhower came to power, a critical majority of middle-class Americans had decided to believe what their government had been telling them about Social Security for more than fifteen years. If Social Security administrators insisted on describing the program as a form of insurance that just happened to pay windfall benefits worth twenty times what it collected in premiums, who were they to argue? Both the politicians and the people had come to love this wonderful, seemingly harmless high provided by getting something for nothing.

3

Hubris

"Alarm spreads over the country," Margaret Mead wrote in 1957. "People are going to have too much leisure." The great danger, the famous anthropologist admonished, was that Americans would soon wind up with too much "unearned time, loose time, time which, without the holding effects of fatigue before and fatigue to come, might result in almost anything."[1]

It was a crisis, a broad range of social critics agreed, without precedent in all of history. "No society has ever been in this position before," Harvard sociologist David Riesman wrote the same year, in an essay entitled "Abundance for What?" The economic problem—the problem of scarcity and competition for material resources that had always defined the human condition—was essentially solved.[2]

So now what?

Riesman had his own ideas for how America could meet the challenge of affluence. One of the more memorable was his recommendations for the establishment of an Office of Recreation, which would be charged with making plans for vastly expanded recreational facilities and personnel. In contrast to FDR's Works Progress

Administration, which had helped put people to work during the depression building public infrastructure, Reisman suggested that in the new economy of abundance, "it may turn out that a 'Play Progress Administration' . . . will be necessary to spend the money fast enough."

By the mid-1950s, the postwar boom was being interpreted in many influential quarters as not just a sustained economic recovery but the dawning of a profoundly new, if long-predicted, age of mass leisure and abundance. Common sense might suggest that as more and more Americans began to enjoy the fruits of such abundance, they would find the wherewithal to become less and less dependent on government transfer programs. But as it turned out, the reverse was true. The conviction that America had become an affluent society not only led to a proliferation of middle-class subsidies but to an increasing willingness to borrow from future Americans to pay for it all.

The ironies here run deep. During the 1930s and 1940s, a chorus of critics from Townsend to Lord Keynes had attacked the middle-class thrift ethos as a source of industrial depression. The popular conviction that excess savings were hurting the economy was behind the stipulation in Townsend's plan that elderly pensioners would have to spend their benefits within thirty days. Social Security itself was also seen by at least some of its advocates as an important device for weakening the thrift ethos. "Nobody is going to spend these accumulated savings if he does not know where next week's income is coming from," argued Social Security expert Eveline Burns in a 1943 address to the Institute of Post-War Reconstruction. But, said Burns, "if a man has a modest assured income, he may be inclined to spend some of these accumulated savings, as the economists hope he will spend them."

Starting in the mid-1950s, however, America's presumed new status as an affluent society served equally well as a rationale for continuing cultural and political attacks on middle-class thrift and for continuing expansion of the middle-class welfare state. The arguments were somewhat different, of course, but the conclusions were the same: thrift had no place in the affluent society. Indeed, the only reason that Americans would ever have to worry about scarcity again, many opinion leaders argued, would be if they didn't maintain a sufficiently high level of consumption. And because each new generation in this "economy of abundance" would be vastly richer than the one that went before, there was no longer any reason for Americans to scrimp and save on behalf of the future. Instead, many economists argued, transfers of wealth in the opposite direction—from the future to the present, or from the young to the old—would bring the greatest good for the greatest number.

FUTURE ENVY

Joseph J. Spengler was among the first economists to spot the connection between affluence, the welfare state, and the so-called contract between the generations. In 1956, Spengler delivered a paper in Gainesville at a conference sponsored by the University of Florida's Institute of Gerontology. The paper attracted little attention at the time, but it later became widely influential in both academia and government.

Spengler departed from virtually all previous thinking about the economics of aging by emphasizing the dramatic upward mobility among the working-aged population that was then occurring in the United States. What accounted for this rapid rise in both income and productivity? The answer, said Spengler, was technological progress. And technological progress, he continued, was primarily the result not of individual thrift and investment but of social spending on the "educational, research, and engineering activities of a very large fraction of our society."

The idea that the technology and the economic dividends that flowed from it were communal property seemed obvious to Spengler. He went on to ask how the elderly of the era could ever get their fair share of the windfalls their taxes of yesteryear had presumably helped to create. "The aged are being deprived of their rights," Spengler charged, "by the fact that they are more likely than not to be denied a share in the fruits of technical and related progress; in the fruits, that is, of a process that is essentially social in that it is unconnected with particular agents of production owned by particular persons to which agents these fruits may be imputed."

As a remedy, Spengler proposed a "social credit for the aged" to enable them "to share in the fruits of technological progress." Under the system, the government would rebate a supplemental return on any fixed-income instruments, such as bonds or savings accounts held by the elderly, with the amount of the supplement rising by age.[3]

This, by the standards of what came later, was an exceedingly conservative proposal. It essentially required members of each generation to save during their middle years in order to be entitled to benefits in retirement. If—and only if—the savings of each middle generation eventually resulted in rapid technological progress, the scheme allowed for members of that generation to share in the dividends—but only in proportion to their previous, individual sacrifice or thrift.

The uses to which Spengler's ideas were put were far from conservative, however. For in the next two decades, they would become an important part of the argument used to justify an explosion of entitlement spending on middle-class retirees, which would lead to a further erosion of both the ability and proclivity of middle-class Americans to save for themselves.

THE POLITICS OF AFFLUENCE

During the Kennedy–Johnson years, entitlement spending on the middle class grew dramatically. Alongside the enactment of Medicare in 1965, which instantly became the government's fastest-growing entitlement program, came significant increases in Social Security spending. Between 1960 and 1968, thanks largely to higher benefits and a lowering of the minimum retirement age for men, the number of Social Security beneficiaries doubled, as did real expenditures—to $30.2 billion.[4] Poverty was still a massive problem among the elderly in the 1960s, and yet more than two-thirds of this entitlement money went to retirees who were not poor.

Today, Lyndon Johnson's "war on poverty" is what most people think of when they consider social policy in the 1960s, but compared to the growth of the middle-class welfare state, the war on poverty was just a cheap sideshow. In its glory days, the Office of Economic Opportunity, the main new institution of the president's declaration of social war, consumed less than $6 billion between 1965 and 1968.[5] Throughout the late 1960s, Social Security payments to the elderly were about ten times higher than federal payments for Aid to Families with Dependent Children (AFDC), the federal government's main welfare program.

AFDC, to be sure, was growing quickly and fostering much resentment and backlash from the middle class, but the hypocrisy factor was overwhelming for anyone who understood how the federal government was actually spending the taxpayers' money. The middle class had become a "standard beneficiary of the welfare state through Social Security, Medicare, unemployment compensation, and so on," notes John J. Broesamle. Accordingly, "The 'welfare crises' of the late sixties and seventies amounted substantially to the fact that many of these same, good middle-class folk resented putting out a few more percentage points of GNP in order to ameliorate conditions for the bona fide poor."[6]

What was driving the growth of the middle-class welfare state? At one level, it was raw politics, of course, as the senior power movement began to gather force and politicians scrambled to buy votes. In accord with one of the iron laws of governance, the very existence of government transfer programs created incentives for interest groups to organize. As Jonathan Rausch points out, "After Social Security and Medicare were in full swing, the elderly had so much at stake in Washington that they would have been crazy not to have organized, both to protect 'their' programs and to agitate for new benefits."[7]

It hardly mattered that, thanks to the spread of private pension plans, rising real estate values, improvements in health care, and other factors, the economic condition of older Americans was improving dramatically on its own. As with the middle class in general, increased affluence led to a demand for more government benefits, not less.

To understand why these efforts to expand the middle-class welfare state were suddenly so successful, one must give full weight as well to the power of ideas, and specifically to the idea of the affluent society as spread throughout different sectors of society. By the mid-1960s, hubris over the potential of the American economy was reaching its apogee. In 1966, Robert Theobald, author of *The Challenge of Abundance*, even went so far as to declare that "money itself is an anachronism." In Theobald's analysis: "Money was needed to ration scarce goods and industrial services in the past, but it is a highly unsatisfactory means of determining priorities in a cybernated era."[8]

This sense of a dawning golden age influenced all policymaking involving trade-offs between current and future consumption. "In the exuberance of the times," notes budget expert Allen Schick, "growth was seen as a good that could be sustained through skillful management of the economy. It was appropriate, therefore, to spend not only current fiscal dividends, but future ones as well."[9]

Believing that future generations would inevitably grow up to be far better off than current taxpayers, many economists even began to conceive of long-term public investments as a form of taxing the poor to benefit the rich. It is no coincidence that between 1965 and 1980, total public capital expenditures declined by 30 percent, from $33.7 billion to less than $24 billion. Measured as a percentage of gross national product, the nation's capital budget fell by more than 50 percent, according to estimates by the Council of State Planning Agencies.

The affluent society paradigm would have an even more profound effect when it came to the nation's social spending. Writing in the *Social Security Bulletin* in 1965, for example, commissioner Robert Ball announced that America had become such an affluent society that there were virtually no economic constraints left on expansion of the system, or on government social spending in general. "Poverty in the past has been basically the result of the fact there was not enough to go around," wrote Ball. "By contrast, today it can be taken as a fact that the abolition of want in the United States is no longer a problem of economic capacity."

The reason, again, was that the next generation was bound to become rich beyond imagination, no matter what. Just follow the trend lines, Ball argued: "Extremely conservative projections of what has been happening in industry lead to almost unbelievable conclusions. If we take not the rate of productivity increases that seems likely to result from the new [automated] approach to problems of production but instead merely the average rate over the past 100 years, our grandchildren will be able to produce in one day as much as we do in a 40-hour week."[10]

What were the implications for Social Security? In a speech the following year to the American Society for Public Administration, Ball described the Johnson administration's vision for the program. The first priority, he said, was to increase benefit levels. Ball conceded that approaches other than Social Security, such as public assistance or a negative income tax, could do a better job of supporting the very poor, but "why," he asked rhetorically, "would we want to limit our economic security objectives to such a goal? A 'minimum income for all' might have been a stirring objective when it was proposed by Sidney and Beatrice Webb about 1910, but we can do much better than that in the United States in 1966."[11]

"Doing better" for retirees, rich and poor alike, became a kind of contest in the Johnson administration. The president was so eager to raise Social Security benefits that, the following year, when his undersecretary of health, education, and welfare, Wilbur Cohen, came to him with a proposal for a 10 percent across-the-board increase, the president's reaction, according to Cohen, was, "'Come on, Wilbur, you can do better than that.'" As Cohen kept returning with successive proposals, Johnson kept repeating the refrain to "do better," until at last Cohen came in with a 15 percent increase to grace the administration's 1967 budget.[12]

FETAL FINANCE

No one much worried about what such generosity would eventually cost the young and the unborn, because everyone knew that future taxpayers in an affluent society could afford it. This idea was given explicit expression by Paul A. Samuelson, among the most influential economists of the era. In a 1967 column for *Newsweek*, Samuelson explained:

> The beauty about social insurance is that it is actuarially unsound. Everyone who reaches retirement age is given benefit privileges that far exceed anything he has paid in. And exceed his payments by more than ten times as much (or five times, counting in employer payments).
>
> How is this possible? It stems from the fact that the national product is growing at compound interest and can be expected to do so for as far ahead as the eye can see. Always there are more youths than old folks in a growing population. More important, with real incomes growing at some 3% per year, the taxable base upon which benefits rest in any period are *[sic]* much greater than the taxes paid historically by the generation now retired. . . . Social Security is squarely based on what has been called the eighth wonder of the world—compound interest. A growing nation is the greatest Ponzi game ever contrived. And that is a fact, not a paradox.[13]

Advocates seeking to expand Social Security, Medicare, and other middle-class entitlements were quick to see the political implications of such utopian predictions. In 1970, the Special Committee on Aging held hearings, revealingly entitled "The Economics of Aging: Toward a Full Share in Abundance." Setting the tone for the hearings, Nelson H. Cruikshank, president of the National Council of Senior Citizens, testified: "Bold new steps are long overdue, steps that would immediately enable today's retirees to share in the abundance they helped to create."[14]

One of the more cunning of those bold steps was a little-noticed change in how Social Security calculated its long-term debts. Casting about for ways to finance a major expansion of the system without raising taxes, Social Security administrators instructed their actuaries to adopt so-called dynamic earnings assumptions. Specifically, the actuaries were instructed to assume in their long-term projections for the system that real wage levels would continuously rise from one generation to the next.[15]

Instantly, the huge deficits that were actually looming in Social Security vanished, at least on paper. And sure enough, with all this "new" money to spend, Nixon and Democratic barons in Congress soon engaged in a bidding contest to see who could raise Social Security benefits the most. In 1972, the bidding finally came to a halt when Nixon signed into law a bill that raised Social Security benefits by 20 percent and for the first time indexed benefits for inflation. Using "dynamic earnings" assumptions, the Social Security Administration promised that the system would still never cost more than 10.2 percent of payroll.

Despite making such reckless bets with the next generation's money, Social Security activists at the time assured everyone that they were actually acting with great conservatism. On the eve of his retirement in 1973, social security commissioner Robert Ball predicted that tax rates then in effect would remain level or even drop slightly over the next forty years. Appearing before a Senate committee, Ball testified that if official projections erred, it was on the conservative side, assuring the senators, "I have a lot of confidence in that."[16]

Even with the Vietnam War going badly, the U.S. trade deficit yawning, and commodity prices beginning to rise ominously, Ball had no trouble finding well-connected economists to back up his optimism. Juanita Kreps, a disciple of Spengler and then a rising star among economists working in the field of aging, reassured policymakers that by 1985, the U.S. economy would become so large and efficient that, without any reduction in overall production, it would provide American society with any one of the following options:

- A universal twenty-two-hour workweek.
- A twenty-two-week standard vacation.
- Retirement at age thirty-eight for everyone.[17]

Ironically, just five years later, Kreps would find herself, as Carter's new secretary of commerce, arguing that American business could not withstand the burden of bailing out Social Security with what became the largest tax hike in history to that date.

The United States was entering a new age of limits in which real wages for the young would not grow, even while the tax bills and debt service charged to their account became unprecedented. Yet for the American political system, facing up to the consequences of the country's economic hubris during the postwar era would prove impossible. Middle-class workers would scapegoat the poor for the mounting cost of government but never admit their own role, or that of their parents, in creating a new deficit state that encumbered their children. New senior power militants demanded to keep "what we've got coming to us"—come what may. As the affluent society yielded to deindustrialization, America became gripped by a new politics of denial.

4

Denial

Ann Cummins, a pretty young widow with two children, received many threats, including one from a woman promising to put a rattlesnake in her home if she did not move. After finding her rented house broken into, the Christmas tree knocked over, and some of the children's gifts beneath it stolen, Cummins got the message and left Youngtown, Arizona, for good in 1995.

Youngtown was no place to be young, anyway—a town without pity. Retirees would chase children down the street with canes.

"It gets to you and it gets to the children," another young mother in town told a reporter. Her seven-year-old boy had been "frightened to death by taunts from some older residents," said Mrs. Fred Schott. "We've had all kinds of calls from people telling us to get out of town and threatening to blow up our house if we didn't. And we get cards and letters saying we don't belong here and should be put in jail."[1]

To the casual observer, Youngtown might appear to be an ideal place to raise a family. Conveniently located fifteen miles from bustling Phoenix, Youngtown in the early 1970s had a population of just 1,900. It was a neat community of two-bedroom homes, many with citrus trees and cactus in the front yard. But the problem for young families attracted to its quiet and seemingly safe streets was who got there first.

Save Youngtown for Retirees (SYR) was formed in June 1974 after a group of residents observed that a school bus was making a stop in their neighborhood. The presence of children living in Youngtown enraged these seniors. They objected that the community's developer had promised, back when he began building in 1960, that the town would be America's first incorporated retirement community. They didn't want to pay for schools or listen to children playing in the street. Wrote one outraged SYR activist to the local newspaper:

> Youngtown was founded for the older American. This is our choice and we older Americans have the right to choose our own lifestyle, which we have earned after two world wars and a depression. Young people should not be allowed to take this right away from us. The few who would upset our lifestyle are *traitors to their own generation* and are not an asset to the community."[2]

The president of the local chapter of the American Association of Retired Persons agreed. "It would be criminal to bring a child to live here," said Eric Robinson, a seventy-one-year-old retired traveling salesman. "We have nothing for them, and we don't intend to have."

The troubles at Youngtown soon became very serious indeed. Before it was over, two members of SYR would be convicted for illegal trespassing and assault. But far from feeling the sting of any opprobrium from the outside world, the town's elders found themselves being celebrated far and wide.

Robinson would later report that he received thirty letters from people from all over the world, all but two of them positive. "Most of them want to come and live with us," he boasted. After a report about young families being run out of Youngtown appeared in the *New York Times*, a New York retiree felt so inspired he wrote a letter to the editor concluding, *"Aux armes, senior citoyens!"*[3]

It was a cry heard throughout Arizona and beyond, as the example of Youngtown inspired a new, militant antichildren's movement.

DENIAL

A group calling itself Adults Only formed in Apache Well, Arizona, in December 1974. Two years later, the group boasted twenty-six dues-paying member organizations representing thousands of individuals in adult communities throughout the state, including Sun Lakes Home Owners Association, Mesa Mobile Estates Association, and Save Youngtown for Retirees, Inc.

Lobbying efforts by Adults Only were highly successful. At the time, Arizona protected families with children by specifically barring age discrimination in housing. But on June 13, 1975, pressed by Adults Only and ignoring the objections of the American Civil Liberties Union, Governor Raul Castro signed a bill making it illegal for persons to rent or sell to families with minor children in areas designated as exclusive adult subdivisions. The penalty for a first violation of the new law was a fine of not more than $500. For subsequent violation the penalty was a $500 fine and/or three months in the county jail. Soon the last of Youngtown's youngsters hit the road.

PULLING UP THE LADDER

During the 1970s, the place of children in American society, particularly "other people's children," suffered a radical devaluation, while the power and the prestige of adults, particularly a new group coming to be known as "our senior citizens," increased dramatically. Arizona's Adults Only movement, though extreme, was a harbinger of a more general cultural tilt away from the interests of the next generation.

Writing in 1977, the historian David Hackett Fischer, who was then completing work on a pathbreaking history of old age in America, cautioned against what he saw as ongoing attempts to reinvent a form of gerontocracy. The agenda of some aging activists of the time reminded Fischer of colonial New England, where sons had been bound to their fathers by ties of economic dependency, and youth was the hostage of age. "Those who seek to solve the 'problem' of old age today by reversing the age bias of modern America might learn from our historical experience," warned Fischer, "that reversal is not the best of remedies. The cult of youth was preceded in our history by a cult of age that was equally destructive of human relations."4

Underlying the rising cult of seniority in the 1970s was a sharp drop in the perceived productive potential of the U.S. economy. After the oil shocks and deep recession of 1973, the economic hubris of leading policy intellectuals quickly vanished. Even Nixon would be reduced to calling the United States a "helpless, pitiful giant." Many economists worried that the U.S. economy had lost its ability to grow without inflation. For the first time since 1893, the country no longer ran a trade surplus. The U.S. textile industry had been the first to collapse. Now strategic industries like steel, auto, and consumer electronics were losing markets both at home and abroad to foreign competition. In the Cambridge boutiques, the talk was no longer of the "challenge of abundance" but rather of a new "age of limits."

In some quarters, these diminished expectations for the future led to a revival of stewardship as a political value. Suddenly it became fashionable to talk of conserving oil and other nonrenewable natural resources "in the interest of future generations" and to warn about an impending "tragedy of the commons." But for the larger culture, the demise of the affluent society paradigm, far from leading to a revival stewardship, created just the opposite political ethos. As the realization spread throughout American society that the U.S. economy could not deliver on the inflated expectations of the 1950s and 1960s, Americans—and members of the middle class especially—sought to preserve their eroding standard of living by securing still more entitlements. Seniors concentrated on expanding direct spending programs like Social Security and Medicare, while working-aged Americans mostly concentrated on securing subsidies through increased tax expenditures and more tax loopholes. But the results were the same: a politics dominated by special interest groups that more and more discounted the interests of the young and future generations.

THE NEW TAX ENTITLEMENTS

During the 1970s, total Social Security benefits rose by 84 percent even after adjusting for inflation, and total Medicare benefits rose by 132 percent in real terms. This striking growth in transfers, made primarily to the elderly, occurred during a period when the population aged sixty-five and older rose by less than 13 percent. Economist Laurence J. Kotlikoff estimates that the totality of new government transfer payments and other policies put into effect during the 1970s resulted in a net windfall of $19,300 for a typical sixty-year-old male.[5]

Yet Social Security and Medicare were by no means the only middle-class entitlements with exploding costs. During the 1970s, as federal income tax rates rose and inflation pushed middle-class Americans into higher and higher tax brackets, another form of entitlement began to assume more and more importance in subsiding middle-class lifestyles: federal tax expenditures.

Such subsidies had long existed. Back in 1918, for example, when patriotic fervor for U.S. troops in Europe was running high, political leaders in Washington felt they should do something dramatic to reward the doughboys. Facing a tight budget, Congress hesitated to raise veterans' benefits directly. But then someone on Capitol Hill took a look at the five-year-old federal income tax system and came up with a nifty idea: Why not "raise" veterans' benefits simply by exempting such benefits from the tax?

Over the years, many more tax expenditures had followed, nearly all of them created entirely off-budget, with no estimation of eventual cost and far from the scrutiny that normally accompanies direct appropriations. Several, including the exemption of certain Social Security benefits from taxation and the exclusion of employer-paid health care, were created not by Congress but by offhand Internal Revenue Service rulings in the 1930s and 1940s. At the time, no one paid them much notice because tax rates were low, Social Security benefits were modest, and company health plans were rare.

But by the 1970s, all this was beginning to change. Among the first to notice was Stanley S. Surrey, a Harvard Law School don who served as assistant secretary of the treasury for tax policy in the Kennedy and Johnson administrations.[6] In the course of his battles with Congress over tax policy, Surrey was struck by the fact that Congress was increasingly using selective tax reductions for specific groups of people rather than direct appropriations as a means of distributing public resources.

Surrey's favorite example was the deduction for medical expenses. He explained that this tax provision had precisely the same impact, on both the budget and the public, as a multibillion dollar benefit program that heavily favored the very rich (because they pay taxes at the highest rates) and that entirely excluded the very poor (because they don't pay taxes at all). There was indeed only one big difference: the same Congress that created the tax provision would never dare to create the benefit program.

By 1979, the Office of Management and Budget had identified more than ninety different federal tax expenditure programs. The total cost in lost revenue of these programs was over $100 billion, more than twice as large as that year's entire federal deficit.[7] And this was only the beginning. Between the 1970s and the 1990s the cost of federal tax expenditures would grow some 60 percent faster than the economy. By 1993 the total bill would reach $400 billion, with the General Accounting Office projecting a future rate of growth at least 50 percent higher than expected economic growth.[8]

BACKLASH AND DEPENDENCY

Along with tax expenditures and "social insurance" programs, means-tested entitlements also grew dramatically during the 1970s. Why did welfare mothers seem to lose any sense of shame in accepting government handouts during this era? One reason was that clients of programs like Medicaid and Aid to Families with Dependent Children could see that the middle class was also on the dole, and so developed their own overweening sense of entitlement.

Recalling her days as a welfare recipient and rights activist in the late 1960s and 1970s, Theresa Funiciello, for example, writes, "There was a distinct sort of patter that peppered meetings. . . . Virtually everybody in the country was on some sort of welfare (farm subsidies, corporate bailouts, college scholarships, social security and the like) but they all pretended not to be. . . . In this context, welfare recipients were insiders, everyone else was outside. I liked that."[9]

Many liberals of the era also saw the same parallels and sought to take ideological advantage of them. Indeed, one of the earliest uses of the term *entitlement* as a political concept came from liberal law professors and judges who used it to stress that welfare recipients had at least as much right to subsidies as the rich and middle class.

One such was Charles Reich, a Harvard Law School professor. In the early 1970s, Reich would attain celebrity status for his groovy, best-selling book, *The Greening of America.* In liberal academic circles, he was revered for his formulations about welfare and property rights. Reich argued that the welfare state had altered the status of all American citizens to the point that our very concept of property had to change. Entitlement to welfare, Reich argued, was as much a property right as entitlement to Social Security, or for that matter entitlement to land that one may have bought and paid for. Benefits such as unemployment compensation, public assistance, and old age insurance were all alike, Reich maintained, in embodying the "concept of right."[10]

By the early 1970s, Reich's analysis had entered the mainstream of legal theory. Indeed, it became the basis for a landmark U.S. Supreme Court decision that first established the term *entitlement* as a legal concept. The case was *Goldberg* v. *Kelley,* which pitted New York City and state welfare authorities against a beneficiary who had been cut off without a hearing because he refused counseling for a drug addiction that he denied having.

In 1970, Justice William Brennan, in writing for the majority in the *Goldberg* case, made use of Reich's arguments. Noting that much of the wealth Americans enjoyed now came in the form of tax exemptions, Social Security, and unemployment compensation and other "rights that do not fall within traditional common-law concepts of property," Brennan went on to argue that therefore "it may be realistic today to regard welfare entitlements as more like 'property' than a 'gratuity.'"[11]

This position was amplified by Justice Potter Stewart, who held (in *Board of Regents of State Colleges* v. *Roth,* 1972) that "a person's interest in a benefit is a 'property' interest for due process purposes if there are such rules or mutually explicit understandings that support his claim of entitlement to benefits."[12]

The Court still allowed Congress the right to cut benefit programs—welfare and Social Security alike—across the board at any time. But it also held that so long as such programs were in place, bureaucrats and social workers could not simply cut individuals off the rolls without offering them the chance to prove their eligibility, or "entitlement," to benefits under current law.

MIDDLE-CLASS VICTIMOLOGY

So it was that the expansion of the middle-class welfare state during the 1970s encouraged and legitimated the growth of entitlements for the poor, both politically and legally. But the opposite was true too: as poverty programs grew in size and cost, middle-class resentment did as well. In 1960, 7.1 million people received public assistance. By 1974, their number had more than doubled to 14.4 million.[13] This tidal wave of welfare dependency deepened the middle-class's resolve to collect "back" more of the money it was sending to Washington, if not through direct government spending, then through tax breaks and subsidies.

In the vanguard of this spreading sense of suburban victimization were the middle-class elderly. In 1970, a Cape May, New Jersey, widow, testifying before the Senate Select Committee on Aging, advanced the then-still-radical idea that it would be helpful if she and her set didn't have to pay school taxes. "My husband and I have always had our own home," she testified, "and we have helped build so many schools that I think it's about time that something is done for us."[14]

By the end of the 1970s, that idea was mainstream. Communities all over the country began adopting "circuit breakers" and other devices for granting preferential property tax rates to older home owners at the expense of everyone else.

California's Proposition 13 was the most massive example of the phenomenon, and again middle-class seniors were in the vanguard of the movement to secure its passage. There was no mystery why. The measure promised current home owners that their property assessments would be rolled back and frozen at 1975–1976 levels, except for a token 2 percent annual hike for inflation. New homes and newly bought homes would be assessed at current market values.

This disparity would be compounded over time as market values continued to rise. The result, as Robert Kuttner wrote shortly after Proposition 13 passed in 1979, was a massive shift of the tax burden from the old to the young. "Mom and Pop, who bought their house in the fifties, already enjoyed a housing bargain," Kuttner noted. "Their mortgage payments, perhaps $200 a month, reflected the low housing prices of those years, while the kids paid $700 and $800 a month to amortize mortgages upward of $60,000, at interest rates topping 10%. Now, to add insult to injury, Proposition 13 would grandfather the longtime homeowners' taxes as well, while the new buyer would be taxed at ever-increasing rates."[15]

Shifting costs to latecomers was now an institutionalized value in American politics, and the politicians cleverly continued to think of more and more new mechanisms for borrowing from the next generation. The age of entitlement was in full flower.

5

The Big Crack-Up

What's in a word? The power to define an age.

The first use of *entitlement* in its modern sense came in 1974, in the context of the winding down of the war in Vietnam. Many Americans, including federal budgeters, were hoping that the end of the war would bring a large peace dividend, as had occurred after World War II and Korea. But the peace dividend never came. Instead, federal spending each year rose to unprecedented new heights, driven primarily by the cost of Social Security, Medicare, and other transfer payments.

Something fundamental and structural had changed. For the first time in American history, federal spending, some budget experts realized, was out of control.

Historically, the federal government spent most of its money financing its own projects and operations. The biggest budget shares went to the military. Most of the rest went to agencies like the Interior Department, which spent virtually all of their funds on salaries, supplies and equipment, travel, and other purchases of goods and services. So long as this was true, controlling the budget was relatively easy. As budget expert Allen Schick notes: "The tools for cutting expenditures were simple but adequate. Budget makers would estimate available resources and could scour the lists of items requested by agencies to determine where savings could be obtained."[1]

But by the 1970s, the composition of federal spending had changed dramatically. With the growth of programs like Social Security and Medicare, more and more of the federal budget consisted of transfer payments from one group of citizens to another. In the case of such programs, huge sums flowed through the federal government on their way from taxpayers to beneficiaries, in accord with complex tax and spending formulas. But few of these sums were subject to any formal budget process, much less to control by the White House or federal administrators. In 1974, when President Nixon announced the first budget ever to reach $300 billion, he lamented that 90 percent of the increase in spending over the preceding year was mandatory.[2] He could not legally have avoided it without getting Congress to repeal at least some of the benefit promises it had made in the past.

The proliferation and growing expense of such benefit promises in the early 1970s created a need among budget experts for a term to describe them generically. It also created a need for some mechanism that Congress could impose upon itself to try to contain their growth. Both came in the form of the Budget and Impoundment Act of 1974, in which the term *entitlement* was first used in a legal document to describe a whole category of federal spending.

The authors of the Budget Act sought to curtail what they referred to as "legislation providing entitlement authority." To make it more difficult for Congress to pass runaway spending programs, the act required that any bill making a promise of future benefits also specify that these benefits be funded through annual, as opposed to open-ended, appropriation.[3]

In other words, Congress forbade itself from writing just another blank check for whatever turned out to be the cost of new social programs, and instead resolved to debate and appropriate funds formally for their cost each year. The measure may have actually helped slow the growth of new entitlements in the years that followed. But unfortunately the genie was already out of the bottle, as the cost of existing entitlement programs skyrocketed out of control.[4]

REALITY CHECK

This history helps explain why today the term *entitlements* refers to both social insurance and welfare programs alike. From a budgeter's perspective, there is little difference between the two types of programs. Both must be funded out of current tax receipts or federal borrowing, and both have costs that are driven by forces outside government control, such as how many children welfare recipients decide to have or how many older Americans elect for early retirement on Social Security.

Appropriately enough, the first mention of *entitlements* in the mainstream media came in the form of quotations from government officials explaining why they couldn't control federal spending. A 1974 article in the *New York Times*, for example, quoted President Ford's budget director, Roy Ash, describing why the administration would be unable to balance the fiscal year 1976 budget. Entitlement programs, Ash noted, had grown to consume more than 50 percent of the budget and yet could be altered only through new legislation.[5] A month later, the *Times* reported on a new study by Ash that attempted to analyze the budget's "uncontrollability." A central factor in driving the budget out of control, the *Times* reported, was the cost of "entitlement programs."[6]

Budget wonks were worried about more than just the current costs of entitlements. The biggest source of concern, for those who followed the budget closely (and comparatively few Americans—in or out of government—did in those days), was the effect of unexpected economic and demographic trends on future entitlement spending.

One of the most significant and long-lasting of these trends was the end of the baby boom. By the mid-1970s, fertility rates had been declining for almost two decades and were now dropping precipitously below replacement levels. In 1974, when Social Security actuaries finally revised their fertility assumption to reflect current reality, the result was a very large projected long-term deficit for the program. By simply counting heads, it was clear that there would come a period in the next century when the number of retirees would grow much faster than the number of workers and that current tax rates would be nowhere near sufficient to cover the extra cost.

Meanwhile, life expectancy among the elderly continued to improve dramatically. Just between 1970 and 1977, the decline in mortality rates among the elderly ranged from 4 percent for men over age eighty-five to 16 percent for women aged sixty-five to seventy-four.[7] And as Americans were living longer, they were retiring earlier. During the 1960s, the labor force participation rate for elderly men fell from 33 to 27 percent. During the 1970s, it plummeted further to 20 percent.

The implications of these trends for federal spending were ominous, as a few farsighted demographers and budget analysts realized. By 1975, per capita expenditures for the elderly, at all levels of government, already exceeded the amount spent on children seventeen and under—including the total spent on public education—by more than three to one.[8] Given this extreme budgetary bias in favor of the elderly, any increase in the retired population would drive up social spending geometrically, even if Congress enacted no new benefits.

Meanwhile, after the hard recession of 1973–1974, a new unfavorable trend began to emerge. Even as the economy recovered, productivity growth did not return to the levels achieved during the 1950s and 1960s. Some economists blamed the trend on inadequate investment, others on the influx of women and young people into the job market, but whatever the cause, there was one clear implication: unless the trend reversed itself, not only would there be fewer workers to support each retiree in the future, but those workers wouldn't necessarily grow up to be as efficient as policymakers in the 1950s and 1960s had planned on their becoming. In 1967, Paul Samuelson had justified increased spending on the elderly by declaring, "A growing nation is the greatest Ponzi game ever contrived." But by the 1970s, the rapid rates of economic and population growth that Samuelson had assumed would always pay the bills were starting to fade.

And finally there was a third trend driving entitlement spending out of control: inflation. Ironically, when Congress enacted automatic cost-of-living adjustments (COLAs) for Social Security beneficiaries in 1972, the Nixon administration and many Republican congressmen saw it as a cost-containment measure that would help take the politics out of the program. The thinking was that by tying benefits increases to an automatic index, the Democratic majority in Congress would be prevented from raising benefits faster than inflation, as it had done consistently since the end of the 1950s.

Democratic barons in Congress, meanwhile, were sure that indexing wouldn't impose any fiscal burden on the program, since the nation was bound to solve its modest inflation problem in short order. "We are not going to let the cost of living go up," Ways and Means chairman Wilbur Mills reassured Social Security's chief actuary during hearings on the feasibility of indexing. "We are going to stop it here one of these days. . . . We are already committed to that."[9]

MAINLINING COLAS

History would reveal the futility of such talk in short order, as the inflation rate shot up to 12.2 percent by 1974. The problem with indexing wasn't just its unfortunate timing. The formulas used to set the new COLAs would also turn out to be deeply flawed. As a result, beneficiaries received far more than the actual rise in their cost of living, thereby giving those receiving the checks a stake in the very inflation that was impoverishing younger taxpayers.

One reason for this was that the consumer price index (CPI), upon which COLAs were based, was itself deeply flawed in those days. The CPI attempted to measure inflation by tracking increases in the price of selected goods and services, weighted according to the consumption pattern of a typical consumer. That was a sound enough approach for measuring inflation in any one year, but over time, as prices of different items change relative to one another, so do consumption patterns. For example, as energy prices rose in the 1970s, Americans found ways to use less energy through conservation and increased efficiency. But in calculating the overall cost of living, the

CPI continued to give the same weight to energy prices year after year, as if Americans were continuing to use the same amount of energy as they had before the OPEC oil crisis.

Another way the CPI overstated the real change in the cost of living was by giving too much weight to housing costs. Until 1985, the CPI failed to account for the fact that while rising real estate prices might be hard on renters, they were great for home owners. As millions of middle-class Americans found out in the 1970s, if you own your own home, a rise in home prices brings a rise in home equity and an automatic shrinkage of your mortgage, not any real decrease in your standard of living.

The CPI, precisely because it exaggerated the real cost of living for home owners, substantially exaggerated the cost of living for most Social Security beneficiaries as well. Already by the 1970s, three-quarters of the elderly owned their own homes, and two-thirds owned them outright. In contrast, only 12 percent of all adults under fifty-five owned a fully paid-off home. The excessive housing "push" to the CPI thus benefited precisely those Americans least likely to be paying for a first-time home. Meanwhile, of course, no price index—not even a realistic one—protected the incomes of younger Americans, then or now.

The cumulative effect of overindexing on federal entitlement spending was enormous. From 1970 through 1982, the CPI rose about 21 percent faster than actual inflation.[10] This meant that, over and above the substantial benefit increases actually voted into law by Congress, all cash beneficiaries who began collecting in 1970 saw their monthly benefit checks go up by an extra one-fifth during the next twelve years.

And that was only part of the windfall inflation brought. Automatic indexing of benefits to the CPI kept all current beneficiaries ahead of inflation, and new retirees got a double boost. That was because initial Social Security benefits have always been determined by a formula that multiplies a worker's average monthly wages times a certain percentage. The more you make over your lifetime—even if only because of inflation—the bigger your benefit.

This formula in itself ensured that new Social Security retirees would receive benefits that reflected the effect of inflation.[11] On top of this came the overly generous COLAs. At a time when real wages weren't growing at all, this double indexing meant that Social Security was becoming progressively much more generous, and much more of a burden on the working population—even without Congress's so much as taking a vote. From the early 1950s to the late 1960s, Social Security paid workers retiring at age sixty-five between 31 and 32 percent of their last year's earnings. After a series of steep benefit hikes enacted by Congress in the late 1960s and early 1970s, this so-called replacement ratio rose to 38 percent. Starting in 1975, the double-indexed COLAs caused automatic giant jumps in the replacement ratio: from 45 percent in 1979 to 47 percent in 1980, and to 51 percent in 1981 (the best year ever to retire at age sixty-five on Social Security).

All these trends together drove Social Security into the ground in short order. As we've seen, the system was on the verge of bankruptcy by 1977, and Congress and the Carter administration were forced to enact a bailout package that constituted the largest single tax hike in history until that time. But the same reckless optimism that had driven the program into insolvency continued even after this massive reality check. Social Security's actuaries dutifully projected that with payroll taxes now rising to an "ultimate" scheduled rate of 12.4 percent of taxable payroll by 1990, the system could easily meet its obligations for at least the next seventy-five years. Instead, in just five years, the cost of Social Security outgrew its revenue base again, creating the biggest political and economic crisis in its history and the need for an even more massive bailout—this time under a Republican administration.

REAGAN'S PSEUDO-REVOLUTION

The breakout of the term *entitlements* into the mainstream culture occurred in the early 1980s. On April 9, 1981, *U.S. News & World Report* referred to the "revolution" in "entitlements." (In a feature on transfer programs a month earlier, the term was not used.) Later that year, *Time, Business Week,* and other magazines also referred to the problem of entitlements, surrounding the still-new term with quotation marks to signify its nonstandard usage.[12]

Soon media interest in entitlements intensified. In the spring of 1981, when the Reagan administration released its annual budget forecast, it did what no other administration had ever done before: for years ahead, it predicted a smooth, robust return to national prosperity, yet it still projected budget deficits that would hover in the vicinity of $100 billion a year.

Reagan's tax cuts, and his proposed military buildup, were part of the reason, of course. But those who understood what was driving the budget knew better than to ignore the single largest factor behind all the red ink. Seeking to explain the new reality of structural deficits stretching as far as the eye could see, sophisticated political commentators, most notably James Fallows of the *Atlantic Monthly*, began popularizing the concept of entitlements as it had come to be used and understood by federal budget wonks.[13]

Soon the press was full of talk about entitlements, both pro and con. In an interview with *U.S. News & World Report*, the conservative philosopher Robert Nozick complained, for example, "There's too much emphasis on so-called entitlement rights."[14] William Safire, meanwhile, in explaining the sudden popularity of the term in one of his "On Language" columns, noted that it still contained some ambiguity. Safire concluded: "Liberals take care to divide funds transferred to people by the Government into public assistance—welfare—and entitlements, which carries the connotation of 'earned, deserved.' Conservatives tend to lump the two together and demand that a cap be placed on it."[15]

Conservative usage carried the day, and entitlements, defined to include middle-class social insurance programs, came to be widely seen as a major cause of the deficits. By 1982, the number of articles in the *New York Times* mentioning both "entitlements" and "deficits" in their copy shot to 122, up from just 19 two years earlier. But amid all the new talk about the "problem of entitlements," there was no action, not even from a conservative administration that claimed to be bent on smashing the New Deal order.

One reason was that moderate Republicans were up to their ears in complicity for the runaway cost of entitlement programs. Between 1956 and 1977, Congress had passed thirteen major acts expanding or liberalizing the social insurance programs. These included the creation of the Social Security disability program in 1956, Medicare in 1965, and the big benefit increases in the early 1970s. Over two decades an average of 80 percent of House Republicans and 90 percent of Senate Republicans had voted for these expansions.[16]

Even after Reagan and the New Right captured the party in 1980, ascendant forces within the conservative movement continued to declare entitlement cuts off-limits. In 1980, Irving Kristol, a leading conservative thinker of the day, was a guest speaker before the House Republican caucus. Dispensing what he took to be "political realism," the great intellectual told Republican politicians: "Don't be foolish! Your constituents are the elderly, the farmers, and the veterans. Don't alienate them, don't cut their programs."[17]

The Republican party obviously took his advice. But there was one problem with what Kristol had to say that day: these three constituencies accounted for two-thirds of the entire cost of the welfare state. How could Reagan deliver his giant tax cut, finance an arms buildup, and still exempt two-thirds of the welfare state from spending cuts? Kristol didn't explain.[18]

The Reagan administration did manage to trim the growth of some obscure middle-class entitlement programs. For example, the administration succeeded in capping the COLA in the railroad retirement program at slightly below the inflation rate, which reduced overall spending by 0.0001 percent.[19] But Reagan shrank from taking on the real entitlement monsters, such as Social Security, Medicare, and other social insurance programs from the middle class.

The result was that Reagan's vaunted income tax cuts were just make-believe for most Americans. Even before the tax cuts were fully phased in, working people were socked with a tax increase much larger than what they had supposedly just been given. In 1983, to cover the cost of bailing out Social Security one more time, Reagan and Congress struck a deal under which they raised payroll taxes on working Americans by roughly $200 billion—more than erasing any gain they might have anticipated from the Reagan income tax cuts.[20]

"Why did the conservative, anti-spending party (GOP) end up ratifying a half-trillion dollar per year welfare state?" Reagan's budget director David Stockman asked several years later after he'd safely left public office. "In the answer lies the modern dirty little secret of the Republican Party," Stockman noted. "The conservative opposition helped build the American welfare state brick by brick during the three decades prior to 1980."[21] After one term of George Bush—during which real federal benefits grew 50 percent faster than during the term of Jimmy Carter—it's only appropriate to update Stockman's remark to include the four decades prior to the early 1990s.

Could any party have taken on the growth of the middle-class welfare state and still remained in power? Perhaps not until the true cost of these programs became more apparent to the rising new generation of middle-class Americans. Even today, the self-serving myths, the hidden subsidies, the organized interests, and the cults of victimization that surround most middle-class entitlement programs make reform painful indeed, no matter how inevitable in the long term. In Part II of this book, we examine seven case studies of the middle-class welfare state, to see how the major programs actually work and how they reflect broader trends and attitudes in American society that cannot be sustained into the next century.

PART II

CASE STUDIES

6

Manufacturing Social Security

D-day minus 2. Inside a vault over three hundred feet long, scores of U.S. Treasury Department workers, screened by both the Secret Service and the FBI, scurry as the clock counts down. Acoustical devices implanted in the ceiling listen for any sound out of the ordinary, such as a pistol's report. At the loading dock outside, armed guards stand at the ready, as a forty-four-foot, eighteen-wheel tractor-trailer slowly backs into place to receive its half-billion-dollar load.

This is the so-called Boston truck, named for its final destination. A specially trained twelve-member crew immediately goes into action, loading, sealing, and locking the trailer as quickly as possible. As the rig pulls away from the Treasury Department's production plant on Townsend Avenue in Philadelphia, it begins a twenty-four-hour journey through the northeastern United States, following a route and schedule that must not be broken. To protect against the threat of an inside job, the truck's driver has been told that at any point he may be trailed by special agents in unmarked cars.

These and other security measures are more than justified. The

73

cargo transported by this semi is literally worth more than twice its weight in gold.

It isn't bullion the Boston truck hauls: it's government benefits. On board are roughly 600,000 Social Security checks, due in beneficiaries' mailboxes by D-day, less than forty-eight hours away. Neither flat tires, nor riots, nor leaking air brakes, nor even collapsing bridges along Interstate 95 can keep this truck from swiftly completing its monthly journey. Social Security recipients expect their checks and expect them on time; it's a matter of entitlement.

Just who exactly along the Boston truck's route will get a check, and for how much, was determined many days before. The mainframes at Social Security headquarters in Baltimore hum seven days a week, twenty-four hours a day, adding new beneficiaries' names, taking the dead off the rolls, adding cost-of-living adjustments and making other "postentitlement changes" to the Social Security Administration's (SSA) so-called master payment file. Every twenty hours, SSA technicians transmit another updated batch of the master file to SSA's regional processing centers, located in Philadelphia, Birmingham, Chicago, Kansas City, and San Francisco. And from each of these centers, every twenty hours, vans pull out carrying racks of 2,400-foot computer reels, plus accompanying paperwork, bound for the nearest Treasury check-writing plant.

As the delivery date for Social Security draws near on the third working day of each month, postal trucks bearing checks fan out from Philadelphia. On D-day minus 4, vans run for the airport, bearing fliers for the 20 percent of all check recipients who have moved out of the region to distant locations since their younger days. On D-2 the Richmond truck heads south, stopping at postal distribution facilities in Baltimore and northern Virginia along the way, while the Pittsburgh truck heads west and the Boston truck moves north. During these key final days, the Philadelphia plant will mail a total of 9 to 10 million checks. Then, on D-0, its computers transmit an impulse into the U.S. banking system that sends another 9 to 10 million checks to recipients who elect for direct deposit.

With the completion of each month's production cycle, a wave of spending power washes over the American economy. Social Security accounts for more than one out of five dollars the federal government spends and amounts to some 5 percent of the gross domestic product. Only a small portion of this money flows to people in poverty. While only about 14 percent of Social Security dollars go to households with income below $10,000, more than 20 percent goes to households with income above $50,000. For such middle- and upper-class households, Social Security provides an average boast of income of around $12,000 to $14,000 a year.[1]

The multiplier effect is felt from the strip malls of Las Vegas and surrounding Clark County (whose retired population grew by 121 percent during the 1980s), to the car dealerships of Sun City, Arizona, to the mountain craft shops of Asheville, North Carolina, to the condo canyons of south Florida. In Monroe Township, New Jersey, where more than half the population lives in sprawling, age-segregated retirement communities, Santo Intravartolo, owner of Corkscrew Wines and Liquors, Ltd., enthuses: "Most of our business is seniors; we deliver and we cater to them. It's very stabilized. We aren't affected by plant layoffs or what-have-you."[2]

THE FLOPPY IN YOUR FUTURE

It's nearly impossible to overstate the influence of Social Security on American life. Every month the system sends out $25 billion in checks to about 47 million Americans. The money runs like the mighty Mississippi through the heartland of American culture, its currents transforming the nature of work, family, and the economy itself. Its effects on behavior dwarf those of such comparatively tiny programs as Aid to Families with Dependent Children. Between 1957 and 1992, for example, the percentage of American men aged sixty-five to sixty-nine remaining in the workforce dropped by half, from 52.6 percent to 25.9 percent, a trend largely attributable to the retirement subsidies provided by Social Security.[3] Oddly, ordinary Americans know little about how Social Security actually works, largely because of the web of myth and propaganda that has surrounded the program since its inception.

As we have seen, Social Security officials have long characterized the program as a form of insurance. They are also fond of such insurance-related terms as *trust funds, reserves,* and even *surpluses.* There is no mystery why the program's advocates choose to speak this way. As Martha Derthick has pointed out, insurance has always been the central symbol of all Social Security messages, "and it was stressed precisely because it was expected to secure public acceptance. Because insurance implied a return for work and investment, it preserved the self-respect of the beneficiaries; because it implied a return in proportion to investment, it satisfied a widely held conception of fairness; and because it implied the existence of a contract, it appeared sound and certain."[4]

But in reality, Social Security is not an insurance program. Moreover, it isn't financed by a trust fund. Indeed, what are known as the Social Security trust funds are really just bookkeeping entries designed to keep track of how much of a burden the system is imposing on the next generation of taxpayers.

To understand how Social Security really works, it's helpful to be as literal as possible about the program's operations so as not to be misled by mere words. Don't think about trust funds and reserves; think about postal trucks in motion.

Begin, then, with a simple question: Where does the money come from to pay for each month's Social Security benefits? Actually, it comes from the same places all the government's other money comes from. Each day, roughly $4 billion flows into government accounts maintained by the Federal Reserve in Washington. About $3 billion of this comes from taxes and user fees of every variety: income taxes, cigarette taxes, payroll taxes, gas taxes, admission tickets to the national parks, grazing fees, landing fees, copying machines at the Library of Congress, gift shop sales at the Statue of Liberty, tariffs and import duties, and so forth. The other billion or so dollars a day comes from federal borrowing.

As fast as the money builds up in these accounts, federal agencies draw it out. Social Security extracts its take each month starting on D-0, drawing out just enough over the next several days to cover the float on the $25 billion worth of checks it has just sent around the world.

MANUFACTURING SOCIAL SECURITY

Once the checks clear, there is never any money left over. But months after the fact, government accountants will update a special ledger, or memo account, showing the difference, if any, between what the Social Security Administration has been spending for retirement and disability benefits and what the Internal Revenue Service has been collecting in payroll taxes.

The last time I checked, the keeper of this ledger was Ronald Iroff. A friendly, bearded man in his forties who peers out at the world through bispectacles, Iroff works in an obscure back office of the Funds Management Division of the Financial Management Service, located in the Treasury Department building on Fourteenth Street in Washington, next to the Bureau of Engraving and Printing.

There, in a cubicle outside his office, sits an aging IBM-clone 386-chip personal computer, loaded with an antiviral program that runs as it is booted up and an off-the-shelf small business accounting program called Solomon III. Iroff and his small staff use the machine for many general office purposes, including updating the ledger periodically. They keep the ledger filed under its official Treasury Department code name, 20X8006, and store it on a 5 1/4-inch floppy disk, which is usually kept in the disk holder on top of the Hewlett-Packard monitor.[5] This disk is the only reality behind what is called the Old Age, Survivors and Disability Insurance Trust fund.

Why does the government bother to keep this memo account? Obviously Social Security officials enjoy the image of probity and fiduciary responsibility derived from being able to refer to the existence of a "trust fund." But the ledger does actually serve one useful purpose for those who know how to interpret its true meaning: it provides a rough measure of how much the next generation will have to pay (in addition to currently scheduled payroll taxes) in order to fulfill all the Social Security benefit promises that are being made today. For the number that appears as the "surplus" in the OASDI "trust fund" would—in the event that future Social Security benefits are not cut—become the amount of new revenue that future taxpayers have to raise in order to keep the system from collapsing.

So what's happened to all the money you've paid into Social Security over the years? It's gone, spent, vanished. For most of the program's history, each month's take in payroll taxes was barely enough to meet the cost of each month's benefits. Currently, because the baby boomers are all of working age and because payroll tax rates have been hiked dramatically in recent years, the government is indeed collecting more from this particular revenue source than it is currently paying out in Social Security benefits. But make no mistake about it, this does not mean there is any surplus in Social Security. The government is still spending every dime it collects in revenue from you and all other taxpayers, including all payroll taxes—and doing so the moment the money comes in the door. In fact, thanks to the overall budget deficits, the government is spending that much and more each month, making up the difference by borrowing.

Quite literally, the government is setting absolutely nothing aside to pay for anyone's future benefits, regardless of all the rhetoric about "trust funds" and "surpluses." When the baby boomers reach retirement age, every dollar they receive in benefits will be a dollar some taxpayer at the time will do without. Assertions to the contrary are nothing short of a classic big lie. As Paul Hewitt of the National Taxpayers Union has noted, "At the core of every private insurance plan exists a sinking fund, a pool of capital that has been built up to pay expected benefits. But the core of every social insurance plan is an unfunded liability, a debt that reflects money that should have been saved, but was not."[6]

ROBIN HOOD IN REVERSE

Social Security isn't an insurance scheme; it's a transfer program. Who does it transfer money from? Mostly from today's workers to today's retirees, and not just from year to year but over the life cycles of entire generations.

The program provides huge windfalls to current beneficiaries. Consider a typical middle-income, one-earner couple who retired at age sixty-five in 1980. Reflecting the common wisdom of their friends at the senior center, of the propaganda put out by various senior power groups, and of decades of misleading information disseminated by the government itself, such a couple is likely to believe that when it comes to Social Security, "We are only getting back what we put in."

But however much it may please them to think that they are paying their own way, it's just wishful thinking. In reality, such a couple has typically paid in only about $51,000 in Social Security taxes during their working years, even after adjusting for inflation and for the interest they might have earned if they had deposited all their Social Security dollars in the bank. In return for these taxes, such a couple became entitled on the day they retired to a stream of future Social Security benefits with an annuity value of $209,900, or more than four times the real value of their previous Social Security contributions. Couples of this age with high lifetime earnings receive even greater amounts of windfall benefits.[7]

If Social Security could continue to offer such fabulous deals, the program would be no less marvelous than the goose that laid golden eggs. But Social Security is in reality like all other deals that sound too good to be true: it may provide enormous windfalls for a lucky few, but over time it will swindle most participants.

One of the great secrets of the program is how harshly it will treat most middle-class Americans in the future even if the program is *not* cut or eliminated just as they reach retirement age. Given current life tables and benefits formulas, a single man with average wages who turned fifty in 1995 can expect to receive a Social Security entitlement worth $115,200 (adjusting for inflation) if he retires at age sixty-five in 2010. That's actually a larger benefit than is received by such men who retire today. But it's still a swindle; in order to become entitled to such a benefit, the man who was fifty years old in 1995 will wind up, under current law, having paid a lifetime average of $151,000 in Social Security taxes. That makes his lifetime "return" a dead loss of $36,300. By comparison, if such a man had retired in 1980, he would have become entitled to $39,000 *more* in benefits than he ever paid in taxes.[8]

Today's thirty-year-olds are generally promised an even rawer deal under current law. Consider a typical upper-middle-class couple of this generation with a husband whose lifetime annual wages average $60,000 (in inflation-adjusted dollars) and a wife whose lifetime wages average $24,444. At current tax rates, such a couple will wind up paying Social Security taxes totaling $671,000 (in today's money) before reaching age sixty-five. In return for these taxes, this couple is currently promised Social Security benefits with an annuity value of $498,000, which represents a loss of over $173,000 on their investment. (And this is not even counting the taxes they will then go on to pay on their benefits.) By comparison, if such a couple were fortunate enough to have retired in 1995, they could expect to receive windfall benefits in excess of $37,000.[9]

The reason different generations get treated so differently under Social Security is that payroll taxes stayed so low for so long. For the first eleven years of the program, the maximum annual Social Security was just $30. It stayed below $100 until 1959 and had risen to just $824 as late as 1975. That means that for a senior who paid the maximum payroll taxes in effect between 1937 and 1975, for example, the maximum he or she could have contributed to the system was just $6,864.60. Today, workers paying the maximum Social Security tax "contribute" that much to the system in just nine months.

THE END OF THE CHAIN LETTER

Since the government spends all of this money and more even before you can take your paycheck to the bank, the long-term solvency of Social Security depends on future taxpayers and the world they inherit. Leaving politics aside, the key determinates of Social Security's long-term financing are future rates of mortality and morbidity, immigration and emigration, the fertility rate, the rates of inflation in prices and wages, the unemployment rate, and trends in workforce participation and retirement decisions. Rising real wages help expand the revenue base for Social Security, but since Social Security benefits are set higher for high-wage workers than for low-wage workers, an improvement in real wages becomes a negative trend for the system's long-term finances unless the trend is never broken.

You don't have to be an actuary to see that most of these factors are working against the long-term solvency of Social Security—for example, the trend toward longer life expectancy. Most Americans would consider this good news, but not those who tend to Social Security's finances. Improving mortality rates are the single most important demographic factor eroding Social Security's solvency.

Part of the "problem" is that "too many" people are living to retirement age. Back in 1940, a twenty-one-year-old man stood only a 53.9 percent chance of surviving long enough to collect Social Security. Today's twenty-one-year-old males, by contrast, stand better than a 72.3 percent chance of living to age sixty-five, while twenty-one-year-old women stand better than an 83 percent chance.[10] What this means for Social Security is that the living can no longer count on large subsidies from the dead. In financing Social Security, we can no longer count on nearly half of all taxpayers dying before they reach retirement age. The same principle holds true for all private pensions and health care plans. As life expectancy improves among the working-age population, the economy's "ghost dividend," as it were, disappears.

Meanwhile, the average age of retirement keeps falling. As recently as the early 1950s, retirement as we now know it did not exist as an institution. Most Americans, when polled, said they aspired to work for as long as possible and viewed retirement as suited only for the disabled.[11] But Americans today look forward to retirement as a positive time of life—as a chance to travel, pursue hobbies, and otherwise indulge their interests—and most get started the moment they think they can afford to quit their jobs. Between this new pro-retirement ethos and structural changes in the economy that have dramatically shrunk employment opportunities for middle managers and many experienced blue-collar workers, it is no longer uncommon for Americans to end their careers in their mid-fifties, and the average age of retirement has now dropped to age sixty-two.

As we retire earlier and earlier, we are living longer and longer; life expectancy improves not just among the working-aged population, but especially among the old. In 1940, the average remaining life expectancy for those who had survived to age sixty-five was 12.7 years for men and 14.7 for women. Today sixty-five-year-old men can expect to live another 15.3 years and women of that age another

19.6,[12] and there is no end in sight to this progress. Although some researchers have speculated that there may be inherent limits to how many times human cells can divide and that improvement in human life spans is therefore inherently finite, there is little empirical evidence yet available to support the claim. Indeed, studies of mortality rates among Mormon high priests, Seventh-Day Adventists, and other straight-and-narrow types suggest that, even without further medical breakthroughs, dramatically higher life expectancy rates (up into the low-one-hundreds at birth) are available to those who adhere to optimal lifestyles.[13]

Moreover, it's not particularly far-fetched to assume that the U.S. population as a whole will adopt healthier lifestyles as information about the opportunities for increased longevity filter through society. As the demographer Samuel Preston points out, since the 1950s, per capita tobacco consumption has declined by 40 percent, saturated fat consumption has declined by more than a third, seatbelt use is increasing, and at least 30 million Americans regularly practice aerobic exercise. Even AIDS has proved to be a much less deadly scourge than originally feared, due almost entirely to behavioral changes.[14]

Meanwhile, as more and more Americans live into their one-hundreds, fewer and fewer are getting around to having children. The birthrate has been on a long-term decline in the United States for over two hundred years. The big exception to the trend was the post–World War II baby boom, but the socioeconomic conditions that spawned the boom show no signs of returning. Despite the comparatively small size of the "baby bust" generation that follows the boomers, real wages of young Americans continue to decline faster than for any other age group. And today's young women are far from aspiring to the social roles played by women of the 1950s. In recent years, there has been a modest increase in the overall fertility rate, but it has been largely confined to unmarried women.[15]

Dramatic increases in the illegitimacy rate and the poverty it creates raise further questions about how many productive, taxpaying citizens will be available in the next century to support the swelling ranks of Social Security recipients. Fifty years ago, 5 percent of

American births were to unmarried women. By the early 1990s, nearly a third of all babies born in the United States were illegitimate, including over 20 percent of all white babies. Lee Rainwater, a Harvard sociologist, predicts 40 percent of American births and 80 percent of minority births will be out of wedlock by the turn of the century.

Illegitimate children are far more likely than those in husband-and-wife families to grow up in poverty. In 1991, for example, the poverty rate for children of unwed mothers was 66 percent, compared to just 8 percent for children of married couples.[16]

Given these realities, the trend toward out-of-wedlock births, and the rise of childhood poverty generally, is likely to swell the ranks of the underclass in the next century. Out of the pool of new taxpayers the Social Security Administration is assuming will be available to pay for benefits in 2020–2030, about one out of four is now living in poverty. Far from supporting the elderly in the next century, these poor children are more likely to compete with the retired population for public resources.

Defenders of Social Security often point to immigration as a panacea for all the negative demographic trends. Increased immigration, all else being equal, would indeed be somewhat positive for Social Security financing, particularly since immigrants tend to have higher birthrates than the existing U.S. population. But even if immigration could be maintained at the high rates the United States has experienced over the past fifteen years, the long-term impact would be minor compared to other economic and demographic trends. To erase even one-quarter of the projected growth in tax rates needed to fund Social Security through 2040 (under the SSA's so-called best-guess projection) would require a net increase in immigration to 2 million a year. This is about twice the number of immigrants who arrived annually on U.S. shores at the turn of the twentieth century, when immigration was at its all-time historical high.[17] With feelings against immigrants already running high in California and many other parts of the country, any attempt to ameliorate Social Security by importing more warm bodies would likely inspire even greater economic insecurities and political backlash.

Recognizing how indeterminate any projection of the system's long-term financing must be, the SSA always publishes in its annual report a range of projections for the future of the system. It is the so-called intermediate-range forecast that is supposed to be the government's best-guess estimate of what the future holds in store for the system. According to the 1995 forecast, here's what will happen to the system's main pension and disability program in the next century:

• After running huge deficits in the early 1990s, Congress bailed out the disability program in 1994. Still, SSA actuaries project the program could start running a deficit again as early as 1999 and be bankrupt as early as 2004. Expenditures are projected to soar from $38.9 billion in 1994 to $73.2 billion by 2004 under the actuaries' best-case scenario and to $110.5 billion under the worst-case projection.[18]
• The long-term outlook for the combined pension and disability programs looks even bleaker. The actuaries project that OASDI will run out of money to write checks in 2025 under its intermediate-range assumption, and possibly as early as 2015.[19]
• To keep benefits flowing, taxes would have to rise dramatically. Today the OASDI program costs the equivalent of little more than 11 percent of all wages subject to Social Security taxes. Under the comparatively optimistic economic and demographic assumptions used by the SSA in its intermediate-range forecast, the cost of benefits as a percentage of taxable income would have to rise to more than 17 percent by 2030. Under its more realistic high-cost projection, that figure would rise to 20.5 percent by the time children born today entered midlife. By 2070, a payroll tax as high 28 percent would be necessary to keep the checks flowing.[20]

Some people might argue that such a levy would not be an impossible burden to place on the next generation. By itself, it wouldn't be. But consider first that it is probably based more on denial and wishful thinking than on observable reality. For example, the intermediate-range projections assume that net immigration will rise over the next several years to an ultimate level of 900,000 persons per year by the year 2000, including 650,000 net legal immigrants and 250,000 illegals.[21] That might happen, but most Americans would hardly welcome such a trend, and the current movement for stricter immigration controls makes it seem less than inevitable.

Similarly, this projection assumes that improvements in life expectancy will come much more slowly in the next twenty-five years than they did in the past quarter-century. For example, whereas male life expectancy at birth increased by 5.2 years between 1970 and 1995, the projection calls for it to increase by only 2.7 years over the next twenty-five years.[22] Over the past twenty years, average male and female life expectancy at age sixty-five has grown by 0.95 year per decade. Under this projection, the improvement is assumed to be just 0.44 percent per decade, less than half the historical pace.[23] The projection also assumes modest but consistent real wage increases in the coming decades, even though real wages have been generally flat since 1973.

The Social Security Administration's so-called high-cost projection is a more likely forecast, and in any event is a more prudent and appropriate model to use for planning purposes. Yet even this pessimistic projection contains assumptions many older Americans would recognize as far from the worst that might be expected of the economy in the future. For example, the pessimistic projection assumes that inflation will average less than 5 percent in the next decade, which is well below the 7.75 percent average annual inflation rate of the 1970s.[24] It assumes that real wages will rise consistently every year after the turn of the century, which would be an improvement over the experience of the past twenty years.[25] As for life expectancy at birth, it assumes it will rise by the year 2040 to 78.3 years for men and 84.8 years for women, which hardly seems the "worst" we might hope for.[26]

Some Americans might object that the next generation can and should pay for the rising cost of Social Security. This rationalization ignores the reality that the problems in Social Security, as dire as they may be, are only part of a much larger encumbrance being created by our overall system of entitlements. Add in just the future projected cost of Medicare hospital insurance, for example, which is part of the Social Security system, and the cost of providing these combined benefits to the elderly and disabled of the next century ultimately rises to 29.22 percent of taxable wages under the SSA's intermediate projection, and to 48.09 percent of taxable wages under its more pessimistic scenario.[27]

Those who say we can easily afford the rising cost of Social Security are thus like an alcoholic in denial who refuses to admit how much he really drinks. The effect of Social Security itself on the body politic might only be equivalent to drinking three or four martinis a night—not healthy, but sustainable at least in the short term. The problem is, however, that Social Security is hardly the only bottle out of which middle-class America is sipping these days, and the cumulative effects are poisonous indeed.

7

Hair of the Dog

Two forms of "stinking thinking" pervade the health care debate in America today.

The first, more common among conservatives, is denial. The health care crisis will solve itself, we hear, maybe with just a few insurance reforms here and there. If programs like Medicare are spiraling out of control, then we'll just pay doctors and hospitals less or lower the subsidies to affluent retirees a notch.

Then there are those who think another drink is the solution. A classic subconscious ploy played by the alcoholic is to invent a crisis, such as a fight with his wife, for which, he tells himself, drinking is the only recourse. Mainstream liberal opinion on health care is equally obtuse. Faced with a health care system that is overdosing on too many middle-class subsidies, the liberal solution is to order up another hair of the dog that bit us.

The root cause of America's health care crisis is, once again, our expanding ethos of entitlement. It is a curious feature of our time that a culture that so insistently celebrates relativism, pluralism, and situational ethics should be so adept at discovering absolute rights (and the entitlements that putatively follow from them). But such is the case, and nowhere more so than in the realm of health care. Because Americans now habitually think of health care as a right to which they are entitled regardless of cost, they have difficulty even thinking about how health care should be allocated, paid for, or rationed. No one can put a price tag on what's mine by right, after all. And rights are not divisible.

But regarding health care as a right or entitlement is particularly inappropriate and unhelpful, primarily because proclaiming a right to health care begs the question of what we mean by health care, or even by health itself, and therefore distracts us from the real and difficult choices that confront us. Indeed, the effect of "rights talking" about health care is as obfuscating as a three-martini lunch.

A sober look at the health care debate must start with this reality. Health today does not have the same definition it had a hundred years ago, or even twenty years ago. Instead, it's a fluid and ever-expanding concept. A century ago, for example, the only people who were mentally ill were those who were stark-raving mad. Since Freud, good mental health has come to mean freedom from neurosis, and the ranks of the mentally ill accordingly continue to swell. A 1993 study by the Institute for Social Research at the University of Michigan found, for example, that under current definitions, nearly half the U.S. adult population suffers significant mental illness at least once in their lifetime, and a third of the adult population is mentally ill at any one time—with conditions ranging from alcohol dependency, to social phobia, to simple phobia, to generalized anxiety and panic disorders.[1]

The process also goes the other way. One hundred years ago, homosexuality was a disease; since the 1970s it has been officially declassified and become a mere lifestyle. Thanks to this particular social reconstruction, health care spending (for mental therapy anyway) is perhaps lower than it otherwise would be.[2] But usually the tendency is in the opposite direction—toward higher thresholds of what it means (and what it costs) to be in good health. Twenty years ago, female infertility was a condition of women who could not become pregnant after a year of unprotected intercourse. Today female infertility is a condition of women who cannot become pregnant after repeated in-vitro fertilization and gamete intrafallopian transfer operations costing $8,000 a try. Similarly, twenty years ago an elderly person who became forgetful wasn't thought to be ill, only to be aging. Today such a person is likely to be diagnosed as stricken with a terminal illness called Alzheimer's disease, the cure for which now inspires frenzied, government-subsidized competition among university researchers and drug companies.

Just as slippery as our concept of health is our concept of life itself. Once, when a man's heart stopped, so did his experience with the health care system. Today hospitals routinely use cardiopulmonary resuscitation, for example, to try to revive patients who in a previous age would have been declared dead. The cost of this particular heroic measure is huge. Among the 5 percent of patients whose hearts resume beating after CPR, most never breathe on their own again, yet typically consume $82,000 to $189,000 in intensive care expenses for each year of life gained.[3]

Our concept of disability is no less elastic. When the first workers compensation programs began late in the last century, a disability was a work-related injury, such as the loss of a hand or a leg. Today statements offered by friends or family members that a person is having difficulties in social functioning can be sufficient to qualify him or her as disabled for the purpose of collecting Social Security Disability Insurance.[4]

Similarly, alcoholism and drug dependency are now thought of as diseases rather than moral failings. As such, these diseases, if severe enough, can create entitlement to disability insurance, and even, if the dependency is abject enough, to special protections under the Americans with Disabilities Act (ADA).

This can lead to some paradoxical results. In 1994, for example, John Hartman, a founding member of the Doobie Brothers rock group, sued under the ADA after twenty northern California police departments blocked his dream of becoming a police officer. Local law enforcement officials held that Hartman's admitted recreational drug use during the 1970s disqualified him from being a police officer. Hartman countered that his drug use was a form of disability and as such couldn't be used as a basis for discriminating against him. Though the federal district court judge hearing Hartman's complaint dismissed the suit, his reasoning was revealing of the perversity of current cultural and legal norms concerning addiction, disability, and entitlement. The judge ruled that while Hartman had established proof that he was once a casual drug user, he had failed to show that he was a drug addict and therefore entitled, under the ADA, to become a police officer.[5]

Around the globe, disability is an inherently subjective and ambiguous concept, easily subject to political abuse. In Costa Rica, for example, there is no reason to believe that true disability rates are out of the ordinary. And yet 20 percent of all Costa Rican pensioners receive disability pensions, and more than a third of all social insurance spending is for disability payments.[6] In the Netherlands, where until recently workers complaining of stress could collect up to 70 percent of their salaries in disability payments, the ranks of the disabled similarly exploded, eventually forcing the government to change its definition of disability to control costs.[7]

Further evidence of how elastic our concept of health care is, and of the open-ended nature of health care entitlements, comes from the dramatic variation from city to city in per capita Medicare costs. Because doctors and hospitals in different cities vary greatly in how they treat specific illness, from the number of tests they order to the kinds of operations they perform, the dollar value of a Medicare entitlement varies greatly from one city to another as well. A Medicare patient in Miami with kidney stones will typically wind up costing the government far more than if he or she lived in Minneapolis. The *New England Journal of Medicine* reports that in 1989, after adjusting for differences in age and gender, Medicare payments for a doctor's care, per beneficiary, varied from lows of $822 in Minneapolis, $872 in San Francisco, and $954 in New York City to highs of $1,493 in Detroit, $1,637 in Fort Lauderdale, and $1,874 in Miami.[8]

In a culture that has no fixed sense of what it means to be healthy or even of what appropriate health care is, talking about a *right* to health care is close to meaningless. An entitlement to a pension, food stamps, or crop supports is an entitlement to a specific benefit, with a specific value, determined by a specific formula. An entitlement to health care, by contrast, is often just a blank check.

SURVIVAL OF THE FRAILEST

Adding to the confusion of our debate is the well-established reality that the more money a society spends on health care, the "sicker" it becomes by many measures—and not just in some subjective sense. As the demographer Eileen M. Crimmins has pointed out, "As mortality declines, those saved from death do not tend to be persons of average constitution but a weaker and frailer group who would have perished under a more severe mortality regime. Thus, with more mortality declines the population becomes more heavily weighted with a frailer group more susceptible to a whole host of diseases and conditions than the average survivor in the population."[9] In other words, good medicine keeps sick and frail people alive, thereby increasing the number and proportion of sick and frail people in the population.

In recent years, for example, there has been an alarming rise in the incidence of people suffering from sepsis, a complex, costly, and often fatal disease. In 1992, the number of hospital patients diagnosed with sepsis increased by nearly 7 percent, adding a projected $1.1 billion in brand-new hospital charges. The cause of the epidemic: doctors, who now routinely save critically ill patients who only a few years ago were untreatable.[10]

This same dynamic occurs even when we come up with outright cures for diseases or find ways to prevent them. Children who would have died of diphtheria or whooping cough had they been born a century ago are now easily saved, but by surviving, they thereby automatically incur a heightened statistical risk of contracting AIDS, heart disease, cancer, and ultimately Alzheimer's. That is not an argument for abandoning the fight against childhood disease, of course, but a demonstration of how our health care system can become the victim of its own success.

Adding to the compounding cost of health care is the fact that even as good medicine produces more old people, old people insist on still more health care to keep them feeling young. As Willard Gaylin, a physician, has pointed out, Americans, having learned what modern medicine can do for them, are increasingly unwilling to live with the natural effects of aging. Americans now routinely undergo knee or elbow operations, for example, not so they can continue to work (most of us, after all, do not work at jobs requiring physical strength) but so they can continue to play golf or ski. Notes Gaylin: "Dying in one's sleep at ninety-two after having won three sets of tennis from one's forty-year-old grandson that afternoon and having made love to one's wife twice that same evening—this is about the only scenario I have found most American men will accept as fulfilling their idea of death with dignity and growing old gracefully."[11]

If money were no object, none of this would matter. But in the real world, the money we spend on our ever-expanding health care sector eventually comes at the expense of other pressing social needs, including the need for investments necessary to finance the health care sector itself. During the 1980s alone, federal health care spending increased more than 50 percent, even after adjusting for general inflation. During the same period, federal spending on education and science declined 22 percent. In 1965, for every dollar that states spent of their own money on health care, they spent $1.70 on transportation, including roads, bridges, and public buses. By 1990 states were spending only 41 cents on transportation for every dollar on health care.[12] At all levels of government, health care entitlements have become like those voracious creatures in the old Pac-Man video game, gobbling up public resources with no sign of diminishing appetite.

In announcing his 1996 budget, President Clinton noted that 40 percent of the total projected increase in federal spending over the next five years came from the rising cost of health care entitlements. He also noted that the deficit could be eliminated in less than a decade if per capita spending on Medicare and Medicaid increased no faster than consumer prices in general.[13]

But given current policies, there is no reason to believe that that will happen. Worse, the combination of an aging population and new technology will make today's health care costs seem like mere pittances by the time the baby boom generation approaches retirement age. No other nation has been able both to control medical cost and subsidize access for the mass of its citizens without creating mechanisms that compel physicians and patients to weigh the costs and benefits of various treatments—in other words, to make hard choices. Neither can the United States.

All of our major health care entitlements are unsustainable: Medicare, Medicaid, and the massive tax subsidies that prop up and inflate the cost of employer-provided private health insurance. To know just how large the health care crisis of the next century is really becoming is to realize just how phony and disconnected our current debate over the "right to health care" remains.

THE SICKNESS IN MEDICARE

Consider Medicare, the federal government's premier health care entitlement. So far, it has proved to be a fabulous deal for its beneficiaries. When Medicare started in 1965, it was supposed to be another one of those social insurance programs under which beneficiaries "earned" their own benefits by paying "premiums." The original Medicare payroll tax was set at 0.35 percent and was officially projected at the time to top out at 0.8 percent in 1987. Retirees who enrolled in Medicare's voluntary supplementary medical insurance plan, which underwrites the cost of doctor and outpatient visits, paid a premium of $3 monthly, matched by a government contribution from general funds.[14] But as with Social Security, those modest contributions hardly began to pay for the real cost of the program, and Medicare quickly degenerated into a Ponzi scheme financed by borrowing from the future.

Medicare beneficiaries have never even begun to pay for the cost of their benefits. A person turning sixty-five and retiring in 1967, for example, received approximately $38,000 on average in Medicare provider payments while contributing only $3,000 in postretirement insurance premiums, for a net subsidy of $35,000.

Later retirees made increasingly greater payroll tax contributions to Medicare. Still, the size of their subsidies continued to grow be-

cause benefit payments shot up even faster. For example, someone retiring in 1990, even though contributing nearly $18,000 in Medicare
taxes, will receive an $82,000 subsidy as the cost of his or her future
benefits shoots past an average of $100,000 (in 1991 dollars). Ameri-
cans who retired in 1990 can expect to receive more than $4 in health
benefits for every $1 they paid in to the Medicare system.[15]

Such windfalls are not sustainable over the course of more than
one generation. What would happen if Medicare's outlays per en-
rollee continued to grow at their historical pace? Using rather optimistic economic and demographic assumptions, the program's
trustees estimate that the cost of Medicare would hit 54.1 percent of
payroll by 2040. With more adverse (but entirely plausible) demographic and economic developments, a straight-line extrapolation of
the historical trend in real per-beneficiary spending would push
Medicare costs in 2040 all the way to 85.9 percent of payroll.[16]

Even if the average growth rate in real Medicare outlays per en-
rollee turns out to be just *half* of the historical rate, the program
would still wind up costing tomorrow's workers *nearly one out of five
dollars they earn.* Would that ever happen? Of course not. One way or
another, Medicare spending will continue to be cut back—if not
eliminated outright.

THE GENTRIFICATION OF MEDICAID

Medicaid, established along with Medicare in 1965, is a means-
tested entitlement program run by both the federal government and
the states. Like Medicare, its costs are racing out of control. The
general inflation in health care costs is one reason. Expanded eligibility for the poor and near-poor is another. A third factor, with particularly ominous implications for the program's future costs, is its
gradual gentrification. Originally intended to provide medical benefits primarily to the welfare population, Medicaid is being transformed these days—with the help of a cottage industry of clever
lawyers—into a program that picks up the nursing home bills of
more and more middle-class families.

"The middle class has come to view Medicaid as an entitlement when it comes to long-term care coverage," says Robert Kane, chair of long-term care and aging at the University of Minnesota School of Public Health. "The social stigma previously associated with going on Medicaid has been largely replaced by a sense that it's OK, I paid taxes, and defrauding the government is perfectly appropriate."[17]

If you doubt this, just fire up your web-browser and do a bit of surfing on the Internet, as I did one Sunday afternoon in October 1995. I entered the keywords: "Medicaid," "asset transfers," "middle class." My computer's browser raced toward the edge of the info universe, looking for matches, and in seconds, up popped the World Wide Web site run by D. Victor Pellegrino, Esq., a New York "elder law" attorney. Pellegrino helpfully posts a file on ten frequently asked questions about how middle-class people can qualify for Medicaid and then invites readers to e-mail him "to explore this area in greater detail."

A little ways down the infobahn, an enterprise calling itself "Entitlement Management, LLC" (EM) has hung a shingle. "Hello Visitors!" the good folks at EM exclaim: "We decided to become a presence on the World Wide Web in order to assist people to:

- protect their hard-earned assets;
- successfully apply for Social Security Disability; and
- successfully apply for Medicaid."

Just to make sure I understood what was actually being advertised here, I dashed off an e-mail letter asking if it is "really necessary for a person to spend down all his assets to qualify for Medicaid." A short time later came e-mail from Eileen McMullin, senior partner at EM. "No, a person does not have to spend-down/reduce," she responded. "There are a number of ways to transfer assets to children and still qualify. Your questions indicate that I can most likely help you. I will be glad to discuss fees with you once I know what your exact needs are."

How much do the pretend-paupers on Medicaid cost the taxpayers? No one knows, for many of the techniques used to disguise the assets of people applying for the program do not create any paper trail in the public record. But the sums involved are substantial.

Bentley Lipscomb, secretary of Florida's Department of Elder Affairs, estimates that 30 to 35 percent of the Medicaid nursing home patients in that state have not actually divested their assets. If Lipscomb is correct, then non-poor Medicaid beneficiaries are consuming nearly as much as the entire Florida Medicaid nursing program cost just eight years ago. There is no reason to believe the situation is much different in other states.

If you think it's those people on the other side of the tracks who are responsible for Medicaid's fiscal meltdown, consider this: Middle-class and affluent families who figure out how to get Medicaid to pay for Grandma's nursing-home needs receive an annual subsidy of about $30,000—roughly equivalent to the price of a brand-new, well-equipped Lexus ES-300.

In many states, loosely written eligibility standards and lax enforcement mean that affluent seniors and their children hardly even need to lie in order to qualify for Medicaid. A study released in 1995 of Illinois' Medicaid program found, for example:

> . . . someone with a home worth $200,000, plus home furnishings of reasonable value, plus a car worth $50,000, plus a term life policy with a $100,000 death benefit, plus $72,660 (or more under court order) to transfer to a community spouse would qualify routinely for Medicaid nursing home benefits in Illinois.[18]

Only 4 percent of seniors have purchased private long-term care insurance, despite its now being widely available. Why? One reason, of course, is simply denial. Who wants to dwell on the prospects of developing Alzheimer's or becoming incontinent, no matter how common such conditions? Another reason is that many Americans erroneously believe that Medicare will cover their chronic long-term care needs. But a final, and increasingly important, reason is that more and more middle-class and wealthy seniors and their children are learning how to get Medicaid to pay for their nursing-home bills and still preserve their assets.

"If people feel that all they have to do is get a lawyer and pay a couple of thousand dollars in order to get on to Medicaid, the private long-term care insurance industry can never compete," notes Erwin

HAIR OF THE DOG

Bodo, director of reimbursement and statistical programs for the Florida Health Care Association, which represents the state's nursing homes industry. Tellingly, Bodo, who is 47, has not purchased private long-term care insurance for himself. Nor, with a single exception, have any of his colleagues at work, despite being exposed daily to the realities of chronic disability. Even those who criticize Medicaid's de facto transformation into a middle-class welfare program act on the assumption that one way or another, the government will pay for their own nursing-home care, too.

By taking advantage of numerous loopholes, it's easy for middle-class and wealthy people to qualify for Medicaid. "I have numerous clients that I have sheltered hundreds of thousands of dollars for," boasts Julie Osterhout, an elder-law attorney practicing in Florida.

Stories about spouses having to impoverish themselves in order to qualify an ailing partner for Medicaid are still commonly heard, but the reality has been quite different for many years now. For example, under a federal law passed in 1988, a healthy spouse can retain not only a homestead of unlimited value, but financial assets of up to $74,820. Income tests for Medicaid eligibility aren't difficult to pass. In most states, a sick spouse with up to $1,300 in monthly income can qualify for Medicaid-funded nursing-home care; of that income, his or her healthy spouse can keep up to $1,200 without sharing some of the nursing-home expense.

Even these comparatively mild restrictions are easily avoided. To begin with, anyone, regardless of wealth, can qualify for Medicaid nursing-home benefits simply by transferring assets to children or other beneficiaries at least 36 months before applying for assistance. If this time restriction proves too cumbersome, it is also easy to get around. For example, one can pay down a mortgage, put in a new pool or addition, or buy a bigger, more expensive house. These are commonly used ways to shelter assets, since homestead property is not counted as wealth by Medicaid's means-test.

Automobiles are also exempt property in many states. This means, for example, that you can get Grandma to buy a Mercedes for you, a Lexus for your brother, a Cadillac for your sister and still have Medicaid pick up her nursing-home bills. Moreover, virtually unlimited amounts of assets can be sheltered in Medicaid's means-test through the purchase of annuities. "Under the current rules, annuities count as income, not assets," explains attorney Osterhout. "So that way you can shelter $200,000 in just five minutes." Larger sums can be sheltered through the creation of Charitable Remainder Trusts and other sophisticated devices.

Osterhout belongs to a burgeoning cadre of elder-law lawyers who make a substantial living by counseling middle- and upper-income families on how to take advantage of such loopholes. One measure of the growth of this kind of practice is the membership of The National Academy of Elder Law Attorneys, which has grown from zero to 2700 since its founding in 1988.

Predictably, many elder-law attorneys are quite self-righteous about what they do. First, they insist it's all perfectly legal. Sheltering assets to meet Medicaid's means-test, they say, is no different than claiming the home mortgage deduction or taking advantage of some other legal loophole when you do your taxes: Under current law, this is something middle-class and wealthy people are entitled to do even if it adds to the deficits and leads to cuts in other programs.

Moreover, many elder-law attorneys argue, it is sound public policy to allow the middle class on to the Medicaid rolls. For example, in his book, "How to Protect Your Life Savings from Catastrophic Illness and Nursing Homes," Harley Gordon, a founding member of the National Academy of Elder Law Attorneys, argues: "True, Medicaid was designed to provide for the poor who have no other means to pay for long-term care. But that's the point—there is no system for the middle class. Does that mean that it makes sense to drive millions of elderly Americans into poverty before we lend them a hand?"[19]

Some elder-law attorneys also evoke a kind of moral relativism in justifying their work. Why is it, they ask, that middle-class people who use Medicare to pay for acute illnesses face no opprobrium, but those who use Medicaid to cover the cost of chronic illness are condemned as unethical? If it's O.K. to have the government pay for your heart attack, they ask, why is it not O.K. for the government to pay for having your bedpans changed? "Find the high moral ground

HAIR OF THE DOG

anywhere," says Charles F. Robinson, one of Florida's most prominent elder-law attorneys. "Nobody can climb mountains and raise flags on this issue."

Since more and more middle-class families are becoming convinced that they are indeed entitled to have the government pay for their nursing-home needs, it's worth examining these claims. True enough, the current law of the land does allow middle-class people—and even millionaires—to take advantage of many loopholes in qualifying for Medicaid. So long as this is true, individuals can hardly be faulted for legally pursuing their economic interests. But is the law that allows middle-class and affluent families with clever lawyers to qualify for Medicaid itself really fair or in the public's long-term interest? Why haven't our political leaders closed these loopholes long ago?

OUT OF THE MOUTHS OF BABES

Note, to begin with, how this policy serves to redistribute resources. Middle-class and wealthy families on Medicaid have not paid for the benefits they receive. The program is funded on a pay-as-you-go basis by general revenues coming from both state and federal governments. So when the Smith family, say, gets Grandma on Medicaid, and thereby preserves her savings, that's not just the Smith's private business. As soon as she goes on Medicaid, you and all other taxpayers wind up subsidizing not only Grandma herself, but also her heirs through the extra inheritance she's thereby able to bequeath.

And taxpayers aren't the only losers. Families trying to pay for their own nursing-home care take an additional hit. Explains Mary Ellen Early, director of public policy for the Florida Association of Homes for the Aging: "If Mrs. X deliberately spends down her assets to qualify for Medicaid, that means everyone else who's paying with their own money must pay more." Nursing homes in Florida, says Early, lose $240 to $300 a month on every Medicaid patient, so that cost is shifted to private-pay people. The situation is similar throughout the country.

CASE STUDIES

Is there really no moral difference, as attorney Robinson claims, between the middle-class entitlement to Medicare and its (de facto) entitlement to Medicaid? At least by design, Medicare is a social insurance program under which beneficiaries help pay for the cost of their own benefits through payroll taxes collected during their working years, as well as through premiums, copayments, and deductibles collected during their retirement years. True, the federal government has so mismanaged the program that, as we've seen, the average Medicare recipient receives many times more in benefits than he or she ever paid in taxes. True, as it careens towards insolvency as a result, Medicare has degenerated into something approximating a straightforward transfer of wealth from young to old. But the fact that politicians over the years have used Medicare as a means of buying votes with windfall benefits is hardly an argument for why some middle-class and wealthy Americans should now receive windfall Medicaid benefits as well.

Generational equity is another reason Medicaid shouldn't be a middle-class and wealthy entitlement. Because of the aging of the population, the U.S. General Accounting Office predicts that by 2018, even after adjusting for inflation, total long-term-care costs will be three times higher than in 1988. By 2048, long-term-care spending will triple again, to $350 billion, or roughly the cost in real dollars of the entire Social Security system today.[20]

Medicaid now pays for nearly half of all nursing home care in the United States. Even if that ratio doesn't increase in the future, taxpayers are obviously exposed to an enormous unfunded liability.

Much of this burden is unavoidable—the result simply of the aging of the population. But the public expense deriving from middle-class and affluent families who have simply neglected to insure themselves against long-term care cost *is* avoidable and indeed *must* be prevented if the country is to avoid generational warfare in the next century.

With its large elderly population, Florida provides a case study of what other states can expect to experience in their own Medicaid programs during the next two decades. Already, more than 30 percent of the money distributed by Florida's Medicaid program goes to persons age 66 or older. Only 3 percent of Florida's Medicaid caseload resides in nursing homes, but this population collects 24 percent of the program's resources just for the cost of their nursing-home beds alone. Meanwhile, the threshold for children receiving Medicaid is as low as 31 percent of the government's own official poverty line. The state's day-care program for the working poor has a waiting list of 25,000, and its Child Abuse and Neglect Prevention program has a waiting list of 2,100.

As the number of Americans requiring long-term care continue to grow dramatically, the cost of a Medicaid program that pays out benefits to the poor and non-poor alike could easily crowd out virtually all other social spending, particularly for groups that are not politically powerful. So what is the solution? The federal government could create a social insurance program like Medicare that covered long-term care, but frankly, its record in managing Medicare, Social Security, and other social insurance programs does not inspire confidence. Any taxes collected for the purpose of pre-funding future long-term-care costs would likely wind up going to defray the current cost of government, as has happened with all the so-called assets of the Medicare and Social Security trust funds.

The only real solution is for middle-class and wealthy people to take responsibility for their own future long-term-care needs by purchasing private long-term-care insurance. And the only way this will ever happen on a sufficiently large scale is if government sends a very clear signal that Medicaid will not pick up your nursing-home bills unless you are truly needy.

This could be done without imposing undue hardships on Medicaid beneficiaries. For example, state governments could implement a kind of "pay-after-you-go" plan. Medicaid beneficiaries could continue to hold on to the types of assets that are currently exempt from Medicaid's means-test, such as homestead property and annuities. In fact, spend-down requirements for currently non-exempt assets such as bank accounts could be greatly liberalized. But the states would place liens on these assets, which they would exercise after the beneficiaries' death to recover the value of their Medicaid benefits. In this way, Medicaid nursing-home benefits would essentially become loans, not grants. Medicaid patients could have the psychic satisfaction of not having to spend down their assets during their waning years, but the taxpayers would not be responsible for indemnifying their heirs.

Several states, such as Oregon and Florida, already have modest asset recovery programs in place, but for the most part they are concerned with recovering unreported windfalls received by Medicaid beneficiaries such as inheritances from siblings. The real challenge is to close the legal loopholes in Medicaid eligibility rules and then make sure the new law is enforced.

How much money would a "pay-after-you-go" plan for Medicaid save? No one knows for sure, but to the extent that such a policy encourages the middle class and wealthy to purchase private long-term-care insurance rather than relying on government, the savings could be substantial, especially over time. State governments could further discourage middle-class and wealthy dependence on Medicaid by mandating long-term-care riders on private and public employee group health policies. This way, today's workers would begin to prepay their generation's huge future liability for long-term care. As many elder-law attorneys themselves admit, the middle class cannot count on the government's continuing ability to deliver long-term care as an entitlement; in the end, the middle class and the wealthy must pay their own way, and not just for nursing-home care, but for all their health care needs.

BACKDOOR SUBSIDIES

As we will see in greater detail in subsequent chapters, the federal government operates many other middle-class health care entitlements, including expensive subsidy programs for veterans, military retirees, and civil servants. All are careening toward insolvency. But the cost of these subsidies pales next to the cost of a health care benefit nearly all middle- and upper-income Americans receive. It's the tax subsidy provided to everyone who receives group health insurance through his or her employer.

Here's how this tax subsidy works. Suppose you earn $30,000 a year working for an employer who offers you no health insurance. If you want to buy a car, or food, or even health insurance, you must first pay taxes on that $30,000 and then use whatever is left over.

Now suppose your neighbor also makes $30,000 a year, but $5,000 of that comes in the form of an employer-sponsored health care plan. Who is better off? Your neighbor, because that $5,000 received in the form of health care benefits is entirely tax free, even from Social Security and Medicare taxes, as well as from state income taxes.

This amounts to a major subsidy, with economic effects no different than if the government just mailed checks to people with employer-provided health care. For an employee in a 33 percent marginal tax bracket, $100 of employer-provided health insurance effectively costs only $67 in terms of after-tax income, for example. And, of course, the higher your income and tax bracket, the bigger the health care subsidy you receive—up to 50 percent or more after the exemption from state income tax is taken into account.

This tax subsidy creates huge distortions in the health care market. It is the basic reason, for example, that group health care plans now routinely cover incidental health care costs. Few people buy insurance to protect themselves against other incidental costs in life such as, say, their microwave oven's going on the blink. Why? Because most of us could easily afford to pay the $200 or $300 it would take to replace the appliance. So why then do most of us carry health insurance that covers $100 doctor visits or $40 prescriptions? Because by using tax-subsidized insurance to pay for such incidental costs, we effectively receive a 30 to 50 percent discount on such expenses as compared to paying with cash.

Congress had good intentions when it created this tax preference, back when the income tax was first enacted in 1913. The measure was designed to expand access to health care by encouraging employers to set up health care plans. But the actual effect of this subsidy has been to price more and more Americans out of the health insurance market by fueling health care inflation.

Americans who enjoy this subsidy consume more health care insurance, and more health care than they otherwise would, thereby driving up prices for everyone. This is in part because those who receive the subsidy get to purchase their health care with tax-free dollars. It is also, in part, because the existence of the subsidy encourages people to use insurance for underwriting their routine health care expenses. When people use insurance to pay for eyeglasses or prescription drugs, they're less inclined to resist high prices than if they were paying with their own cash up front. When such purchases are covered by insurance, it seems at least as if someone else is paying the bill.

As Patricia M. Danzon, professor of health care systems and insurance at the Wharton School of the University of Pennsylvania, observes, this tax subsidy plays a critical role in the inflation and the inequities of the U.S. health care system. "High tax-induced levels of health insurance," notes Danzon, "have made consumers insensitive to prices, fueled demand for . . . cost-enhancing technologies and undermined demand for cost-reducing technologies."[21]

Predictably, the cost of this subsidy is exploding along with the cost of health care in general, making it one of the federal government's fastest-growing entitlements. From 1980 to 1991, its cost soared by 90 percent.[22] By 1993, the loss to the federal Treasury alone exceeded $46 billion. The U.S. General Accounting Office predicts that between 1994 and 1998, the average real increase in the cost of the exemption will run at 5 percent per year, for a total of $199 billion.[23]

THE WORST OF ALL WORLDS

Faced with these unpleasant realities, many people go looking for scapegoats. There are plenty of potential candidates in the American health care system. Every year, for example, about two hundred physicians are suspended from participation in Medicaid and Medicare because of fraudulent and abusive practices.[24] According to a study by the General Accounting Office, fraud and abuse, including overcharging, billing for services never performed, and the like, accounted for an astonishing 10 percent of all U.S. health care spending in 1991—or about $70 billion.[25] But don't believe for a moment that clamping down on waste, fraud, and abuse will solve Americans' health care crisis. Even if it were possible to do so, that $70 billion is less than the average annual growth rate in U.S. health expenditures. In other words, even if we could eliminate all waste, fraud, and abuse with the stroke of a pen, total health care spending would be right back where it was to begin with in about twelve months.

The same is true when it comes to the cost of red tape. There is no doubt that both government and the insurance industry expend tens of billions in processing claims. The General Accounting Office estimates that the cost of claims administration came to $67 billion in 1991.[26] But again, even if we could somehow eliminate all this expense, costs would be right back where they were within a year.

Simply mandating that doctors and hospitals adopt more efficient practices doesn't provide a long-term cure either. Promoting health maintenance organizations, setting fee schedules for specific procedures performed under Medicare, and similar efficiency measures enacted over the past fifteen years may have created a one-time drop in utilization and spending trend lines, but such measures treat only the symptom of the health care crisis, not the disease itself. The overall rate of growth in health care expenditures continues unabated.

The conclusion is inescapable: real cost containment will require altering the underlying upward trend in health care spending. The only way to do this is to make hard decisions about who receives what procedures at what price. Everything else amounts to short-term palliatives or smoke-and-mirrors cost shifting.

As it approaches the twenty-first century, the United States faces a fundamental choice on health care. It could use market forces to allocate health care. But so long as the majority of Americans are insulated from the real cost of their health care through entitlement programs and tax subsidies, a market-based solution will never work, no matter how promising in principle.

In theory, the United States could also achieve universal access and cost containment by nationalizing its health care system, as all other advanced industrialized nations have done to one degree or another. But this approach requires more than just declaring every American *entitled* to decent health care. As virtually every other country has learned, it requires making hard choices about which procedures will be covered and which won't, about how long patients must wait to receive certain procedures, and about the total amount of resources a nation can afford to devote to health care. In other words, it involves rationing health care through the political process rather than through markets, with all the downfalls that such an approach seems inevitably to bring in the long term.

In the last two chapters of this book, we'll explore ideas for containing health care costs in greater detail. But for now, it should suffice to note that there are no quick and easy cures and that even under the best of circumstances, the real cost of health care costs is going to rise.

You will pay. Thirty years ago, when the total cost of health care was comparatively small and hordes of baby boomers were on the verge of entering the labor force, it was easy to create and finance middle-class health care entitlements like Medicare and the exclusion for employer-provided health care. No longer. Regardless of how the American health care system winds up being reorganized, middle-class Americans will inevitably wind up paying for far more of the cost of their own care.

The implications for middle-class culture are clear. The spread of AIDS and other sexually transmitted diseases has already led many Americans toward neo-Victorian ideas about sexual promiscuity. But the new realities of health care finance in the twenty-first century create an objective need to reinvent many other bourgeois values of the last century as well, particularly thrift, temperance (applied to all substance abuse), and clean living generally. Modern technology may provide for liver transplants and advanced cancer treatments not available to Victorians. But like Victorians, those who want access to the latest medical breakthroughs will have to use their own resources. And at a time when life spans are lengthening and health care costs are soaring, the inevitable reduction in middle-class health care subsidies makes the economic incentive for living like a thrifty, temperate nineteenth-century bourgeois stronger than it was even 150 years ago.

8

The Private Pension Bailout

Shortly after James Hudson succumbed to the heat wave of early July 1993, official Washington was met with an unexpected embarrassment. The conscientious forty-three-year-old National Park Service foreman had cared full time for the statue of Abraham Lincoln in the Lincoln Memorial for the last eight years. Yet when he died, local newspaper readers soon learned, his widow and seven children were left with no life insurance or pension. Their breadwinner, it turned out, had been officially classified by the Park Service as a "temp" all these many years, and as such was not entitled to any fringe benefits.

The plight of the Hudson family might be extreme, but it certainly isn't unusual. When even a "model" employer like the federal government forces loyal full-time workers to accept the status of temps, it is little wonder that more and more private sector employers do so as well. Experts say there may be as many as 30 million to 37 million temporary or contingent workers today. Richard Belous, senior economist at the National Planning Association, predicts that their ranks will increase to about 35 percent of the U.S. workforce by the year 2000, up from about 25 percent today and 20 percent just ten years ago.[1]

And this is probably a conservative estimate. Indeed, in a very real sense, the vast majority of American workers, and especially younger workers, are "temps" these days. Sure, they may hold down a full-time salaried job and even be promised a pension. But what are the chances of their being able to stay with a single employer long enough to vest into full retirement benefits?

Capitalism, as the economist Joseph P. Schumpeter once observed, is a process of "creative destruction," and never more so than in today's highly competitive world economy. Allis-Chalmers, White Motors, Studebaker, the Milwaukee Road, the Rock Island Railroad, Eastern Airlines: Such American institutions that once offered lifetime employment for generations of workers are now only dimly remembered as fallen flags of American business. In the 1980s alone, 20 million workers lost jobs because of plant closings or permanent layoffs.[2] Given the pace of business failures and consolidations over the past two decades, it's fair to say that most companies doing business in the 1990s will be long gone within twenty years.

And yet, as the majority of American workers struggle to accommodate themselves to these realities, they are encumbered by a particularly ironic burden from the past. Even as more and more Americans lose hope of collecting the pensions and other fringe benefits their fathers and grandfathers came to expect from American corporations, they must pay for the massive subsidies that government still lavishes on the lucky few who still do collect such corporate entitlements.

In the previous chapter, we examined how the huge tax subsidies enjoyed by employer-provided health care plans had driven up the cost of health care across the board while also costing the U.S. Treasury more than $46 billion a year in forgone revenue. In this chapter, we examine a similar, and perhaps still more inequitable, case study of backdoor subsidy: the nation's traditional private pension system.

Unlike say, an Individual Retirement Account, where beneficiaries collect only what turns out to be the actual return on their investment, traditional, or so-called defined-benefit, pensions typically promise to replace some fixed percentage of a worker's pay upon retirement. Since such pension plans may or may not have sufficient assets to make good on such promises, they can easily wind up being underfunded, even when fund managers are acting in good faith, which is often not the case. And when underfunding occurs, the cost of making up the deficit, as often as not, gets shifted to other people, including, ultimately, the taxpayers.

Consider Pan American World Airlines. Once the world's premier airline, it made money in only two years between 1980 and 1991. In a desperate attempt to save itself, Pan Am suspended payments to its three pension funds in 1980, 1981, 1982, and 1985, subtracting $200 million in assets. In 1987, Pan Am won special permission from the Internal Revenue Service and Department of Labor to sell its pension plans a leasehold on its Worldport terminal building at JFK Airport, for what turned out to be an absurdly high price. Soon after, the unfunded liabilities of the pension ballooned to $600 million. With that kind of red ink on its books, no buyer for the airline could be found, and the company was liquidated in 1991. More than twenty thousand workers lost their jobs, while the federal government picked up the cost of honoring most of its pension commitments.[3]

Taxpayers, in fact, wind up subsidizing these traditional pension plans even when they don't go broke. Defined-benefit plans receive over $8 billion a year in federal tax subsidies.[4] At the same time, such plans enjoy federal guarantees against default that have a free market insurance value of about $10 billion.[5]

Yet despite these huge subsidies, one pension plan out of five does not have the money to pay promised benefits, with the total amount of underfunding surpassing $31 billion.[6] Throughout the post–World War II era, the windfall benefits conveyed to the private pension system informed our collective sense of how much discipline and thrift was required to enjoy a middle-class standard of living in old age. Today this chain letter, too, is coming to an end, adding still more to the need for the middle class to adopt a sterner, more self-reliant ethos.

THE CHAIN LETTERS BEGIN

The American Express Company started the first U.S. pension plan in 1875, followed by the Baltimore and Ohio Railroad in 1880. By 1900, a few banks and public utilities had followed suit. Then, in the first two decades of the twentieth century, pension plans burgeoned among railroads, pubic utilities, and large manufacturing firms, particularly in the oil and steel industries.[7]

From the beginning, many of these plans were underfunded. Instead of building up reserves, they ladled out cash on a pay-as-you-go basis, paying current benefits out of current revenues. Money was not stockpiled for future costs, and within a generation, many of these programs were reeling in debt. For example, the Pennsylvania Railroad began its pension plan in 1903, with an annual expenditure of less than $300,000. But by 1925, as more and more Pennsy workers qualified for pensions, the road was spending about $3.5 million, with further increases ahead.

The crisis was industry wide, even before the Great Depression. "How long can American railroads stand the financial strain of their present pension plans?" asked the trade journal *Railway Age* in 1925. "What assurance has anyone that current revenues in 1950 will be sufficient to stand the strain of pension liabilities that are accruing in 1925?" None whatsoever, it turned out. These mismanaged private railroad pensions survived only because Uncle Sam bailed them out in the early 1930s. To this day, railroad pensions are provided by an obscure Federal entitlement known as the Railroad Retirement program.[8]

Few new pension plans were created during the depression, and only about 17 percent of the labor force in 1940 worked at jobs with pension plans. Then, during and shortly after World War II, pension coverage exploded. The primary reason was the increasingly generous tax subsidy Uncle Sam provided for pension plans in that period. As late as 1939 only 5 percent of the population had paid income taxes; by 1946, 75 percent paid them, with corporations shelling out up to 80 percent of their profits in tax. As a result, the special provisions exempting pension trusts from taxation suddenly became very valuable to a broad cross section of the population.

Meanwhile, wage controls imposed during the war limited pay increases but permitted workers to receive pension benefit increases of any amount. In other words, if you wanted a raise during the war, the only way you could get one was in the form of a fatter pension or other fringe benefits. This, combined with the increasing value of pensions funds as devices for escaping high income taxes, led to a huge increase in pension coverage. While only 515 plans existed in 1938, by 1946 there were about 7,000 of them covering about 3.3 million employees.[9]

After the war, pension growth temporarily slowed, but the continued high tax rates and strong interest in pensions by employees, especially organized labor, spurred rapid pension growth in the late 1940s and through the 1950s. Why were unions particularly interested? One reason, of course, is that union leaders like controlling the riches that pass through a typical multi-employer pension trust fund. Another is that union politics tends to be dominated by older workers, and the creation of new pension plans created the opportunity for older workers to receive enormous windfall benefits.

A prime example comes from the United Mine Workers, which in 1946 became the first union in the country to win an employer-funded pension over which union leaders had administrative control. A key feature of the new plan was the generous credit it provided older workers for service performed before the plan's existence. The provision of these so-called past service credits meant that retired miners could receive pensions of $100 a month without anyone's ever having set aside any money to pay for these benefits. Though management tried to persuade the UMW to fund the cost of these windfalls, the union instead wanted the maximum benefits possible for current retirees.

The result, by 1955, was a deficit for current retirees alone that exceeded $1.25 billion, or more than eight years' worth of contributions to the fund. But the UMW's fiery, charismatic president, John L. Lewis, wasn't fazed in the least by the burdens his pension was im-

posing on the future of his union, and on the Appalachian coal min-
ing industry in general. It would be a "crime of the highest order," he
insisted, to deprive those now alive and in need merely to "sequester
and secrete these great sums of money" in a pension fund.[10]

This pattern repeated itself throughout industrial America during
the postwar era. Most of the new pension plans started during this
period were in deficit from day one because of the provision of past-
service credits for older workers. As time went on, the deficits typically became larger and larger, as unions perpetually won higher and
higher pension benefits in successive contracts. Whenever this happened, pension actuaries merely increased the plan's existing debt
for past-service credits and amortized, or stretched the repayment
of, the new obligations over thirty years.

This would not have been a problem if workers had waited that
long to receive the new benefits, but some workers retired right
away, and nearly all would be retired and drawing the new higher
benefits before any cash was committed to paying for these benefits. As a result, pension debt just kept growing. As Steven Sass of
the Federal Reserve Bank of Boston has pointed out in a study of
pension fund finances, by the early 1960s, widespread provisions
for early retirement and dramatic increases in monthly pension
benefits meant that most funds were setting few, if any, assets aside
to defray future obligations. "The equity accruing to the young and
the able," notes Sass, "had become cultural and political rather than
economic."[11]

THE FIRST BAILOUT

So long as the economy and the workforces of most large industrial
companies continued to grow rapidly during the 1950s and 1960s,
the mounting debt in most pension funds could be easily financed.
As with Social Security during that period, most private pension
plans had lots of workers available to pay for each retiree, so the cost
of current benefits could be easily met on a pay-as-you-go basis. But
with the recession that settled across industrial America in the

1970s, all the pension debts built up during the postwar period started coming due.

One of the most politically significant pension failures of that era took place when the Raybestos-Manhattan Co. shut down a plant in Passaic, New Jersey. This just happened to be in the backyard of the powerful chairman of the U.S. Labor Committee. Senator Harrison A. Williams would later be sent to prison as a result of his implication in the Abscam scandal of the early 1980s, but future generations will probably take more affront at his role in making the federal government responsible for the cost of bailing out failed pension funds.

At the same time Raybestos-Manhattan was faltering, Ballentine's, a Newark dairy company, was also on the brink of closing. This made the pressure on Williams to "do something" about protecting workers' pensions particularly acute. As hundreds of similar plants closed throughout what came to be known as the Rust Belt, other members of Congress felt the same heat.[12]

The result was a landmark bill known as the Employee Retirement Income Security Act of 1974 (ERISA), which Gerald Ford signed into law on Labor Day as one of his first acts as president. Ironically, many conservatives went along with ERISA, believing that it would help prevent private pension plans from being nationalized as part of a greatly expanded Social Security system, which then seemed liked a real possibility to many observers.

ERISA had several provisions. It set minimum (albeit, still woefully inadequate) funding standards for private pensions. It set standards for coverage and a maximum of ten years (since reduced to five) for a worker to acquire a vested legal right to his or her promised pension benefits. And finally it created a new federal insurance agency, the Pension Benefit Guaranty Corp. (PBGC), to pay pensions to the beneficiaries of failed plans. Williams and the other authors of ERISA did not expect this promise to cost much. They thought all the regulation created by ERISA would be enough to prevent all but a few isolated claims. But as it turned out, the very existence of federal insurance for failed plans actually led to even more financial recklessness among plan sponsors, because it was now the taxpayers who would ultimately pay for any pension debts that got out of hand.

THE MORAL HAZARD OF PENSION INSURANCE

Insurance tends to change the behavior of those who have it. When the federal government provides flood insurance, more people build on flood plains. When it insures savings and loan deposits, savers pay less heed to how the thrift is run. And when it insures private pension plans, both beneficiaries and plan sponsors tend to become less interested in how future benefits will be funded. This is the fatal flaw in ERISA. The act tightened regulation of pension finance, but not enough to overcome the perverse incentives, or "moral hazard," as actuaries call it, created by federal pension insurance.

Take the example of TWA. At a time when the now-bankrupt airline's pension fund was underfunded by $1.2 billion, it *increased* pension benefits by $100 million. And why not? In the event of default, the PBGC stood ready to pick up the tab, which is exactly what happened when the airline folded.

From the start, financial experts have warned about the long-term consequences of insuring pensions. In effect, the PBGC provides plan sponsors with the opportunity to borrow (via deferred compensation) from their employees on the assumption that if the company fails, the additional debt eventually will be repaid by the taxpayers. As pension expert James H. Smalhout has pointed out, "The existence of such guarantees makes pension promises much more valuable to employees, who in turn become more willing to substitute new pension benefits for wage increases—a tradeoff that has proved particularly attractive to companies with weak balance sheets."[13] This ability to lower total compensation costs by making pension promises with the government's money is known in the financial literature as the "pension put," and in many cases it represents a significant portion of a sponsor's value to shareholders.

What's the total value of this subsidy? With roughly $1 trillion in private pension promises at risk—approximately the size of the thrift industry at its peak—the answer is clearly "a lot." But because no one knows exactly how many plans will fail in the future and at what cost, estimating the precise value of the subsidy is not easy. A 1987 study of six major steel producers and IBM produced estimates of an annual subsidy ranging from approximately $2,000 to $5,000 per participant for various steel companies and $1,270 for IBM.[14] A more recent effort conducted by the White House's Office of Management and Budget estimated the present value of the subsidy at between $30 billion and $60 billion, which translates into an annual subsidy in the $2.6 billion to $5.2 billion range.[15] Outside experts, such as Smalhout, believe the actual subsidy amount may come to $10 billion a year, or as much as $4,000 per participant in the riskiest pension plans.[16]

The PBGC does collect premiums from pension funds, but these don't begin to cover the real cost the program is imposing on future taxpayers. One reason is that the government spends these premiums as fast as they come in the door instead of investing them in wealth-producing assets. The trust funds maintained by the PBGC are just as bogus as those maintained by the Social Security Administration, and for the same reason. PBGC premiums that aren't immediately used for current PBGC expenses wind up being used to buy U.S. Treasury debt, for which future taxpayers are liable.

In effect, the government is using PBGC premiums to fund general operations, just as it is using Social Security funds for this purpose. Indeed, under the budget rules in effect since 1990, PBGC premiums not used for current expense make possible additional spending for programs within the jurisdiction of the congressional labor and education committees.

Moreover, even if PBGC premiums were used to build up real reserves rather than for financing other government activity, they would still be woefully inadequate. Even as the Clinton administration congratulated itself in late 1994 for sneaking a premium hike increase through Congress as a part of an obscure technical provision of a massive trade bill, the maximum premium charged to the riskiest plans was scheduled to rise gradually to a mere $142 per participant.[17]

Because such premiums don't begin to cover the real costs presented by underfunded plans, another negative dynamic is created: adverse selection. When underfunded plans pay too little, they are in effect subsidized by well-funded plans, which pay too much in proportion to the actual risks they present. This creates an incentive for well-funded plans to shut down, a trend that has been gathering force since the early 1980s. "Ultimately," warn analysts Zvi Bodie and Robert C. Merton, "the United States could be left only with bankrupt defined-benefit plans with the benefits financed directly by the taxpayers."[18]

ARE THE SUBSIDIES JUSTIFIED?

America certainly has a long-term interest in reducing poverty and dependence among the elderly in the next century. But are the subsidies for private, defined-benefit pension plans an efficient or equitable means for achieving that end?

The first major problem with these subsidies is that, like so many other entitlements, they flow primarily to a relatively affluent minority of Americans. That is true of the tax subsidies provides for Individual Retirement Accounts as well, but at least in the case of IRAs, any American workers who wants to take advantage of these subsidies is able to do so. By contrast, barely one out of five American workers can even potentially collect defined-benefit pensions—a ratio that will only worsen as more and more employers continue to cancel their defined-benefit plans.[19] Even among those whose who are covered by such plans, only an estimated one third will hold on to their jobs long enough to collect benefits.[20]

Who are the typical recipients of PBGC-insured pensions? More often than not, the beneficiary is male, over fifty, working in a relatively high-paying job for an employer he has served for a long time, and living somewhere in the North Central states or the Northeast. Most such folks are certainly patriotic Americans, but is there any particular reason for singling them out for expensive pension subsidies?

There is no doubt that federal pension insurance allows weak firms to retain workers they otherwise could not afford. But to the extent that PBGC subsidies ultimately benefit such weak firms while providing comparatively little value to strong firms, the question becomes why that is an appropriate public policy? By disproportionately lowering the cost of labor for firms that lack strong demand for their products, PBGC subsidies reduce the overall efficiency of the economy.

Another consideration is that many of the recipients of PBGC-insured pensions are far more affluent than the average taxpayer. In 1993, the maximum benefit guaranteed by the PBGC stood at $2,420 a month, or $29,250 a year. Counting Social Security, this produced a government-guaranteed retirement income of as much as $42,796—more than eight times the social minimum the government pays to needy elders under its Supplemental Security Income program.[21]

Not only is class equity a problem; generational equity is as well. Given the shrinking number of employers even offering defined-benefit plans, young people are far less likely to receive any benefit over their lifetimes from the subsidies these plans consume than are members of the current older generation. Yet disproportionately it is the young who will pay for the huge unfunded liabilities building up within the federal pension insurance program.

Even when defined-benefit plans don't intentionally run up big debts, they often degenerate into a mechanism for permanently transferring wealth across generations. For example, Bethlehem Steel in 1978 had 101,000 workers; today it makes the same amount of steel with just 24,000 workers. Throughout this period, Bethlehem Steel's pension fund has carried a debt of $2.4 billion. But now, with a dramatically shrunken workforce, the burden of carrying this debt approaches $100,000 per worker.[22]

This is not an uncommon story. Any company that carries a substantial pension debt and then downsizes faces a similar problem. Ultimately the debt must be paid, or the plan will go broke. Firms can make up such a deficit only by holding down wages, cutting reinvestment, cutting dividends, or some combination of all three. However the bill winds up being paid, the next generation as a whole is worse off.

That can happen even when everyone involved has the best of intentions. Because these plans promise benefits without regard to the actual future performance of their investment portfolios, many disparate demographic and economic trends can unexpectedly

throw them into insolvency. A round of layoffs and forced early retirements, for example, will unexpectedly raise pension debt by
shrinking contributions and swelling benefit costs. Similarly, when
the return on the plan's investment portfolio is lower than expected,
or when costs rise due to retirees' living longer than anticipated, the
prospects for default grow inordinately. A Labor Department study
indicates that for each decline of one percentage point in interest
rates earned by a corporate pension plan, the plan's total unfunded
liability rises by about 10 percent.[23]

Although ERISA establishes minimum funding rules, the financial position of an underfunded plan often deteriorates dramatically
in the years shortly before actual termination, particularly if the
number of retirees covered by the plan is increasing rapidly while
the number of active workers is shrinking. According to PBGC, the
funding level of a typical underfunded plan plunged to about 40 percent of liabilities at actual termination from a level of 60 to 80 percent only five years earlier.[24] In short, even the best-run plans are in
effect riverboat gambles.

THE WAY OUT

The government could never raise premiums enough to compensate
for the full risks to which it exposes future taxpayers through the
PBGC. At that level, the cost of PBGC insurance would quickly
force huge numbers of marginal plans to go under. And a premium
that shifted all the risk to other sponsors, instead of taxpayers, would
cause healthy plans to leave the defined-benefit system. That leaves
only one practical alternative: cut the insurance.

Most people in America who are striving to save for their retirement don't receive federally subsidized pension insurance. If you invest your IRA in a mutual fund that goes broke, it's your loss. If
your 401(k) pension plan at work buys worthless annuities or gets
bitten by derivatives, Uncle Sam says you should have diversified.
So how long will the federal government go risking hundreds of millions of your tax dollars insuring defined-benefit pensions enjoyed
by a minority of relatively well-off workers concentrated in a few
heavy industries?

If private industries or unions want to protect against loss of their pensions, they can buy private insurance, as is the normal practice for private pension plans even in such European welfare states as Sweden, Finland, and Germany. But the days of taxpayers as a whole subsidizing these plans are rapidly drawing to a close. Just as was the case for most Victorians, neither your government, nor your employer, is going to do your retirement saving for you.

9

Subsidizing Suburbia

When future historians look back on our era, they will no doubt concentrate on a few choice examples of inequity and dysfunction of the American welfare state. When they do so, they will no doubt mention first and foremost the federal government's largest housing subsidy: a program that by 1991 was providing an average of $3,000 a year to each of the 6 million wealthiest households in America, while offering nothing to the 36 million Americans in poverty.

To qualify for this particular benefit, citizens had to borrow using their primary residence as collateral. And the more they borrowed, even if it were to finance a vacation home in Aspen—or just a ski trip to Aspen—the more subsidy they would receive from other taxpayers. By 1991 the cost of this benefit had risen to $36 billion, of which 80 percent went directly to households with incomes over $50,000.[1] Meanwhile, economists bemoaned the anemic U.S. personal savings rate, which in the early 1990s fell to its lowest level since the 1930s.

The name of this extraordinary federal entitlement program? The home mortgage deduction.

After veterans' benefits, it is among the nation's oldest and most sacrosanct of entitlements. Its origins date back to the first income tax experiments during the Civil War. In the Revenue Acts of 1864 and 1865, Congress permitted taxpayers to deduct interest expense (including mortgage interest payments) as well as local tax levies (including property taxes).[2]

When the federal income tax became permanent in 1913, Congress again provided for a mortgage interest deduction. It was a trifling benefit at the time. The top income tax rate was a mere 7 percent, and only the top 2 percent of the labor force was even required to file a return.[3] But over time, as federal income tax rates climbed and American home owners simultaneously began carrying more and more mortgage debt, the mortgage interest deduction became ever more expensive. By the early 1990s, its cost was more than double the budget authority of all housing assistance programs for the poor run by the U.S. Department of Housing and Urban Development (HUD).[4]

Today not only is the mortgage interest deduction the largest federal housing subsidy, it is also straightforwardly the most "entitlement-like." In contrast, many HUD programs in effect work like lotteries, benefiting only a lucky few among those who might qualify. Indeed, less than a third of renter households with very low incomes (below 50 percent of median income in their areas) receive any federal housing assistance whatsoever.[5] Most public housing authorities have long waiting lists, and even many of HUD's loan guarantee programs are available only to those who show up early to grab a place at the head of the line. But the mortgage interest deduction is a maximum entitlement: if you qualify, you get your benefit, no matter who else is in line or what it costs the government.

The same is true of the three other major housing subsidies distributed through the tax code: the deductibility of local real estate taxes (established in 1913), the deferral of capital gains on home sales (established in 1951), and the forgiving of up to $125,000 of capital gains on houses sold by those over fifty-five years of age (established in 1964).[6] Together with the mortgage interest deduction, these entitlement-like subsidies cost the Treasury $76.8 billion in 1993.[7]

This doesn't even count the largest tax subsidy flowing to home owners. If you invest $100,000 in stocks or bonds, you have to pay taxes on any return they yield. But if you invest the same money in buying your own house, the very substantial return your house will bring you in the form of rent-free living is exempt from any taxation whatsoever.

Who benefits from these tax subsidies is far from clear. On paper, upper-middle-class home owners receive the largest benefits. According to the congressional Joint Committee on Taxation, for example, the average value of the mortgage interest deduction for taxpayers with incomes over $100,000 was $3,469 in 1991. In contrast, the same deduction was worth an average of only $516 for taxpayers in the $20,000 to $30,000 bracket who qualified to take the benefit— and, of course, many, including renters and those who opted for the standard deduction, did not.[8]

Many middle-class home owners have also learned how to use the home mortgage deduction to finance vacations and other forms of consumer spending. Between 1987 and 1991, the interest paid on consumer loans gradually lost its deductibility, while interest paid on loans secured by a home mortgage, including home equity loans, remained tax deductible. Some banks even offer credit cards for conveniently borrowing against your home—and getting a tax break too.

But the same people who enjoy these subsidies also pay a price for them. The government must make up the cost of the home mortgage and other housing subsidies somehow. It does this in part by running up the national debt, setting overall tax rates higher than they would otherwise be, and closing other loopholes, such as the deductibility of Individual Retirement Account contributions, that might otherwise remain open.

What you subsidize, you tend to get more of. In the long run, subsidizing middle-class home ownership may well lead to serious overbuilding and a bust in home prices, particularly as changing demographics shrinks the ranks of home buyers. But before that day comes, there can be little doubt that housing subsidies continue to prop up home prices higher than they otherwise would be. Today the market value of a house is determined not just by its utility as a shelter from the elements but also as a shelter from taxes. The tax benefits become, in other words, just one more amenity—like built-in curio cabinets or convenience to shopping—for which you must pay when you buy a house.

The same point applies to other tax breaks available to home owners, such as the deferral of capital gains, which Congress passed at the height of the Korean War with the stated intention of alleviating wartime hardships. Those who owned houses at the time certainly received a net benefit, but everyone since has simply paid a little more for residential real estate, in accord with its increased value as a capital gains tax shelter.

And, of course, having paid for these loopholes when you bought your house, you understandably don't want Congress to take them away—at least not without offering compensation. So it is that the nation's addiction to these entitlements, which were once no more than obscure and insignificant details of the tax code, becomes more and more chronic each decade. Every time either federal tax rates or average home prices go up, the value of these tax breaks increases, causing new home owners to become even more dependent on government's continuing them forever. But as with any other addiction, this one can't go on forever. Indeed, given the enormous budget constraints being caused by the growth of entitlements, it's easy to imagine the home mortgage deduction disappearing, or at least being severely means-tested, within ten years.

MIDDLE-CLASS HOUSING SUBSIDIES AND DEINDUSTRIALIZATION

Meanwhile, middle-class home owners continue to enjoy plenty of direct housing subsidies that are likely to be cut as well. Two well-known examples are the mortgage guarantee programs run by the Veterans Administration (discussed in Chapter 10) and the Federal Housing Administration (FHA). Chances are you'll be hearing a lot more about the FHA program in coming years. As of September 30, 1992, the FHA held $329.5 billion in mortgages on single homes and apartment houses,[9] of which about $13.8 billion was in default.[10] Alarmed that the cost to taxpayers could go much higher, the General Accounting Office has placed the FHA on its list of "high-risk" programs.

Does America get its money's worth for these subsidies? To answer that question, you have to consider what they really cost in the long run. Along with shortsighted banking and credit regulations, middle-class housing subsidies have served to divert huge capital flows away from productive investment over the past generation. This in turn has led to falling real wages for today's younger Americans, making housing all the less affordable than it otherwise would be.

The competition between housing and industrial competitiveness was particularly acute during the 1970s, when the value of tax subsidies, like the mortgage interest deduction, rose dramatically as inflation pushed Americans into higher and higher tax brackets. Largely because of this increase in the value of home owner subsidies delivered through the tax code, millions of Americans decided that piling on mortgage debt to buy the biggest house they could possibly afford was the quickest route to riches—or at least a far better idea than saving their money in the bank or investing in the stock market.

The result? Not surprisingly, the average stock lost 23 percent of its value during the 1970s, while the average house appreciated 155 percent. Capital that could have gone for retooling American industry at a time of mounting foreign competition went instead for financing the sale and resale of houses and condominiums at ever higher prices. The homes of Grosse Pointe and other suburbs of Detroit came to be far more luxurious than any found in the suburbs of, say, Yokohama or Stuttgart. But in Detroit the suburbs surrounded a burned-out deindustrializing core. The haunting symbol of the new American economy became the abandoned factory surrounded by a sprawling housing development.[11]

In the short run, all the subsidies pouring into the housing sector did help to stimulate economic growth and forestall recession—providing yet another reason why cutting the subsidies became politically impossible, no matter what damage they might be doing to America's future standard of living. As Alan Carlson of the Rockford Institute recalls: "A recession could be avoided, the macroeconomic argument went, only through the maintenance of residential construction at an artificially high level. The American economy was hooked, with a super-heated housing market being its drug of choice."[12]

HOUSING AND BOURGEOIS VALUES

Skyrocketing housing subsidies also had a profound effect on middle-class values during the 1970s, particularly in helping to extinguish the last vestiges of the thrift ethos. "The house became a vehicle for maintaining consumption patterns in the face of stagnating incomes," housing economists George Sternlieb and James Hughes observe. "Homeownership became not only the symbol of the good life, it became a means for financing its continuance. Who needed a formal savings account when the house had become the chief repository of personal stored wealth? The consumption ethic conquered the habits of thrift assiduously cultivated in the original social housing compact. Government policy made losers of savers and winners of speculators."[13]

Another way housing subsidies may have affected middle-class values is by helping to underwrite, or at least accommodate, the breakup of the American family into smaller and smaller households. Since the 1970s, the rate of household formation has far exceeded the rate of population growth. Delayed marriages and an increasing divorce rate are the primary reasons. It's obviously an exaggeration to say that housing subsidies caused these trends, yet they certainly helped facilitate them by making it comparatively cheap to remain single, or for husbands and wives to strike out on their own, or for grandparents to move away to the Sun Belt. As Alan Carlson puts it, "The excess capacity of the residential construction industry resulted in the building of homes that could only be filled by the parts of shattered or never-formed families."[14]

To be sure, many still argue that federal subsidies to home ownership and suburban living make for a more wholesome, virtuous, and civic-minded citizenry. Yet who today would argue that the American middle class, as it is found today amid the strip malls, tract homes, and office parks of America's sprawling suburbs and exurbs, is any more wholesome and virtuous, let alone rooted in the life of the community, than it was a generation ago? In the 1950s, it was still possible to believe that children raised in spanking-new subdivisions would grow up free of delinquency, drug use, and other evils associated with the inner city. But in the 1990s, as suburban high schools grapple with gangs, guns, and mounting teenage suicides, such ideas seem at best utopian. Far from fostering better-adjusted children, suburban sprawl is producing kids widely condemned as "mall rats"—a generation most notable for its weak sense of community and lack of faith in the future.

"No man who owns his own house and lot can be a communist," the developer Bill Levitt declared in the 1940s. "He has too much to do." And so it may be. But the idea that subsidizing Levittown strengthens middle-class virtue has no evidence in its favor today. The typical middle-aged, middle-class home owner may feel he collects little or nothing in the way of direct government housing aid. But with the value of his house propped up by federal tax expenditures and other direct and indirect subsidies worth tens of thousands of dollars, his dependency on government can objectively rival that of many welfare mothers. And in many ways, the results of such an addiction are no less harmful.

10

Everyman a Hero

Throughout American history, soldiers have returned from war feeling victimized, and the public has almost always acknowledged at least some debt of gratitude. In this sense, veterans' benefits are the quintessential entitlement: they are at least perceived to be a reward for valor—a true earned right—not just another government handout or federal employee benefit. And yet in modern times, the definition of just who is a veteran keeps expanding to the point that today, actual combat or even wartime experience has little do with who receives veterans' benefits.

The absolute cost of veterans' payments continues to break new records, reaching $37.7 billion in 1995. But due to the ever-looser connection between veterans' benefits and actual war experience, as well as to the aging of the veteran population, that number will grow rapidly for many decades to come, even if America never fights another war. The Department of Veterans Affairs estimates that the present value of its liability for entitlements promised to ex-servicemen and women comes to more than $189.85 billion.[1] No money has been put aside to pay for this debt from the past, which is as large as a Reagan-era deficit.

CASE STUDIES

Just who is a veteran anyway? For the average American, the label is likely to conjure up images of paraplegics haunted by flashbacks from Hue, or of war heroes from Tarawa or Belleau Wood returning home to ticker-tape parades. A grateful nation asks, How can we ever repay these men and women who have risked their lives in battle to keep us free? And from just such a diffused feeling of guilt and gratitude comes the opportunity for no end of political mischief.

During the 1920s and 1930s, many Americans were shocked by reports of aging Spanish-American War and Great War veterans' receiving free medical care for non-war-related conditions such as obesity, itching, and varicose veins. "Peace veterans" became their derisive epithet. But at least such men had once gone overseas to defend their country. Today, barely half of the 27 million Americans eligible for veterans' benefits have ever served in a war zone, much less seen combat. For purposes of collecting benefits, experience in battle has become irrelevant. Without the public's paying much attention, veterans' payments have evolved into a smorgasbord of social welfare benefits that for no particularly coherent reason go exclusively to ex-servicemen and women.

What makes this set of entitlements even more perverse is that they offer far too little for combat veterans who have truly sacrificed for their country, while lavishing all sorts of unneeded benefits on uniformed office workers. No amount of benefits can ever begin to repay what some men and women lose on the field of battle. But while a young soldier crippled and blinded for life by a land mine receives a total disability benefit of just $1,730 a month, tens of billions of dollars flow each year to enable noncombat veterans to refinance their homes with subsidized mortgages or to receive free health care.

So primordial are the myths surrounding veterans' benefits that many Americans, particularly conservatives, have trouble seeing these entitlements for what they really are. As one reader of an early draft of this chapter wrote: "You will not find a veteran who is in more sympathy with your critique than me. But in looking at all the people on the dole, from the run-of-the-mill poor person to the guy with the FHA loan, you should acknowledge that at least veterans gave *something* in return."

EVERYMAN A HERO

Of course, some veterans have sacrificed far more for their country than can ever be repaid. But this chapter is not about those war heroes. It's about the vast majority of Department of Defense employees who just happen to wear a uniform to work. Yes, these men and women may find themselves in harm's way if a war breaks out. But statistically, most hold jobs that are no more dangerous (and often less so) than those held by many civilians, from police and firefighters to convenience store clerks and taxi drivers—a fact that would remain true even if the United States were engaged in another conflict on the order of World War II.

Yes, some of these Department of Defense employees might have had more lucrative or enjoyable careers in the private sector. But the fact that some have sacrificed other ambitions to serve in the military does not per se distinguish them from other entitlement recipients. After all, many farmers could make more money with less work if they took office jobs; fortunately, some still "sacrifice" to put food on our tables. Similarly all sorts of other public employees—NASA engineers, prosecutors and judges, FDA scientists—could probably also have made higher salaries working in the public sector.

Frankly, most Americans can make just as strong a case as most veterans for having "earned" their benefits. Lifelong civilians who collect the home mortgage deduction, Social Security, Medicare, and Medicaid have all "sacrificed" for their country, after all, if by no other means than the "contributions" they make every April 15. Even welfare recipients, most of whom are only on the dole for short periods, pay all sorts of taxes over their lifetimes. The question, as always, is, Are the benefits one receives proportionate to one's contributions?

Many veterans complain that cutting their benefits would be tantamount to breaking a contract. But legally, veterans' benefits are no more a contractual right than Social Security benefits. And morally, the promises politicians may have made to veterans over the years are no more, and no less, inviolate than the promises they have made to other special interest groups.

The unvarnished truth about veterans' benefits is that they are not a reward for valor. If they were, they would go exclusively to combat vets and would be set high enough to be commensurate with the sacrifice made. Instead, veterans' benefits are a form of political payoff to a large and well-organized special interest whose members politicians have felt compelled to appease from time to time by throwing other people's money at them. In this sense, veterans' benefits are no different from the entitlements that today flow to retirees, farmers, home owners, and other special interests. They are claims on the public purse enforced by pure political power, and like other such claims, their cost has become untenable.

WHEN JOHNNY MARCHES HOME FROM THE OFFICE

Entitlement to veterans' benefits these days depends somewhat on when a person joined the armed services but not at all on what actual sacrifice he or she made while in uniform. In distributing veterans' benefits, the government does not care, for example, if an applicant served as a naval clerk in Key West during the Vietnam War or as an infantry scout in the Mekong Delta. Instead, every ex-serviceman or woman with more than ninety days of active duty between August 1964 and May 1975 is officially classified as Vietnam-era veteran and as such is entitled to all the same benefits as those who actually fought in Vietnam.

Not surprisingly, most Vietnam-era vets never saw Vietnam. Of the 8 million persons who passed through the military while the war in Vietnam was fought, only half were stationed in Southeast Asia, and 65 percent never saw combat.[2]

It's much the same for older veterans. An American who wore a uniform at any time between September 16, 1940, and July 25, 1947, for example, is entitled to special benefits as a World War II–era veteran. That is true even if this person joined the Coast Guard on VJ Day and spent his or her tour filling out forms in New London. On the other hand, merchant marine seamen who faced relentless attacks by Nazi submarine wolf packs in the North Atlantic received no entitlement to veterans' benefits until the 1980s, when most were well into their sixties.

For ex-servicemen who wore a uniform during official no-war periods, there are still plenty of benefits available. Certain health care benefits require official wartime experience, and veterans' education benefits have become less generous since the move to an all-volunteer force in the 1970s. But in most cases, persons leaving the military today are entitled to the same benefits as earlier vets if they've served on active duty for more than six months.

Among the most coveted of these benefits is the Department of Veterans Affairs' home loan guarantee. Want to buy or build a house with no money down, no mortgage insurance costs, no points, and with below-market interest rates? Your banker will tell you to forget it—unless you are an ex-serviceman or woman.

Veterans can purchase homes priced up to $184,000 with no down payment and with other favorable terms unavailable to non-veterans. Banks and other financial institutions know they have nothing to lose in offering such sweetheart deals to veterans because the taxpayers pick up the cost of any defaults. In 1992, the cost to the taxpayers of making good on VA-guaranteed mortgages in default came to over $740 million.[3]

Mortgage bankers and realtors love the loan guarantee program and perpetually clamor to make it even more generous. As a spokesman for the National Association of Realtors told Congress in 1993, it supports an increase in guarantees because it "will provide a much needed economic boost to high-cost housing markets."[4]

The VA doesn't care if you're a struggling first-time home buyer seeking a handyman special or an affluent middle-aged professional trading up to a high-class place on the water. Its only concern is that you once wore a uniform and received an honorable discharge. Veterans can continue to take out any number of new VA mortgages throughout their lives as they move from property to property. Those who default after taking out two or more VA mortgages cost the taxpayers over $15 million a year, according to estimates by the Congressional Budget Office.[5]

Taxpayers also often get stuck when veterans sell their houses. The VA allows any qualified buyer, veteran or not, to assume a VA mortgage and enjoy all its subsidized terms. When that happens, the VA and the taxpayers remain at financial risk for the assumed loan.

A plethora of other benefits also flows to veterans with little or no regard for their actual combat experience or service-related loss. Often it is not just veterans who benefit but a variety of other interests who profit indirectly. One example is VA educational assistance benefits, which can still be substantial, adding up to a maximum of more than $12,600 for veterans enrolling as full-time students. During the 1970s, the high value and loose administration of these benefits caused hundreds of diploma mills to spring into existence and virtually underwrote a dramatic expansion of the nation's vocational-technical schools.

Other veterans' benefits range from preferential processing for Farmers Home Loan Administration loans to the affirmative action mandate on federal contractors to employ and promote Vietnam-era veterans.[6] Veterans also enjoy preferential hiring by the federal government itself. When originally enacted in 1865, this policy applied to disabled men only, but as with so many other veterans' benefits, it now covers everyone who once wore a uniform.[7] Even disability benefits themselves have lost their link to military experience. For example, the Department of Veterans Affairs offers means-tested pensions to disabled veterans who have as little as one day of wartime service and whose disabilities are specifically *not* service related.

Indeed, fully half of VA disability compensation payments now go to ex-servicemen and women whose injuries or diseases are not connected with their military service. More than 390,000 veterans currently receive VA compensation payments totaling $1.2 billion a year for diseases that the General Accounting Office reports are generally neither caused nor aggravated by military service—for example, arteriosclerotic heart disease, diabetes mellitus, multiple sclerosis, Hodgkin's disease, chronic obstructive pulmonary disease (including chronic bronchitis and pulmonary emphysema), hemorrhoids, schizophrenia, osteoarthritis, and benign prosthetic hypertrophy. Recipients of VA disability compensation payments remain entitled to Social Security disability payments as well.[8]

A wide range of government agencies besides the Department of Veterans Affairs also deliver benefits specifically targeted to ex-servicemen and women, often at the direct expense of other citizens seeking services. Consider the case of the Department of Labor's Veterans' Employment and Training Service program (VETS). Labor Department staff detailed to VETS are legally prohibited from serving nonveterans, so if a local employment service office is crowded with nonveterans seeking job training, these specialists cannot help out, even if they have no veterans to serve.[9]

By far the single most expensive, and fastest-growing, category of veterans' benefits is medical care. The Department of Veterans Affairs administers a vast health care system: 171 hospitals, 131 nursing homes, 371 outpatient clinics, and 36 domiciliaries. Spending on VA health care equaled $14 billion in fiscal year 1992, which amounted to 41 percent of total veterans' programs that year. VA health care program outlays have more than doubled since 1980.[10]

Originally, only veterans disabled in the course of military duty had entitlement to free health care, but under pressure from the American Legion and other veterans' groups, Congress broadened eligibility over the years to include public medical care for all who have served in the armed forces, regardless of whether the need arises from service-connected causes.[11] Veterans with service-related disabilities still are first in line for access to the system. But today, the VA estimates that well over half of its hospital, outpatient, and nursing home patients are being treated for non-service-related conditions.[12]

When treating veterans whose disabilities are not related to military service, the VA is supposed to collect copayments from those who can afford to pay. But due to lax administration, the VA forfeits millions each year by not checking on veterans who lie about their income in order to avoid copayments. According to a 1992 General Accounting Office study, the number of veterans inappropriately receiving free VA health care for non-service-related conditions exceeded 100,000 annually in the early 1990s. The cost to the taxpayers was over $120 million a year.[13]

The mass migration of retired veterans to Sun Belt states means that VA hospitals in many other parts of the country have trouble keeping their hospital beds filled. Still, Congress goes on authorizing the construction of new VA hospitals throughout the Rust Belt even where patients are scarce and beds plentiful. One 500-bed VA hospital under construction in 1993 was going up in an area that already had 1,350 beds unoccupied on a typical day. Suggestions by reformers that the health care needs of veterans could be better met by contracting with private or community hospitals provoke charges of heresy from the VA. With 90 percent of the VA's staff involved in running its medical system, the bureaucratic imperative says to keep building more hospitals.

At the same time, the veterans' lobby strongly resists the idea of allowing nonveterans access to empty VA hospital beds. President Bush's VA secretary, Edward Derwinski, once suggested allowing nonveterans to use VA hospitals in rural Virginia and Alabama, where there were more VA hospital beds than veteran patients. For his trouble, veterans' groups, utilizing their vaunted ability to deliver more than a million letters to Congress on any given issue, forced his resignation in September 1992.[14] Veterans, for all the benefits they enjoy, see themselves as a unique and underappreciated tribe that has been repeatedly abused by an unfeeling bureaucracy and an ungrateful or indifferent public. The idea of allowing civilians to share in their privileges, even if at no cost to themselves, was thus an ultimate insult and abomination.

Despite the declining percentage of the U.S. electorate with military experience, the strength of the veterans' lobby remains difficult to overestimate. Most veterans' groups are small, and essentially fraternal, organizations, each with its own curious rites and rituals and bonds of shared memory. They range from the Navajo Code Talkers Association, a group of fifty Navajo Indians who helped pass secret messages for the Marine Corps during World War II, to Vietnam Veterans Against the War, which these days holds tearful support group meetings in the pews of a lower Manhattan church, to the United Spanish War Veterans, which in 1990 boasted a surviving membership of one. Other veterans' groups, however, while still essentially fraternal societies, have memberships in the millions whom they can easily mobilize for dramatic raids on the public purse.

LEGIONNAIRE'S DISEASE

In the twentieth century, the American Legion has been the dominant veterans' group. Founded by a group of officers and enlisted men in Paris during February and March 1919, the Legion soon gained unprecedented power. Its chief lobbyist, John T. Taylor, had a formidable reputation during the 1920s and 1930s for intimidating officials. At the end of his career, it was said of Taylor that he had "rammed 630 bills through Congress, forced three Presidents to their knees and obtained $13,000,000,000 worth of benefits for ex-servicemen."[15]

By 1932, twenty-four cents out of every dollar Americans paid in taxes was going to support veterans' benefits. The demands by "bonus marchers"—Great War veterans who marched on Washington in 1932 demanding early payment of a budget-busting "bonus" payment—combined with the growing hubris of groups like the American Legion, eventually led to a public backlash.

Early in his presidency, Franklin Roosevelt tried to capitalize on the growing public reaction against Great War veterans with a tough and well-remembered address to the American Legion convention in Chicago in 1933. FDR dared to suggest to the Legionnaires that the government owed veterans no further compensation for their service beyond aid for their war-related disabilities. "No person, because they wore a uniform," Roosevelt stated, "must thereafter be placed in a special class of beneficiaries over and above all other citizens."[16]

It was a courageous stand, particularly in the context of the times, but one from which FDR eventually retreated. By his last term in office, Roosevelt was signing off on the GI Bill of Rights, a cornucopia of preferential welfare legislation, drafted by the American Legion itself. Nothing was too good, the American public decided, for the rising new generation of veterans. Even ex-servicemen who had served as little as ninety days in uniform, and with no combat experience, were eligible for the GI Bill's benefits. These benefits ranged from privileged ocean travel for wartime brides, to subsidized college tuition worth up to $26,400 in today's dollars, to no-money-down home ownership through subsidized 4 percent fixed-rate, thirty-year mortgages. In selling the GI Bill to Congress, Roosevelt proclaimed in a 1943 address that veterans were indeed a special class after all. The boys beating back the Axis were "entitled," he stressed, "to definite action to help take care of their special problems."[17]

And so, the question of why exactly veterans are entitled as a special class remains. If contribution to the war effort was the rationale for the GI Bill, for example, civilians as a group were as deserving as ex-servicemen as a group. Nearly a third of all World War II–era veterans were either stationed outside war zones and/or never saw combat.[18] Meanwhile, nearly 300,000 factory workers died in accidents during the war (compared to 292,000 soldiers killed in battle), and another 1 million workers were permanently disabled (compared to 670,846 soldiers wounded in battle).[19]

But war workers, unlike World War II–era veterans, were not organized. Today the American Legion continues to be the nation's largest veteran group, boasting 3 million members. It builds membership, which costs just seventeen dollars a year, by offering discounts on a broad range of goods and services, from life insurance to rental cars. North American van lines offers a minimum 40 percent discount to Legionnaires making interstate moves. Marriott, Choice Hotels International, and a host of other lodging chains offer similar discounts.

The Veterans of Foreign Wars, which claims 2.1 million members, is even more sophisticated in attracting members by offering its own forms of private entitlements. For example, it boosts membership by offering a plethora of benefits: discount travel services, discount eyewear, a VISA card, discount moving services, and "VFW-Sponsored Purchase Power Benefits" that allow members to "get special perks when you buy products for your household or for gifts," including major appliances and home electronics.[20] Like associations representing the elderly, civil service retirees, and all the other major entitlement tribes, veterans' groups are above all mass merchandising organizations.

Other major veterans' groups include the Disabled American Veterans—now enjoying new influence with the appointment of its former executive director as Clinton's secretary for veterans affairs—as well as Paralyzed Veterans of America, and AMVETs, a comparatively liberal group formed by World War II veterans more interested in introspection than boisterous convention antics. Despite their differences, these groups work closely together in lobbying Congress. In recent years, they have combined with the VFW to present Congress with their own unified "independent budget" for the Department of Veterans Affairs.

Together, veterans' groups have been remarkably successful at defending and even expanding their political power and claims on the budget, despite declining membership and mounting federal deficits. In 1978, they pushed for and won a new, non-service-connected disability pension program; in 1981 they secured protection in the overall budget cutting by President Reagan; and in 1988 they won cabinet status for the Veterans Administration.[21]

Since then, powerful friends in Congress continue to make veterans a politically privileged class that remains largely exempt from fiscal reform measures. In 1989, House Veterans Affairs Committee chairman G. V. "Sonny" Montgomery of Mississippi steamrolled Budget Committee chairman Leon Panetta into approving a $525 million increase in veterans' medical benefits by making creative use of some of his constituents. "I sent a brigade of wheelchair people to see Panetta," Montgomery later boasted. "He saw that we weren't 'just whistling Dixie.'" Two years later, Montgomery, working in concert with veterans' groups, again rolled Panetta as well as the Bush White House. This time he did it by pushing through an exemption to the 1990 budget summit that gave $1 billion in deficit-financed new benefits for Persian Gulf War–era veterans.[22]

Like other special interest advocates, veterans' groups often defend preferential benefits for all their members by pointing to the hardships faced by a deserving minority. The logic of such arguments is always tenuous, but in the case of veterans, the implied premise is also particularly weak.

OLD SOLDIERS

Since World War II, the percentage of veterans with combat or even war zone experience has continued to decline. Just 5.3 percent of veterans from the post–Vietnam War era have seen action or been even remotely near a shooting war.[23] Certainly, then, reward for valor is hardly the rationale for across-the-board veterans' benefits such as subsidized mortgages and free health care. Nor are VA benefits necessarily an acknowledgment of honorable character. Even prisoners and parolees remain entitled to benefits.

Similarly, since the move to an all-volunteer force in the mid-1970s, it has become difficult to use the hardships of the draft as a rationale for granting special privileges to ex-servicemen as a class. Economic need doesn't work either. In 1990, for example, one fifth of all veterans enjoyed a family income of $50,000 or more.[24] As a group, veterans are considerably more affluent than nonveterans. The 1990 Census showed that median income for male veterans that year was nearly twice that of male nonveterans age twenty and over ($24,630 for veterans compared to $12,414 for nonvets). Female veterans, meanwhile, had a median income of $12,598, compared with $9,024 for female nonvets.[25]

The greater age and seniority of veterans compared to the adult population as a whole explains much of this difference. With half of all veterans now over age fifty-six, veterans' benefits are largely an intergenerational transfer of wealth. Yet even when compared to nonveterans of the same age, ex-servicemen have done as well, if not better. Today, Vietnam-era veterans with low levels of education significantly outearn their nonveteran counterparts, for example, and those with high levels of education do just as well.[26] Only 5 percent of veterans have a disability that prevents them from working.

Will the cost of veterans' benefits fade away so long as America avoids another war? Hardly. The veterans' population is aging much faster than the population as a whole, thereby driving up health and pension costs for vets even faster than for nonvets. In the 1990s, dramatic increases are occurring in the age seventy-five to eighty-four group as the World War II population moves through the age spectrum. During the first ten years of the next century, the population of veterans eighty-five and over will begin to expand, growing from 210,000 in the early 1990s to 1.3 million by 2010. By then, the population of veterans age seventy-five and over will have nearly tripled, and half of all veterans, according to projections by the VA, will be over age sixty-five.[27]

If veterans' benefits were the only middle-class entitlements whose cost was being driven up by the aging of population, they might be sustainable. But of course, vets' programs must compete with Social Security, Medicare, the mounting interest on the national debt, and all the rest, for the taxpayer's dollar. Thus, if you are counting on receiving veterans' benefits in the next century, you had better start putting more money in the bank instead.

Veterans' groups can count on great institutional strength, having inserted themselves deeper into the very structure of the federal government than virtually any other special interest. Both houses of Congress have standing committees on veterans with direct oversight of veterans' programs. The VA's status as a cabinet agency also gives its secretary (and the veterans' groups who have his ear) coveted direct access to the Oval Office. But with most vets no longer able to claim wartime experience, and with middle-class America as a whole suffering withdrawal symptoms as Social Security, Medicare, and other entitlements are inevitably cut, vets will soon find themselves asked to surrender their subsidies as well.

11

Yesterday's Generals

Joseph L. Araneo, advertising director for MILI-BUCK$, has his pitch down cold. "When I say military retirees, you might think they're old and don't have any money. But a lot of these guys are still in their thirties and have second careers, and they get great pensions. They've got big bucks to spend!"[1]

And how. MILI-BUCK$ is a New York–based marketing service that rents out mailing lists of retired military personnel. The lists are in high demand from upscale advertisers because they offer a way to reach one of the most affluent consumer niches in the United States.

"The Few, the Proud, and the Well to Do" is how *American Demographics* magazine describes this tribe.[2] Half of all military retirees are under age fifty.[3] Retiring at an average age of forty-two (and often as young as thirty-eight), nearly all of the nation's 1.6 million career military retirees enjoy income and benefits from a second career while also enjoying one of the world's most generous pension plans.

Most veterans never qualify for this bonanza. Only about 17 percent of all military personnel remain in the service for the minimum twenty years required to receive any pension whatsoever.[4] But for those who do vest into the system, military retirement offers a comfortably subsidized life beginning in early middle age.

Most Americans are instinctively sympathetic to the men and women who have dedicated their careers to military service, as well they should be. But the current military retirement system has little do with just deserts or reward for valor. Indeed, as with veterans' benefits, military retirement offers little or nothing to soldiers who have been disabled by war or by the military's own negligence. Rather, it is a system that conveys enormous windfalls to a lucky few, with the biggest gains going to high-ranking officers. Worse, the system is placing huge financial burdens on the next generation, with long-term debts exceeding that of the entire Vietnam War. With the public for the most part distracted by other matters, military retirement has come to be controlled by an elite cadre of lobbyists who are among the best in the business and don't want you to know any more than you already do about this enormously expensive program.

What do military retirees get? In addition to receiving the usual veterans' benefits, plus a bundle of other expensive perks ranging from subsidized health care to taxpayer-financed discounts at post' exchange stores, today's military retirees receive pensions worth between 50 and 75 percent of their final base pay. For a sergeant major or master chief petty officer retiring in 1993 at age thirty-eight with twenty years' experience, initial pension benefits were $22,932. For a chief of staff retiring that year with twenty years' experience, initial pension benefits were $54,096.[5]

These benefits are indexed automatically for inflation, for life, which is often another forty to fifty years, and sometimes much more. In 1992, there were three military retirement recipients age 101 receiving pensions averaging $53,340 a year, and one 106-year-old veteran receiving a pension of $40,764.[6]

Private sector pensions, by contrast, are far less generous. A typical plan replaces 25 to 30 percent of final pay at age sixty-five and is seldom indexed for inflation. The retirement age for military pensions is so young, and the benefits so rich, that the average officer leaving the service this year at age forty-two with twenty years' experience can expect to receive over $1.1 million in pension checks before reaching age sixty-five, and another $1 million by age seventy-five.[7] On top of this comes Social Security, to which military retirees are also entitled once they reach age sixty-two, as well as Medicare at age sixty-five.[8]

Top brass get even more. Even if General H. Norman Schwarzkopf, for example, could not count on $50,000 speaker's fees or his $5 million book deal, the retired four-star general would still be a pension millionaire many times over. As a general who maxed the pay grade, Schwarzkopf will take home $1,028,953 in federal pension checks in just the first ten years of his retirement.[9]

With the end of the cold war, the number of active-duty military has fallen dramatically. But the number of military retirees continues to swell by more than 67,000 new persons each year. The cost to the Treasury is staggering. From 1980 to 1992, military retirement expenditures more than doubled, from $11.9 billion to $24.5 billion.[10]

Military retirees contribute nothing toward the cost of their own pensions. Instead, taxpayers bear the full expense. In 1994 the bill came to over $26 billion. That is more money than the federal government's entire budget for Head Start, K–12 math and science education, college scholarships, adult education, and all Job Training Partnership Act spending combined.

Military retirement also consumes a major share of the Defense Department's personnel budget, which now accounts for nearly half of all its spending. In 1994, pensions for military retirees and their survivors cost more than $2,270,000,000 a month, which amounted to a staggering 78 percent of the military's total basic pay costs.[11]

The lion's share of this money goes to families that are affluent by any measure, largely because most military retirees continue to work and often vest into second or third pensions by the time they reach age sixty-five. According to estimates by the Congressional Budget Office, in 1990 approximately 50 percent of all military retirement spending went to families with incomes of $50,000 a year or more.

One extreme case is former Congressman Hastings Keith. Thanks to his military service and third career as a federal bureaucrat, Keith is receiving more than $9,000 per month in combined congressional, military, civil service, and Social Security benefits. Since the early Reagan administration, Keith, a thrifty New Englander, has been trying to draw attention to the cause of federal pension reform by repeatedly offering to return a portion of the more than $1 million he's collected. So far, Treasury officials, who look forward to their own supergenerous pensions, have turned him down.

Congress took a halfhearted stab at reforming the military retirement system in 1986. But faced with implacable opposition from the Joint Chiefs (all of them nearing retirement age) and from sophisticated, well-financed pressure groups such as the Retired Officers Association, lawmakers backed down from any meaningful measures. The Military Reform Act of 1986 reduced future minimum pension benefits somewhat, but only for persons retiring after 2006. Persons retiring after that date will still receive at least 40 percent of their peak three years basic pay in pension pay, plus cost-of-living adjustments equal to the consumer price index minus 1 percent.

The savings created by this measure are so small you need a microscope to find them. In constant 1986 dollars, the act saves just $1 billion annually by the year 2017 and only about $3 billion yearly by 2040, a mere 7 percent improvement over the spending increases that would have taken place without the "reform." Current retirees, meanwhile, and all who will retire before 2006, have managed to keep themselves exempt from reform.

Who will pay for their future benefits? The long-term liabilities or debts of the military retirement system make its current heavy costs look puny. As of September 1994, the price of future benefits promised to retirees already on the rolls came to more than $409,900,000,000 in 1994 dollars. That number is far larger than the admitted federal deficit, but no less real so long as current retirees are held harmless from budget cuts. Add to this lien on the future the cost of benefits promised to military personnel who have not yet retired. Federal actuaries estimate the present value of this debt at $303,500,000,000. Together, these liabilities come to nearly $3,000 for every man, woman, and child in the United States.[12]

Apologists for the military retirement system sometimes argue that at least part of this cost will be defrayed by the assets of the so-called Military Retirement Trust Fund, which Congress established in 1984. But even the trust fund's own trustees admit that its existence will do nothing to lower the cost of the system on future taxpayers. The trust fund's assets consist of nothing more than government IOUs, or what the trustees tactfully refer to as "mirrored securities." Every security within the trust fund "mirrors" a security, with the exact same maturity and interest rate that the U.S. Treasury has issued to the global credit markets. In other words, as with the Social Security trust funds, its so-called assets are simply part of the official national debt, and, from the point of view of future taxpayers, not assets at all but liabilities.

Thus, it isn't just the professional military that is receiving a huge subsidy here but you and me. Because of those gold brick pensions, soldiers will work for less wages than they otherwise would. This saves money in the short term but raises the cost of the military in the long term. In effect, by not funding those pensions, today's taxpayers force their children to pay for much of the cost of today's defense. And as we'll see in the next chapter, military retirement is just one of scores of unfunded federal employee pension schemes that are pushing off costs on to the next generation.

PENSION COUPS

How did military retirement spin so far out of control? Throughout American history, particularly during times of war, civilian leaders have always been vulnerable to demands from the professional military for increased compensation.

During the dark days at Valley Forge, as we've seen, officers pressed General George Washington for a plan by which they could be retired on half-pay for life. The measure deeply disturbed the many influential Americans of the day, who feared the creation of a professional military caste. In 1783, James Madison noted in a letter that the "opposition in the New England States to the grant of half-pay, instead of subsiding, has increased to such a degree as to produce almost general anarchy."[13] Republican newspapers of the time generally reviled the officer corps as a collection of decadent aristocrats, Benedict Arnolds, or, at best, members of the distrusted Society of Cincinnatus plotting to seize national power.[14] Reflecting such opposition, Congress declined to fund its military pension promises after the war, and officers wound up being paid off in nearly worthless "commutation certificates." Still, the precedent of compensating nondisabled career officers with half-pay lifetime pensions had been created.

As the number of Revolutionary War veterans declined and the Treasury increased, Congress gradually became more generous with both former officers and ordinary soldiers alike, a pattern that would repeat itself throughout American history. In 1818, Congress provided pensions to every person who had served in the Revolutionary War and who "was in need of assistance from his country for support." By 1832, Congress expanded this benefit into full pay for life, regardless of need. By 1836, Revolutionary War widows came to be included.

At the time, many critics denounced these so-called service pensions, named because they conferred benefits on the basis of wartime service alone, and not as compensation for specific, war-related disability. Gradually, however, the public came to accept the idea of service pensions and other benefits, not only for war veterans but for peace veterans as well. Institutionally, this process culminated in the creation of the Veterans Administration in 1930.

Meanwhile, a separate species of military benefits evolved for career soldiers only. This is a branch of the welfare state's evolutionary tree that leads to today's military retirement system. In 1855, the Navy began offering pensions to officers judged to be incapable but not necessarily disabled. In 1861, Congress passed the first major nondisability retirement act, which provided for the voluntary retirement of regular officers of all branches after forty years of service, at the discretion of the president. In 1885, Congress offered similar retirement benefits to career enlisted men.

By this time, the image of the military in American life was improving dramatically. "For many years previous to secession," General Truman Seymour wrote in 1864, "the profession of arms had, at the North, fallen from disrepute to contempt. . . . To be an officer of the Regular Army was, popularly, to be an idle gentleman, well paid for doing nothing, scarcely worthy of respect, and assuredly not of esteem."[15] But after the Civil War, the image of the career soldier gradually improved, as the "art of war" became increasingly scientific and the military adopted new standards of professionalism, largely inspired by the example of Bismarck's Germany. A modern military pension system was but one of many ideas and values the American military borrowed from the Prussian general staff during this era—and Congress, also enthralled by the example of Teutonic efficiency, eagerly went along.

Career service pensions promoted efficiency, military reformers argued, by providing a humane way to dispose of superannuated soldiers. Another touted advantage of the pension system was that it would lead to greater promotion opportunities among junior personnel. No one at the time imagined the hundreds of billions of dollars of pension debt that would be eventually accrued through such a policy. Nor did anyone anticipate the pernicious effect that career service pensions would come to have on the readiness of the military itself as overgenerous early retirement benefits lured more of the service's most highly trained and difficult-to-replace personnel back to civilian careers just as they were becoming most valuable.

Sheer scale is the most profound change in the military pension system to occur during this century. In 1900, the total number of military retirees was a mere 3,029, and total costs were just $3.5 million. Retirees with thirty years of active-duty experience received up to 75 percent of their basic pay, which sounds generous, except that military pay in that era was still exceedingly low. Throughout the first half of the twentieth century, military pensions remained a fiscally insignificant entitlement. Even as recently as 1945, the number of military retirees was still just 57,443, and per capita benefits, again thanks to the low pay scales, averaged a mere $74 a month.[16]

The current bonanza system was set in motion in 1948 when Congress established twenty years as the minimum requirement for voluntary, nondisability retirement. The Army and Air Force Vitalization Act, as its title suggests, was designed to nudge out the huge cadres of senior personnel left over from World War II and to keep the career military forces young and vigorous. But gradually the entitlement created by this legislation assumed a life of its own, eventually becoming not only absurdly expensive but at odds with the military's increasing dependence on highly trained, experienced personnel.

The sheer number of persons qualifying for military retirement was the first big surprise. In 1948, the active-duty manpower of the U.S. military dropped to just 1.4 million, the smallest military the United States would maintain, even through the Clinton administration. The onslaught of the cold war quickly dashed plans for a permanent reduction in force structure. Instead, the Berlin crisis and the Korean conflict led to a sustained buildup of the U.S. military establishment. Ten to fifteen years later, one result was a huge increase in military pension rolls. During the 1960s, the number of military retirees grew by a full 300 percent, from just 255,000 to over 765,000. In the next decade, pension rolls grew by another half a million retirees, bringing the total up to 1.2 million by 1980.

Costs rose even faster. Regular cost-of-living adjustments, formalized in 1963, more than prevented any erosion due to inflation. Meanwhile, improving military basic pay meant that each succeeding cohort of retirees received higher real benefits without Congress's changing benefit formulas or otherwise making any conscious policy choice. As with so many other entitlement programs, military retirement was on automatic pilot—and pointed straight at the moon.

By 1984, President Reagan's budget director denounced bloated military pensions as a "scandal" and an "outrage." Nine years later, no one receiving a military pension had suffered even a token reduction. Moreover, new retirees were receiving still more generous benefits, thanks to the continuing improvements in basic pay levels, to which pension benefits are automatically linked. By 1993, even a middle-rank officer or senior enlisted member retiring at age thirty-eight with twenty years' experience found himself or herself entitled to a pension with a present, or lump sum, value of over half a million dollars.[17]

MIDDLE-AGED WARRIORS

How have benefits this rich managed to escape the budget ax? Military retirees over the years have offered up a variety of often contradictory rationalizations for their windfalls. The original claim—that the military retirement system promotes youthful vigor in the ranks by offering incentives for senior military personnel to leave—still pops up at congressional hearings from time to time. But these days it makes even less sense than it once did.

When a panel of Army brass tried out the line on Senator John Glenn during a 1985 hearing of the Armed Services Committee, the former astronaut and jet fighter pilot quickly set the generals straight. "I was doing my best work [as a pilot] when I was in my upper thirties," Glenn reminded the room. "I was beyond 40 when I was in the astronaut program and made an orbit of the Earth. . . . You do not just throw the guy into the cockpit because he is young and vigorous and thinks he is a hotshot fighter pilot. It takes years of experience before he gets good at it."[18]

As warfare becomes increasingly driven by high technology, the value of youth per se has declined while experience has come to count for more. Even among flyboys, the middle aged often have more of the "right stuff" than pimply faced recruits. But the same point applies even more forcefully to the vast majority of military jobs. In the modern military, more than eight out of ten of all uniformed personnel are in noncombat positions.

From time to time the Pentagon has considered making distinctions in pay and pensions between true combat soldiers and mere desk soldiers, as many other militaries around the world do. A 1976 Pentagon compensation report even toyed with the notion of factoring in sexual deprivation: "Faced with the immediate possibility of personal annihilation amid the vast impersonal destruction of war, hedonistic drive and socially derived needs combine to make sexual deprivation a major stress fact."[19] In the end, however, the military has resisted targeting benefits such as early retirement to those for whom it is truly appropriate. Instead Pentagon brass have used the real deprivations of some military personnel as a vague rationalization of high compensation across the board.

The weakness of that logic sometimes leads defenders of the military retirement system to offer the alternative argument: that the system actually encourages senior personnel to stay. "The military retirement system is the 'light at the end of the tunnel,'" the chief lobbyist for the Retired Officers Association once told Congress, "which enables many careerists to endure the extraordinary demands of military service: Frozen flightlines in sub-freezing weather; protracted deployment on the open and hostile sea; field duty in jungles, deserts and mountainous terrain; enforced family separations; frequent [transfers], often with minimal advance notice, uprooting families and losing second incomes; abridgment of freedom of speech and political activity; and unconditional obligation to give their lives for their country."[20]

These are the sacred tribal myths of military retirees—the litany proving they too are victims, deserving of their benefits as a matter of earned right. But there are two problems with their worldview. The first is that, as we have seen, most career military personnel serve their country in cubicles, not foxholes. The second is that overly generous pensions harm the very institution military retirees profess to love. The current retirement system creates perverse incentives for military personnel still in the prime of life. By not retiring, a thirty-eight-year-old with twenty years' experience will, in effect, pay an extra 50 percent tax on his or her military pay in the form of forgone pension benefits. For most servicemen, no amount of patriotism or love of military life is likely to overcome such financial disincentives for long. Not surprisingly, in 1992 nearly 50 percent of enlisted Army personnel and more than 30 percent of all officers eligible for retirement benefits quit the service.[21]

Another argument used to defend military pensions is that, technically, retirees may be called back at any time into active duty. This is a quaint conceit. It stretches back to the days of George Washington's troubles at Valley Forge with deserting officers. In practice, today's military retirees stand virtually no chance of being called back to duty, even during conflicts such as the Persian Gulf War, when only a handful of recently retired specialists were recalled. For such contingencies, the armed services maintain huge and expensive reserve forces that train regularly (the reserve, incidentally, has its own retirement system). In any conflict large enough to require the secretary of defense to ask significant numbers of career military retirees to try fitting back into their uniforms, civilians would also be undoubtedly subject to a draft as well.

A final argument used by defenders of the military retirement system is that its benefits really are not so generous as they might seem. The objection is that the income formula by which military pensions are set does not include the extensive in-kind benefits (including food, housing and medical care) servicemen received on active duty. If one counts the value of these perks as income, so the line goes, then military pensions actually replace not 50 to 75 percent of preretirement income, but "only" 30 to 60 percent.

This argument ignores the extraordinary perks and in-kind benefits military personnel continue to enjoy after they retire—especially those who settle near military facilities, and they are legion. Around many military bases, particularly in the Sun Belt, huge communities of military retirees have grown up, creating such a market that developers have built special subdivisions targeted directly to them. Patriots Colony at Williamsburg, Virginia, for example, which is conveniently located within easy driving distance of six major military facilities, offers one hundred spacious apartments and fifty villas surrounded by wooded ravines and a perimeter patrolled by security guards. The community's developers describe it as a "premiere retirement community for retired officers of all branches of services."[22] The largest concentration of military retirees stretches between Eglin Air Force Base in the Florida panhandle and the naval facilities in Pensacola.[23] San Antonio's five military bases have attracted a military retiree community of more than 30,000.[24] More than six retirees for every airman on duty had settled in the area around Mather Air Force Base in California before the base closed in 1993.[25]

By retiring near military bases, retirees continue to enjoy access to a broad range of perks and in-kind benefits, ranging from discounted groceries; to morale, recreation, and welfare activities; to free health care. The shopping privileges military retirees enjoy at commissaries and post exchanges amount to a not-inconsiderable entitlement. The discounts offered by these military stores vary from region to region but generally range between 21 and 27 percent.

Who pays for the subsidies? Once again, the taxpayers. The commissary system cost the federal government about $1 billion in appropriated funds in 1993.[26]

But this is pin money compared to the most valuable in-kind benefit military retirees receive. Nowhere else in the annals of the American welfare state is there any stranger case than that of postretirement health care benefits for military personnel and their families. Legally, no such entitlement exists; it cannot be found in any law book. Yet it costs the taxpayers tens of billions of dollars each year and has created accrued deficits that rival those of the military pension fund itself. The present value of the government's unfunded future liability for military retiree health care is estimated by the U.S. Treasury Department to exceed $295 billion.[27]

Congress has never passed a law providing military retirees with access to free health care, and there is no statutory requirement that such care be provided. But as one congressional researcher has written, "Congress is faced with the reality that many military members, retirees and dependents believe that military health care is free and guaranteed for life. While this latter assumption is not true in terms of entitlements actually authorized by statute, this still tends to color the reform debate."[28] That's a fine understatement.

THE STEALTH ENTITLEMENT

The military operates a vast ad hoc health care system that is separate and distinct from the VA medical system. It includes more than 148 hospitals and over 800 medical and dental clinics worldwide, serving nearly 9 million beneficiaries, at a cost of over $15 billion a year. Its staff includes 200,000 military and 200,000 reserve personnel—a force exceeding the size of the U.S. Marine Corps.[29] One of the reasons this system has swollen to such proportions is the free and subsidized care it offers to military retirees.

Before the 1960s, the comparatively small number of military retirees made it easy for military hospitals to adopt the informal practice of treating anyone with previous career military experience, space permitting. But over time, what began as a professional courtesy came to be viewed by military personnel as an inalienable right. Today when military personnel retire from active-duty service, they and their dependents continue to enjoy broad access to the military's health care system. The military allows retirees and their family members to visit physicians in military clinics and have any prescriptions filled for free. As inpatients in military hospitals, retired enlisted personnel pay nothing; retired officers customarily pay only about $4.75 a day and dependents about $9.30 a day.

What about military retirees who do not live near military hospitals? Their consumption of health care services turns out to be an even greater drain on the taxpayers. In 1966, Congress created the Civilian Health and Medical Program of the Uniformed Services. CHAMPUS is a subsidized health insurance plan for military personnel who lack access to military health facilities. Congress briefly considered excluding retirees but soon thought better of it. Today military retirees are eligible to sign up for CHAMPUS, provided they are not yet old enough to qualify for Medicare, as most are not.

This is a major perk. At a time when most of the civilian population is being forced into health maintenance organizations and other forms of managed care, CHAMPUS operates an old-fashioned fee-for-service indemnity plan, allowing participants to visit any doctor or specialist they wish at minimal cost. After beneficiaries pay a deductible of $150 a person or $300 a family, CHAMPUS covers at least 75 percent of allowable expenses, with a limit on out-of-pocket expenses of $7,500. For this coverage, retirees pay no premiums.

How much does this giveaway cost the taxpayers? CHAMPUS is one of the fastest-growing programs in the federal budget, rising by an average annual rate of 28 percent in recent years. Its costs have swollen from just $166 million in 1967 to $3.4 billion in 1992. Says one military analyst: "If a weapons system had a cost over-run like that, we would stop it tomorrow." Retirees are by no means responsible for all of the overruns, but they account for a large share. The Congressional Budget Office estimates that if the government charged retirees just a modest premium of $90 a month for CHAMPUS premiums rather than giving away the insurance, taxpayers would save far in excess of $2.5 billion over five years.[30]

YESTERDAY'S GENERALS

The extraordinary cost of CHAMPUS coverage for military retirees has created a bizarre twist in the politics of base closings. Because CHAMPUS allows access to a virtually unlimited range of private providers, retirees using the program cost the government even more on average than those who use services provided directly by military hospitals and clinics. This fact has placed a unique defensive weapon system in the hands of some communities targeted for base closings. For example, one of the arguments made by Orlando boosters in their attempt to prevent the closure of the Orlando Naval Training Center in 1992 was that closing the 153-bed hospital would result in significant increases for CHAMPUS expenses, due to the large number of military retirees settled in central Florida.[31]

Many military retirees consider any threat by the government to close a nearby base, and particularly its health care facilities and commissary, akin to a breach of contract. "All of a sudden, the quality of life that they had anticipated is gone," explains former Congressman James A. Courter, chairman of the 1991 Base Closure Commission. In 1992, Colin McMillan, assistant secretary of defense for production and logistics, dared to suggest that the military could not afford to keep commissaries and post exchanges open solely for the benefit of reservists and retirees. When a base closed, said McMillan, it would have to close completely. In response, military retiree groups viciously attacked him in an open letter to every member of Congress and President Bush, condemning him for having a "don't give a damn" attitude.

The stridency and overweening sense of entitlement often manifested by groups representing military retirees certainly do not bring to mind images of patriotism and service to country. Here, for example, is Retired Major General J. C. Pennington, president of the National Association of Uniformed Services, warning Congress in 1992 of his power to neutralize all those who dare stand against his legions:

This association has organized in every congressional district in the nation. . . . Coalitions of seniors are also joining with coalitions of military and veterans groups. . . . This is a formidable political force. . . . Members of Congress on both sides of the aisle are now beginning to listen hard and to realize how powerful this force can become since they, together with family members, comprise about one-third of all constituents in each congressional district and the nation at large."[32]

The Retired Officers Association (TROA), founded in 1929, is the most narrowly focused and effective of the many special interest groups that lobby on behalf of military retirees. In 1993 alone, TROA added 12,000 new recruits, bringing its membership to over 393,000.[33] With hundreds of thousands, if not millions, of dollars at stake in the form of their individual pensions, retired military officers have a strong motive to work together as a faction. In late 1993, when the House briefly considered a bill by Congressmen Tim Penny and John Kasich that, along with many other entitlement reforms, would have delayed cost-of-living adjustments (COLAs) for military retirees under age sixty-two, TROA quickly mobilized. Visiting all 434 congressional offices on the day before the vote, TROA's Washington lobbyists created so much political pressure that even before any vote was taken, Kasich crumbled. In a desperate attempt to save the reform package as a whole, Kasich's staff redrafted his bill to include a grandfather clause that would have exempted all current military retirees from any COLA cuts or reductions in benefits. Yet even with this concession, TROA continued to oppose the bill, and it went down to ignominious defeat.[34]

To protect against any future attempts to trim COLAs, TROA has set up a COLA hot line. All a military retiree has to do is call and give TROA operators his or her address. The operators then determine the caller's congressman and two senators and send a "pre-stored COLA message" by Western Union.[35]

To build further unit cohesion, TROA offers members a bundle of its own benefits, suitably targeted to upper-middle-class lifestyles, from discounted cruise ship travel to association-sponsored golf and tennis tournaments. Financial benefits include a tax-deferred program that offers annuities from forty eagerly competing companies, a Gold MasterCard with a $25,000 credit line, and a special "GoldSaver" high-interest money market fund.

The organization's four-color membership magazine, *Retired Officer*, boasts ads from dozens of luxury resort communities and financial services companies. A typical article offers stock portfolio advice to military retirees in their forties and fifties on how to invest their pensions. "Take LCol Bill Wichert, who is 43 years old," reads one recent piece. "With his new civilian job as a computer programmer, his and his wife's combined gross annual income, including his military retirement pay, will be $85,400." Since Wichert plans to continue working at his civilian job for at least another seventeen years, the article advises him and "retirees" like him to "invest aggressively" in growth stocks, with a hedge in tax-free municipal bonds.

The Noncommissioned Officers Association, the Retired Enlisted Association, the National Family Association, and dozens of other groups have carved out niches within the political market created by military retirement spending. The mass veterans' groups, such as the American Legion and the Veterans of Foreign Wars, can also be counted on to lend political support for career military retirees, who typically are among their youngest and most active members. Finally, there are the Joint Chiefs and armed services themselves, which with rare exception will lobby alongside military retiree groups whenever budget reformers propose to trim benefits.

But however much firepower such interests may bring to bear, they have already lost the war. With American children now facing total lifetime tax rates of 82 percent unless entitlement spending is dramatically cut, goldbrick military pensions for thirty-nine-year-olds who've never seen combat won't last long.

Those who retire from a career in the military certainly deserve reasonable pensions. Some deserve early retirement as well. For years, countries such as Great Britain have made distinctions in their military compensation between soldiers assigned to truly physically demanding positions and those who are essentially office workers. The United States must, and will, do the same.

Meanwhile, today's taxpayers will have to pay for whatever pensions they wind up promising to today's soldiers rather than continuing to shift the cost on to the next generation. As with the underfunding of civil service pensions (discussed in the next chapter), the debts of the military retirement system don't just affect a narrow slice of middle-class America but provide a broad, and unsustainable, subsidy to current taxpayers as a whole. When the inevitable reform comes, we will all feel the withdrawal effect from this entitlement as well.

12

Yesterday's Bureaucrats

In December 1895, William Dudley Foulke, the popular author and crusader for government reform, traveled to Washington, D.C., to deliver a stern warning. It had been a dozen years since the great battle to create a federal civil service system. But from this hard-fought triumph over the hacks and "spoilsmen" had come a deep threat to the Republic, Foulke admonished in an address to the National Civil Service Reform League. Already the lack of turnover in federal offices, Foulke observed, was leading to "the evils of superannuation." Protected for life from political firing, the federal civil service, then dominated by long-bearded Civil War veterans, was going gray. Foulke concluded his address with a rousing call for a plan under which the "barnacles might be removed."[1]

How could aging bureaucrats be encouraged to move on? Foulke's idea was to offer them generous life insurance and pension benefits as an incentive to retire. The "economy vote" in Congress, however, objected to the potential costs. The heavy burden of paying for Civil War veterans' pensions convinced nearly all thinking people of the day to resist suggestions for creating another great class of public pensioners. Cynics were even suspicious of plans financed by employee contributions, "for it was always argued," writes one historian, "that if the plan were started and proved insolvent, the government would have to make up the deficit."[2]

The debate went on for more than two decades, as the federal workforce aged in place, but in the end history proved the cynics right—by a margin measured in the trillions. In 1920, Congress at last passed the Civil Service Retirement Act. Seventy-two years later, the present value of benefits promised under the Civil Service Retirement System had grown to more than $1,158,600,000,000. Today, this encumbrance is roughly equal to $4,600 for every man, woman, and child in the United States. About 40 percent of this staggering debt derives from the cost of benefits promised to civil service retirees already on the rolls. The rest is the cost (in today's dollars) of benefits promised to civil servants who will be retiring in the future.

No reserves exist to cover the cost of this liability. Although a civil service trust fund exists on paper, it is, in the words of a Congressional Research Service report, only an "accounting ledger."[3] It contains no actual assets to defray the program's long-term liabilities, which together equal more than 28 percent of America's entire national debt.[4]

How should one think of this pension debt? Don't get mad at the bureaucrats. Precisely because civil service pensions are unfunded, they are effectively, just like unfunded military pensions, a broad-based subsidy for current taxpayers as well. Federal workers settle for lower wages than they otherwise would because of the prospect of receiving generous benefits. This holds down the cost of government in the short run, but in the long run, because these pension promises are unfunded, the next generation winds up paying for our bureaucrats.

MORE CHAIN LETTERS

Remember the next generation? Those are the people who are supposed to pay for your Social Security and Medicare, but their ability to do so will be seriously compromised by the federal employee pension debt we are also expecting them to bear. In addition to the Civil Service Retirement System and the main military retirement system discussed in the last chapter, the federal government today has come to operate more than forty other employee retirement plans.

The Coast Guard, for example, has its own retirement system, which includes coverage not only for uniformed Coasties but, by accident of history, for the surviving widows of lighthouse keepers as well. With no investments or reserves to cover the cost of benefits, the plan costs taxpayers some $450 million a year, or more than 59 percent of the Coast Guard's total payroll. That, however, is just the tip of the iceberg. To amortize the system's unfunded liabilities from the past would require a yearly contribution equal to 153 percent of the Coast Guard's payroll. Because this contribution is not being made, the pension system's debt keeps on growing. The system's unfunded accrued liabilities surpassed $12.5 billion in late 1992 and are growing at a rate of more than $635 million a year.[5]

Then there is the special foreign service retirement and disability fund, run by the U.S. State Department, which offers special benefits to foreign service officers who serve in "unhealthful posts." Pensions start at age fifty with twenty years' experience. In 1991, the system paid out $345 million in benefits. That sum was divvied up among just 11,762 beneficiaries, yielding an average benefit (for retirees and survivors alike) of over $29,000 a year, fully indexed for inflation.[6] Even the Social Security Administration has had difficulty collecting information about this obscure system, but its long-term debts are no secret to the nation's budgeteers: $8.57 billion in accrued liabilities, according to the latest valuation.[7]

Even more secret is the Central Intelligence Agency's pension fund. Its benefit levels and liabilities are classified lest foreign rivals learn what U.S. spooks make when they come in from the cold. The CIA's public information office declines all comment about this black box program. Congressional documents suggest, however, that taxpayer contributions to the CIA's combined retirement and disability fund came to $168 million in 1993.[8] The system's long-term pension debt is undoubtedly much greater. Assuming that the system's benefits are at least as generous, and as underfunded, as those of the foreign service's retirement fund, the CIA's pension debt probably comes to between $3 billion and $4 billion.[9]

Other federal retirement programs are so obscure that few members of the public even know to ask about their finances. The surgeon general and other commissioned officers of the Public Health Service, for example, enjoy their own special plan, which pays benefits equivalent to those of military retirees. The pension plan's long-term debt comes to over $2.551 billion, offset by no assets.

Perhaps the least-known scheme is the United States Tax Court Retirement Plan: investments $0; receivables $0; assets $0. Obscurity from public view has served the system's beneficiaries well. Tax court judges with fifteen or more years of experience who retire at age sixty-five receive an unprecedented 100 percent of their salary in retirement benefits, for life. Since 1953, when the plan was established, tax court judges have contributed nothing toward the cost of their benefits. The last year for which an independent audit of the program is available is 1990. At that time, there were only thirty-four retirees collecting benefits from the program, and yet the plan showed unfunded accrued liabilities of $20,579,139. The cost of financing this debt amounted to 83 percent of the Tax court's total payroll. Who gets the bill? Taxpayers of course, and if they try to wiggle out of it, the tax court knows just what to do.[10]

Not all government pension funds are run as negligently as this. Systems run by the Tennessee Valley Authority and the Federal Reserve are backed by fixed-income securities, common stocks, and other investments in the private economy. Savvy investors would do well to track how the Fed is investing its $2.7 billion-plus retirement nest egg; its asset have done so well that by 1992 they had become worth almost 2.5 times more than the value of the accrued liabilities in its pension fund.[11] Alan Greenspan's golden years are more than fully funded.

Otherwise, however, federal retirement systems are essentially pay-as-you-go schemes, lacking any real assets that will enable future taxpayers to defray their compounding costs. Such pay-as-you-go systems also include special plans for commissioned officers of the Commerce Department's National Oceanic and Atmospheric

Administration, Supreme Court justices, former presidents, and employees of dozens of other federal agencies.

How much is the total burden on the Treasury from these "minor" plans? In part because of the secrecy surrounding the CIA's pension fund, no precise bottom line is available, but the debts of the federal government's lesser-known retirement systems (not including civil service and military retirement) easily exceeded $26.5 billion in 1992.[12]

Even adding up these liabilities, however, is not enough to capture the full public cost of supporting federal retirees. They also enjoy generous health care plans heavily subsidized by taxpayers. Upon retirement, more than 85 percent of federal workers elect to continue their employer-provided health insurance coverage under the Federal Employees Health Benefits Program, the largest employer-sponsored health insurance program in the world, costing more than $11.5 billion a year. It offers about 9 million federal employees, retirees, and their survivors a wide choice of private health insurance plans offered by private companies. Taxpayers pick up 71 percent of the annual cost of health care benefits for retirees covered by this program, 86 percent of whom are enrolled in expensive fee-for-service plans.[13]

As with most other federal pension benefits, no reserves have been set aside to cover the compounding cost of this entitlement, for either today's retirees or federal workers who will retire in the future. The result is another huge debt from the past that future taxpayers must bear in the absence of reform. The General Accounting Office estimates, for example, that just to fund the accrued health liabilities for retired postal workers would require an immediate three-cent increase in the cost of a first-class stamp.[14]

Private companies are required by the Financial Accounting Standards Board to disclose their accrued liabilities for postretirement health care costs on their financial statements, because without this information, it is impossible to determine if a company is solvent. But the federal government has so far managed to keep its own huge unfunded, postretirement health care costs off its books and largely hidden from the public. The best available estimate of how large this health care debt has grown comes from an obscure 1992 Treasury study, which estimated that as of 1991, unfunded liabilities of the Federal Employees Health Benefit Program were already exceeding $115 billion.[15] (This is in addition to the $295 billion in unfunded health care liabilities that has already been accrued by military retirees.)

These debts are not just some abstract encumbrance your kids might bear in the next century. Huge installment payments are already coming due. Largely because of the underfunding of federal pension plans in the past, their current cost has become colossal. In 1993, the cost of civil service pensions alone reached $35.195 billion. To keep this number in perspective, consider that civil service retirees and their survivors constitute less than 1 percent of the U.S. population. Yet the cost of their benefits was $12 billion more than the federal government's entire bill for food stamps that year, and almost $4 billion more than the cost of federal unemployment insurance.[16]

LOSING CONTROL

How could benefits for bureaucrats ever become so monumentally expensive? In 1912, a majority in Congress came up with what would have been a thrifty plan for dealing with the problem of an aging federal workforce. That year Congress passed a law that fixed a seven-year term of office for federal employees. Today the idea would be called term limits for bureaucrats and would probably be wildly popular. But after outraged appeals from civil servants, President William Howard Taft vetoed the bill, and so the issue of how to pay for aging federal workers would not go away.[17]

Federal workers by this point were clamoring for some sort of pension benefits. By 1917 the National Federation of Federal Employees had sprung into existence, becoming the first general union of white-collar workers in the federal service.[18] Together with other newly formed unions, it continued to pressure Congress to create some sort of retirement system for civil servants. Within three years, with strong support from President Woodrow Wilson, the federal employee unions prevailed over strenuous opposition from southern conservatives, winning passage of the Civil Service Retirement Act of 1920.

The law hardly seemed like a budget buster at the time. One reason was that its benefits, by today's standards, were meager. Employees dismissed before reaching retirement age could not receive pensions unless they had served fifteen years or more. Survivors of federal retirees also received no benefits. Employees with at least fifteen years of service could retire only if they became totally disabled for useful and efficient service. The government offered no benefits to federal workers whose disabilities turned out to be the result of their own "vicious habits, intemperance, or willful misconduct."[19]

There was another reason the new pension plan seemed affordable. For several years to come, the payments made by civil servants themselves, who originally contributed 2.5 percent of their base salaries to the system, would more than cover the cost of benefits for the comparatively few retirees then collecting benefits. In fact, the government did not contribute any tax dollars to the Civil Service Retirement System until 1928. But built into the financing of the system was a hidden time bomb: as younger federal workers advanced through their careers, they became entitled to pension benefits for which no reserves were put aside. Worse, Congress kept making these unfunded pension promises more generous. As the population of retirees increased faster than the population of active workers, the cost of current benefits grew over time to be far greater than the value of current contributions.

By 1947, the unfunded accrued liability of the Civil Service Retirement System had already reached $4.37 billion, a substantial sum in those days.[20] By this time, the dramatic growth of government that occurred during the New Deal and World War II had swollen the federal workforce to over 3.8 million, and they were all accruing future pension benefits each day they went to work. The result, fifteen to twenty years later, was an explosion in the civil service retirement rolls. During the 1960s, the number of federal retirees surged by 86 percent; in the next decade, the pension rolls increased by another 75 percent.[21]

Meanwhile, Congress kept improving benefits, again without putting aside any real reserves to cover the future cost of such generosity. By this time, the National Association of Retired Federal Employees, founded in 1921, was evolving into a well-organized, entrenched political force. Federal labor unions, such as the Postal Letter Carriers and the National Treasury Employees Union, were also concentrating their growing strength on securing higher pension benefits. Hoping to control the growing political influence of the federal workers' lobby, fiscal conservatives pressed in 1962 for automatic cost-of-living adjustment for civil service pensions, which they believed would at least limit the growth of benefit levels to no more than inflation.[22] But lobbyists for federal retirees soon learned how to circumvent this attempt to depoliticize the system. Between 1969 and 1977, they even persuaded Congress to go along with a cost-of-living adjustment formula that not only fully protected for inflation but added a so-called 1 percent kicker every time the consumer price index exceeded 3 percent.[23] This runaway indexing, plus ample annuity formulas and escalating salaries, all conspired to push up the average civil service retirement benefit more than 50 percent faster than inflation over the course of the 1970s.[24]

GOLDBRICK PENSIONS

Today, by virtually any measure, civil service pensions are far more generous than those generally available in the private sector. Consider:

• In 1992, the average pension annuity based on private sector employment was about $600 per month. By contrast, the average pension annuity based on civil service employment was about $1,420 per month—2.4 times higher.[25]
• Civil servants tend to collect their pensions longer than their private sector counterparts. The average age at which private sector workers begin to collect an employer pension is sixty-two. In 1993 the average age at which federal civil servants began to collect a pension was fifty-eight.[26]
• Civil service pensions are fully indexed for inflation. In the private sector, this is virtually unheard of.
• Many beneficiaries of civil service retirement are not retired at all but are engaged in second careers. This is a particularly attractive op-

tion because civil service retirement, unlike Social Security, imposes no "earnings test" penalty on beneficiaries who decide to continue working. Reflecting the ease with which civil servants move into private sector jobs after taking early retirement, some three-quarters of all civil service pensioners over age sixty-two also receive Social Security pensions.[27]

• For the declining percentage of workers in the private sector still covered by pension plans, benefits after thirty years of service are usually equal to about 30 percent of wages prior to retirement. For civil service retirees, by contrast, the replacement rate is 56 percent, nearly twice as high.[28]

• Because of indexing and benefit raises, federal pensioners commonly wind up earning far more in retirement than they did during their peak years in the workforce. An extreme example is Albert Gore, Sr., who was defeated for reelection in 1970 after thirteen years in the House and eighteen in the Senate. Gore had the recompense of seeing his son, Al Gore, Jr., follow in his footsteps to the Senate and beyond. But his federal pension must have eased the transition as well. By 1991, Gore's pension had risen to $93,346, more than twice his salary during his last year in Congress.[29]

This last example provides one huge clue as to why Congress has allowed federal pensions to grow so far out of control. Members of Congress are themselves covered by the Civil Service Retirement System, and they act accordingly. Consider the case of Dan Mica, a Florida congressman who retired in 1989 after nineteen years in the House. When Mica returned almost immediately to his old stomping grounds to serve as a consultant on the payroll of the House Foreign Affairs Committee, Washington insiders snickered that it wasn't because of his fondness for the Senate's famous bean soup. Instead, he had come back because of the one additional year of federal employment he needed to vest into a twenty-year pension, worth $36,054 a year at the time. Mica was then just forty-five. If his remaining life is of average length, he can count on at least a $2.5 *million* government pension, regardless of what other careers he pursues or what other fortunes he amasses.[30]

PSEUDO REFORMS

In 1984, Congress created a second-tier pension plan for newly hired employees, called the Federal Employees Retirement System (FERS). Conventional wisdom in Washington holds that the creation of FERS remedied the major flaws of the original Civil Service Retirement System (CSRS), but nothing could be further from the truth.

First, because FERS covers only workers hired since the mid-1980s, it will be many years before it attains any real fiscal significance. More than 98 percent of all federal civil service retirees today collect under the old pension plan. As late as 2032, CSRS will still account for at least one-quarter of all federal pension outlays.[31]

Meanwhile, FERS itself remains quite generous and doesn't address the most glaring flaws of the CSRS: early retirement and liberal definition of disability. "Normal" retirement is still age fifty-five with thirty years of experience, increasing only gradually to age fifty-seven for newly hired employees born after 1949. This is a full ten years earlier than private sector workers of the same age group who may retire and still receive full Social Security benefits.

Not that employees covered by FERS won't eventually collect Social Security themselves as well; indeed, they are automatically covered by Social Security, unlike today's CSRS retirees. Since most FERS participants are still young, their participation in Social Security is for now a boon to the system, which is happy to collect and spend their Social Security taxes. But eventually, under current law, FERS retirees will become entitled to Social Security benefits, for which, as we have seen, no reserves are available to cover the cost.

FERS itself will also impose major accrued unfunded liabilities on future taxpayers. Employees pay only 0.8 percent of their own salaries toward the cost of their FERS pensions. But even these modest contributions will not be available to cover the cost of future benefits, because they are commingled with other government revenues and spent as quickly as they are collected. By the end of 1992, FERS's accrued liability for future benefits had already passed a present value of $128 billion. Virtually all of this still-growing debt will be financed by taxpayers.[32]

CREATURES OF GOVERNMENT

Why can't Congress enact meaningful reform? Aside from self-interested participants in the pension racket themselves, members of Congress also have to contend with the strength of the civil service lobby. The National Association for Retired Federal Employees (NARFE) has grown to include more than 490,000 members organized into 1,740 chapters in all fifty states and most U.S. territories. When the Bush administration considered paring civil service cost-of-living adjustments in 1989, NARFE quickly beat back the proposal by becoming the fifth-largest contributor (of the nation's 4,263 political action committees) to federal campaigns during the ongoing election cycle. This put NARFE just behind such mega-political lobbies as the National Association of Realtors and the American Medical Association.[33]

To build membership further, NARFE offers its rank and file not only an unyielding lobbying force to obstruct civil service retirement reform measures but also a broad range of personal perks. These range from discounts on rental cars, insurance, and credit cards to 50 percent price breaks on worldwide cruises aboard Cunard, Prince, and Royal Caribbean ships.[34] These companies know NARFE's mailing list is a great target market for their luxury liners. In 1990, for example, families with incomes above $50,000 received about one-third of federal civilian pensions, according to the Congressional Budget Office.[35]

Civil servants are not only well organized, they are creatures of government who know how to lobby, and who indeed often look forward to applying political pressure on Congress. An article in the *Federal Employee*, the newsletter of the 150,000-member National Federation of Federal Employees (NFFE), begins:

> If you ask many NFFE members what they think of when they think of March, chances are it won't be the NCAA basketball tournament or weather that comes in "like a lion and goes out like a lamb." No, ask NFFE members what March means to them and watch their eyes light up with anticipation. At NFFE, March means Lobby Week. It's a time

for getting together with friends and acquaintances from around the country and taking the NFFE message to Capitol Hill.[36]

Upon arrival in Washington for Lobby Week, NFFE members receive posters, issue briefs, and a list of members of Congress to lobby, all prepared by NFFE legislative staff. Tribal custom calls for Lobby Week to culminate in a grand victory bash, which in 1994 took the form of a Mardi Gras banquet at a Capitol Hill hotel. The theme of the night: *Laissez les bontemps roulez* "let the good times roll."

To make sure their message receives proper attention from Congress, NFFE passes money around too. "There's an old cliché that says money talks," explains a newsletter article. "This cliché certainly applies to PACs and more specifically to our NFFE-PAC fund."[37]

But of course, the final reason Congress can't reform the system is the same reason it can't balance the budget: the broad middle class benefits from unfunded federal employee pensions in the short term, by using them as yet another mechanism for shifting much of the cost of government on to the next generation. It has been a great racket for most of the twentieth century, helping to boost middle-class living standards beyond what they would otherwise be. But its compounding cost, combined with that of all the other entitlement chain letters discussed in this book, ensures that—in the absence of fundamental reform—all these schemes will collapse before long.

PART III

SOLUTIONS

13

What the Country Must Do

At least as far back as Aristotle, political thinkers have expounded on the desirability of a strong middle class. "It is plain," Aristotle counsels in his *Treatise on Government*, "that the most perfect political Community must be amongst those who are in the middle rank." Societies dominated by a strong middle class, Aristotle went on to observe, are the "least liable to those seditions and insurrections which disturb the Community."[1]

Over the centuries, even the most hoary radical critics of the "bourgeoisie" have generally acknowledged its role in promoting economic development and the world's overall standard of living. "The bourgeoisie," Marx and Engels wrote in the *Communist Manifesto*, "has created enormous cities, "it has "drawn all nations, even the most barbarian, into civilization," and thus "rescued a considerable part of the population from the idiocy of rural life."[2]

Today there are few people left on the planet (and especially in those parts that have endured Marxism) who will dispute the value of building a strong middle class—as both a source of political stability and an engine of economic growth. And yet as strong and justified as this global consensus is, it often leads to a completely false conclusion: that the way to empower and enlarge a nation's middle class is to subsidize middle-class consumption.

In the United States, this line of thinking dates back to the New Deal and was particularly prevalent during the 1950s. We've already seen how developers like William Levitt promised that subsidizing middle-class home ownership would cause the mass of Americans to become too tied to their homes and communities to engage in communism. Activists have used variants of this argument as rationalizations for virtually all middle-class entitlements at one time or another—from Social Security to veterans' benefits—and it is still heard today from those who seek to expand middle-class subsidies.

Behind the debacle of the Clinton health care plan, for example, was a strategy, promoted by Hillary Clinton and White House pollster Stanley Greenberg, that some have characterized as the "Suburban New Deal." In theory, the strategy was supposed to strengthen America (and, incidentally, win more votes for the Democrats) by providing more transfer payments to the middle class. Greenberg argued, to considerable effect, that the administration's most important domestic priority should be "defending and enlarging social insurance initiatives that reach the lower and middle classes rather than constructing safety nets that protect only the poor."[3]

This tradition of argument has two major flaws. The first concerns the true meaning of membership in the middle class. Today we tend to think of the American middle class as defined by a certain income level or standard of living. And so long as one holds to this purely financial definition, it might seem at least superficially plausible that one could expand the American middle class by subsidizing the common man's consumption. Build the proles tidy tract houses in the suburbs, so the reasoning goes, and they will become respectable middle-class citizens.

But this conception is misplaced because it ignores the essential characteristics of the middle class that have historically made it worth promoting. What was it about the "bourgeoisie" of the nineteenth century that caused even Marx and Engels to acknowledge its positive contributions to world history? It was not that the bourgeoisie consumed at a certain level—that its members owned their homes, shopped in department stores, or ate off chinaware. It was, rather, that the bourgeoisie embodied certain habits and disciplines—most notably thrift, honesty, and self-reliance—that allowed its members to become exceptionally productive in building national economies.

Where exactly this ethos came from has always been somewhat mysterious. The bourgeoisie who came to dominate Western life in Marx's time were materialistic, but so were such prebourgeois types as crusaders and conquistadors; men have always lusted after treasure. The difference with the emerging bourgeoisie of the eighteenth and nineteenth centuries, noted the German sociologist Max Weber, was a "certain ascetic tendency"—a view that work was its own reward. This ethos found its best-known expression in the homilies of Ben Franklin, America's foremost champion of bourgeois values.

Searching for antecedents to the Franklin mind-set, Weber famously concluded that the bourgeois spirit derived somehow from the Protestant Reformation.[4] Since Weber's time, cultures around the world, particularly in Asia, have demonstrated that one hardly need be Protestant to be bourgeois, but one constant remains: true middle-class status is a matter of spirit, drive, and ethos, marked by a willingness to delay gratification. It cannot be achieved simply by having the taxpayers provide you with transfer payments. Indeed, to the very extent that the American middle class has become addicted to entitlements, it has lost its bourgeois character and ceased to be a dependable source of either political stability or capitalist spirit.

Some middle-class subsidy programs, most notably the GI Bill enacted after World War II and certain educational grants and scholarships, undoubtedly have helped foster the growth of the middle class, and the country is richer for them. But the reason these programs worked was that, in contrast to virtually all other middle-class entitlements, they subsidized productive behavior, not consumption. The GI Bill had its faults, but it did allow hundreds of thousands of young Americans to realize their quintessential bourgeois dreams of self-improvement through higher education.

By contrast, the Social Security system—to the extent that it discourages thrift and rewards early retirement—does not encourage the spread of true bourgeois values; it does the opposite. The same is true of Medicare, the home mortgage deduction, and virtually all other entitlement programs that subsidize middle-class consumption. These programs may allow some individuals to enjoy a middle-class standard of living who otherwise would not, but the provision of these subsidies actually erodes the bourgeois spirit in American life, creating in its place a mass of dependents who look to politicians to fulfill their expectations of the good life.

The second fatal flaw of the middle-class welfare state is the problem of who winds up paying its bills. Put aside any notions that "the rich" can be made to pick up the tab to any significant degree. Just to close the current cash flow deficit in the budget (never mind the long-term deficits in Social Security, Medicare, and other major entitlement programs) would require taxing away *all* of the income of every American earning more than $175,000 of adjusted gross income—and that's assuming that no one changed his or her behavior as a result of such a confiscatory tax.[5] The top-earning 1 percent of Americans may receive 13 percent of all income in the United States, but that is still not nearly enough to pay for even a small portion of the real cost of the middle-class welfare state.

Don't count on cuts in defense spending to pay the bill either. America has already clipped the long-awaited peace dividend from the end of the cold war and spent most of the proceeds financing the growth of existing entitlements. On its current projectory, defense spending will soon decline to a smaller share of gross domestic product than in any other year since 1940, when Franklin Roosevelt first tried to bestir America into becoming the "Arsenal of Democracy." Even if by some good fortune we find ourselves able to disband the Department of Defense and become a neutral state like Switzerland, this would save considerably less than the annual cost of Medicare alone in the early years of the next century.

So who does pay for middle-class entitlements? For the past fifty years, the answer has always been the next generation. The huge windfall benefits conveyed to early Social Security and Medicare beneficiaries, as we've seen, were financed by ever higher taxes on the latecomers. The rest was financed by deficits. If, even after adjusting for inflation, entitlement spending had grown no faster than the growth of the population and the economy between 1965 and 1995, annual federal spending would today be $466.6 billion less than it actually is. This would have been nearly enough to balance the 1995 budget deficit three times over.[6]

This borrow-and-spend strategy is hardly sustainable through the next century. Even if, over the 1995–2010 period, workers enjoy a rate of wage growth that is more than eight times faster than that experienced between 1973 and 1993, the rising cost of entitlements will tax away virtually all of their gains. If real wages grow only five times faster than during the 1973–1993 period, real *after-tax* income will drop by 59 percent by 2010.[7]

Sure, it is always possible to assume that some breakthrough technology will so vastly improve human efficiency that any amount of debt will eventually seem insignificant, but only fools would bet their own finances on such an outcome. A nation saving less than 1 percent of its income, as the United States currently does, cannot expect to realize rapid increases in productivity. Moreover, if we have learned anything as a society in the last thirty years, it is that affluence is not automatic and that growth of the economy does not necessarily eliminate growth of the underclass, the national debt, or other compounding claims on the next generation's wealth.

A GLOBAL REFORM

The ultimate solution to the crisis of the U.S. welfare state, as we'll see in the next chapter, will be a cultural revolution among the American middle class that will elevate the prestige of such bourgeois values as thrift, work, and family. But such cultural change does not occur in a vacuum. Public policy must change as well, both as a catalyst to cultural change and as a reflection of the new *embourgeoisement* of the American middle class.

The resolution Congress has recently made to balance the budget by early in the next century is a step in the right direction. Unfortunately, however, it is only a baby step, the first of many that must, and will, lead to the effective dismantlement of the middle-class welfare state within the next ten to fifteen years.

As much as the deficits may dominate our politics today, this is the calm before the storm. Today, as the baby boom generation cruises through its prime productive years and as women join the labor force in record numbers, the percentage of Americans working and paying taxes has never been higher. Also, due to the comparatively low birthrates of the 1930s, the rate of growth among the elderly population has tapered off. Meanwhile, the collapse of the Soviet Union has dramatically cut the need for military spending and the economy continues to deliver moderate yet consistent noninflationary growth. With such favorable trends at work, balancing the budget over the next seven to ten years should be a comparatively easy exercise. But as the baby boom generation reaches retirement age, a debt storm will rise that will ruin the American economy and sunder our culture unless we prepare for it.

The time is long overdue for Congress to apply a global means test to all existing entitlement programs. In a 1992 article for the *Atlantic Monthly* entitled "The Next New Deal," Neil Howe and I sketched out how such a means test would work.[8] Since then, the idea has been taken up by the Concord Coalition (a bipartisan organization headed by former members of Congress that focuses on fiscal policy) and has attracted significant political support. Given the increasingly unpleasant choices lawmakers will face in the coming decade, the chances of Congress's actually passing a global means test in the next ten years are quite strong.

Here, in brief, is a how a global means test could work.

The essential idea is to direct U.S. social spending, from whatever source, away from the affluent, and to do so with the passage of a single law that is easy to administer. Under this proposal, low-income Americans, whose benefits are already subject to numerous welfare reform proposals, would not be asked to make any additional sacrifices. And even families with incomes as high as $40,000 would be exempt from any reduction in benefits. But more-affluent families would see the value of their total entitlements reduced according to a graduated scale.

Such a scale might be set up as follows: For families earning between $40,000 and $50,000, entitlement benefits would be reduced by 10 percent of the amount that entitlements contributed to their income above $40,000. So, for example, a family who received $30,000 of nonentitlement income and $15,000 in Social Security benefits would lose $500 of its benefits (because entitlements contributed $5,000 of their income above $40,000, and $500 is 10 percent of that amount).

More-affluent families would sacrifice progressively more of their subsidies. For every additional $10,000 in income above $40,000, families would surrender 10 percent of the benefits that caused their income to exceed $40,000. The means test would be capped, so that even the most affluent families would still receive at least 15 percent of the original value of their entitlements. Thus, a family that received $15,000 in Social Security and $120,000 or more of nonentitlement income would lose $12,750 of its Social Security benefits (because $12,750 is 85 percent of $15,000, which is the amount of their entitlements that contributes to their income above $40,000).

How much money would such a scheme save? The Congressional Budget Office applied this formula to the following programs: Social Security, Railroad Retirement, unemployment compensation, veterans' compensation and pensions, Aid to Families with Dependent Children, Supplemental Security Income, food stamps, Medicare, and Medicaid. For the last two of these programs, it calculated their insurance value minus any premiums paid by individuals. Had such a plan been put into effect on January 1, 1995, it would have saved $189.8 billion by the turn of the century.[9]

Even greater savings could be realized by applying a global means test to entitlements conveyed through the tax code. For example, limiting the home mortgage deduction to a maximum of $12,000 for an individual, $20,000 for a joint filing couple, and $10,000 for separately filing couples (which would effectively means-test the deduction) would instantly raise $6 billion a year, and $30 billion a year by 2020.[10] Tax subsidies for defined-benefit pension plans and for employer-provided health insurance similarly should be included in a global means test, if not eliminated.

SOLUTIONS

A global means test could also be applied to federal employee pensions. In deference to the quasi-contractual nature of these entitlements, the formula for adjusting federal pension benefits could be made considerably less stringent. If the maximum reduction of benefits was held to 25 percent for households earning over $70,000 and the withholding rate set at 7.5 percent, savings of around $7 billion a year would still be possible.

Any means test can be difficult to administer. Witness the virtual industry that has sprung up to advise Americans on how to disguise assets in order to qualify Grandma or Grandpa for Medicaid-financed nursing home care. But a global means test could be comparatively easy to make work. It could be achieved exclusively through tax returns, much as we now handle the limited taxation of Social Security. Each filer would be required to enter all benefits received, which could be checked against federal records. Above certain limits the total would trigger a "benefit-withholding" liability, which the filer would send back to the Internal Revenue Service along with any outstanding income tax liability. As a practical matter, federal benefits could be withheld just as wages are withheld, based on a tax filer's previous experience.

This approach has several political advantages as well. Because all the savings would be collected through the tax code, for example, a single piece of legislation, falling under the jurisdiction of the tax committee in each house, would be sufficient to implement the reform. Moreover, no benefit group could complain that it was being singled out for sacrifice. While affluent retirees would receive less Social Security, yuppies would receive fewer tax subsidies for their mortgage debt. These features give the proposal more public support than one might imagine. When pollsters asked Americans in 1994 whether "you favor or oppose" a global means test (after explaining how this test "would gradually reduce benefits to well-off households and eliminate nearly all benefits going to very high-income households"), 62 percent favored the idea while 36 percent opposed it.[11]

A global means test would treat all Americans according to individual circumstances. This is untrue of most other reform proposals, such as cutting cost-of-living adjustments across the board. For a widow receiving no income other than one large Social Security check, a cost-of-living adjustment may be essential to keep food on the table. For a triple-dipping federal pensioner receiving the minimum Social Security benefit, that same cost-of-living adjustment may be just enough to cover the annual rise in greens fees at the club.

Ultimately, means testing the benefits of current beneficiaries is the only way the United States can afford to privatize its Social Security system or to provide needed tax incentives for savers. This becomes clear when one realizes that privatizing the Social Security system for current workers while continuing to pay full benefits to all current retirees would in effect require today's workers to pay for two retirements: their parents' and their own. Come what may, the cost of supporting the poor and frail elderly will create an unprecedented burden for today's young, who will also face trillions of dollars in other debts and unfunded liabilities from the past. But at least that burden can be alleviated somewhat if affluent members of the current older generation surrender at least some of their windfall benefits.

Make no mistake about it, however. A global means test, while a good start, is no panacea. Applied only to Social Security and other direct entitlements flowing to nongovernment employees, for example, it would eliminate only a small fraction of the expected increase in the national debt between 1995 and 2000. Much more has to be done.

HEALING HEALTH CARE

Also required will be a wholesale restructuring of the U.S. health care system. Just under one-third of all direct entitlement spending goes for just two health care programs: Medicare and Medicaid. Meanwhile, indirect health care subsidies consumed by the middle class, such as the exclusion of employer-provided insurance premiums from income tax, which costs the Treasury more than $47 billion a year, are also a major component of total entitlement spending. As the population ages and new medical procedures and treatments expand our very definition of what it means to be in good health at any given age, the cost of these and other health care subsidies will escalate dramatically. Only by systematically overhauling not just the way health care is financed but how it is delivered can we even hope to contain the growth of health care spending within reasonable bounds.

The first principle of all health care reform should be to make individual consumers, as well as society as a whole, aware of the true cost and trade-offs involved in all health care decisions. This means, in effect, ending health care subsidies except to those who are truly in financial need. And there is no more appropriate way to start that process than by phasing out the tax subsidies to affluent Americans for employer-provided insurance premiums.

Ever since some faceless Internal Revenue Service bureaucrat ruled in 1944 that compensation provided in the form of health insurance is tax free, we've had a huge and growing backdoor subsidy undermining the efficiency of the health care market as well as driving up the national debt. Expect Congress eventually to deny this entitlement to the affluent. Limiting the exclusion to $410 per month for family coverage and to $170 per month for individual coverage (about the average cost of insurance) would save $24 billion a year by 2000. By 2020, such a cap would save $105 billion a year.[12]

In a similar spirit, Medicare premiums and deductibles and co-payments should and will be significantly increased. There is an appropriate role to be played by government in providing Americans with financial protection against catastrophic illness when such protection cannot be purchased on the private market. But there is no reason taxpayers should be subsidizing the routine health care costs of middle- and upper-income Americans, regardless of their age. Doing so not only costs the Treasury money it doesn't have; it also reduces the cost consciousness of many retirees and thereby causes them to overconsume health care.

At the same time, at least some of the insurance value of Medicare benefits ought to be taxable as regular income. This is the least sacrifice we can ask of a population whose members are currently entitled to receive lifetime Medicare benefits worth an average $82,000 more than the value of their lifetime contributions in Medicare taxes.[13]

There is also no reason why the federal government shouldn't ask the recipients of its health care subsidies to participate in managed care networks, such as health maintenance organizations. After all, the people paying for these subsidies (by and large, younger workers) are now generally required by their employers to receive their own health care through managed care networks, which, despite occasional horror stories, are demonstrably effective in holding down health care costs without compromising quality.

The federal government also needs to tighten the loopholes that millions of middle-class families now use to acquire free nursing home care under the Medicaid system. One possible approach is to put a special surtax on family members who have received assets or inheritances from Medicaid patients. The potential savings, particularly over time, are enormous, according to the Congressional Budget Office.[14]

THE POLITICS OF RISK

Removing these and other distorting middle-class subsidies from the health care system will go a long way toward containing costs and making the system operate more efficiently. But even without any direct subsidies whatsoever, it is far from clear whether in the long run the private market for health insurance can be preserved as we currently know it. Pointed at its heart like a stiletto is the ever more precise technology available for diagnosing an individual's inherent tendency to contract certain illnesses. As it becomes possible for an insurance company to determine through a simple physical examination that your unborn child will develop leukemia, or that you carry a gene that puts you at elevated risk for breast cancer or schizophrenia or alcoholism or other expensive diseases, health care may well become uninsurable in any conventional sense. Insurance companies won't be in the business of spreading risks, because for every individual, future health care costs will be close to knowable.

Private insurers already have a pronounced tendency to cherry-pick the best risks (based on age and other demographic factors) and to deny coverage to anyone with "preexisting conditions." The conventional solution to this problem is to propose a requirement that carriers insure anyone who asks for a policy. But such a so-called guaranteed-issue rule by itself is only likely to make matters worse by encouraging more Americans to go bare. Why buy health insurance when you are healthy, for example, so long as you know that if and when you ever get sick you can always run out and buy "guaranteed-issue" coverage? Private health insurance won't work if the only people who buy it are ill or fear they soon will be.

Mandating that every American purchase a minimum health care policy might solve that problem, but it still doesn't necessarily preserve the conditions under which private insurance can operate. This is because political decisions still have to be made about how knowledge of preexisting conditions and likely future illnesses are used in pricing insurance. When we know that young people consume far less health care than old people in general, charging all age groups the same price for health insurance amounts to providing a large windfall to the old. Similarly, when we know that certain individuals carry genes that elevate their chances of contracting certain expensive diseases, charging them the same price as people who don't carry such genes is also in effect a transfer of wealth. The same is true when we fail to charge smokers higher insurance premiums than nonsmokers or fail to impose surcharges on people who engage in other risky behaviors.

This is not to suggest that society shouldn't in some cases provide for such subsidies to achieve various public purposes. But it is to suggest that such decisions are essentially political. And with ever better information about who is going to become sick and who isn't, there are going to be more and more such political decisions needing to be made, regardless of how much government does or does not formally control the health care sector. Health care insurance is inevitably becoming less a matter of shifting risks, and more a matter of shifting costs. Free markets alone will never decide for us what is the best way to do that.

As with entitlements in general, the resolution of the health care crisis is thus fundamentally a question of political culture and values. Regardless of how the provision of health care is organized in the future—whether by government, private enterprise, or some combination—Americans will have to decide as citizens and voters what the ground rules will be for who pays what to whom.

If the answer that comes back is that generally the young must always pay for the old and that the middle class is due the same subsidies as the poor, then America's prospects in the next century will be dim indeed. Instead, individual Americans will have to rediscover the values that propelled the United States as an industrial power in the last century: they will have to reinvent themselves as sturdy, independent, and thrifty bourgeoisie.

14

What You Should Do

The implications of this book for your own finances should by now be clear. You can go on living your life as if you could count on Social Security, Medicare, and other middle-class entitlements. But the younger you are, the more foolhardy it is to risk your future on such a dubious assumption.

Remember the official government projections for entitlement programs we examined in Chapter 1? In order for these programs to continue on their current course, the federal government would either have to eliminate all other forms of spending, including defense, over the next thirty-five years, or else raise taxes on today's children to well over 50 percent.

Anyone who believes that scenario will come true is still in deep denial. Your benefits are going to be cut, if not outright eliminated. The question is not if but when. Are you ready to face consequences? In this chapter, we'll undertake several case studies of Americans of different ages and in different financial circumstances in order to discover how much you must save in a world in which no one can count on middle-class entitlements.

WHAT YOU SHOULD DO

CASE 1: THE SPENDTHRIFT BOOMER

Let's start with a single man we'll call Bob. Born in 1945, Bob as of this writing is already fifty. Like many other leading-edge baby boomers, Bob has never been much of a saver. He did manage to buy his first house in 1985 and has now seen his home equity build up to $100,000. But Bob has always placed a low priority on financial savings. When he changed jobs ten years ago, he spent the modest sum he had managed to build up in the company 401(k) plan on a new car and a prolonged vacation. Since then he's been contributing just 3 percent of his income to the 401(k) plan at his new job, and so has accumulated a retirement nest egg of just $20,000.

Busy with his career as a journalist, Bob hasn't spent much time thinking about when he might retire. But when asked point-blank, he says he figures he might hang it up at about the same age his father did, which was sixty-two.

How much income does Bob expect to have in retirement? Well, again, he hasn't really thought about it, but off the top of his head he says he guesses he'd like to be able to spend about $35,000 a year, or whatever its inflation-adjusted equivalent turns out to be.

Bob also doesn't dwell very often on the question of how long he'll live, but when he gives the question a second's thought, he figures he has a pretty good chance of living at least as long as his father did, which was age ninety.

What must Bob do to realize his casual expectations for retirement? To answer that question, we first have to make an assumption about the real rate of return Bob is likely to earn on his savings both before and after he retires.

For now, let's assume that Bob invests his savings aggressively in the years before he reaches age sixty-two and manages to a realize 6.5 percent return after inflation on his portfolio of mutual funds. This was the average real rate of return for all common stocks between 1871 and 1992, so it's not unreasonable to expect that Bob might do this well, though there are no guarantees.

For the years after he retires, let's assume Bob will be able to achieve 2 percent real return. This is in line with the historical averages for a conservative portfolio invested primarily in bonds, such as a typical retiree would want to guard against loss of principal.

Now, given those assumptions, what exactly is Bob up against as he ages? Of course, he's never done the math, but if he had he'd be in for quite a shock. In order to be able to retire at age sixty-two and enjoy inflation-adjusted purchasing power of $35,000 annually through age ninety, Bob has to start saving $42,898 a year beginning immediately.

Since Bob makes only $40,000 a year, obviously he can't do that. What are his options? Of course, he can always hope to get a raise substantially above the rate of inflation, but like most other Americans, Bob hasn't had one in years and doesn't expect that to change anytime soon.

So realistically, Bob has to give up the hope of retiring comfortably at age sixty-two. Of course, due to layoffs or poor health, Bob may well be forced out of the workforce in his early sixties, but he had better hope he can find a way to make a living until at least age seventy. If he can hang on that long, the size of the retirement nest egg he will need drops dramatically, and with it, the amount he must save each year he remains at work. If Bob can count on working until age seventy, and living no longer than ninety, then his annual savings requirement drops to $13,267.

This is still far more than Bob can save without dramatically changing his lifestyle. Does he have any recourse? Fortunately, Bob can tap into his home equity by making do with a more modest house. In Bob's area, home prices aren't appreciating above the rate of inflation, so his home has little value as an investment. But by moving to a smaller home, he can free up to $40,000 in equity and put it to work in the stock market. Doing so reduces his annual savings requirement down to $9,541 a year, assuming the stock market continues to go up at an average real rate of 6.5 percent.

That's still an awful lot to save, given Bob's $40,000 income. Can he do it? Yes. After all, Japanese families routinely save 20 percent of their income. Does he want to do it? No. "For crying out loud," Bob rationalizes, "I may well die of a coronary when I'm fifty-eight." So Bob decides to hell with the future and goes on living his

WHAT YOU SHOULD DO

life just as he had when the whole subject of retirement first came up. Through his 401(k) he continues saving just $1,200 a year. The likely result: after working until age seventy, Bob will spend the last twenty years of his life living on the equivalent of just $6,000 a year in today's dollars.

CASE 2: THE DIVORCEE

When Ellen married Jack ten years ago, she thought she was set for life. An analyst with a local utility company, Jack brought home a great salary and great benefits to boot, including a generous pension. So Ellen never worried about setting aside money of her own for retirement.

Then came the divorce. She got the two kids, the house, and $40,000 a year in child support for the next twelve years. He held on to most of their savings and his pension. At age forty, Ellen found herself with $40,000 in savings, home equity of $150,000, two kids to put through college, and no retirement plan.

What are her expectations for the rest of her life? She knows she'll have to work to make ends meet, but she doesn't want to work until she drops. If she could retire at age sixty-five, with the ability to spend $35,000 a year in today's money for the rest of her life, that would suit her.

For a woman used to a comfortable middle-class lifestyle, these are seemingly modest expectations but still not easily realized. With her mother still kicking at age ninety-five, Ellen has to assume she'll live at least this long as well. This means that over the next twenty-five years, she'll have to save enough to live on for at least the following thirty years. Assuming that she earns the same real returns on her savings as we assumed for Bob, that turns out to be no easy feat. It requires that Ellen sock away $10,205 toward retirement every year, starting immediately.

What can Ellen do to reduce that number? Assuming that her house is not appreciating in value at a rate commensurate with the stock market, moving to a more modest house may make sense. Because she is much further away from retirement than Bob, she'll get a bigger total return than he did by converting some of her home equity into more lucrative investments. For example, if she took $40,000 of her home equity out of a house that was appreciating only at the rate of inflation and put it to work in the stock market, she would, under our assumptions, reduce her annual retirement savings need from $10,205 to $6,870.

Saving $6,870 might still be too much of a strain for Ellen, especially with college tuition to pay for and her own mother to help support. If she can resign herself to putting off retirement until age sixty-seven, she can still enjoy an inflation-adjusted retirement income of $35,000 a year until age ninety-five by saving just $4,521 a year. That is still quite an encumbrance, but it's manageable. Fortunately, Ellen forced herself to go through these calculations while she was still just forty. If she had waited until age fifty to begin saving for retirement, her annual savings requirement, even after moving to a smaller house and delaying her retirement age, would have jumped all the way up to $17,951.

CASE 3: THE BABY BUSTERS

For Heather and Jason, there's good news and bad news. The bad news is that, having been born in 1970, they don't stand a chance of collecting Social Security and Medicare when they reach retirement age in the 2030s. And their chances of collecting a private, defined-benefit pension are almost equally dim. But the good news is that this couple is still young enough that they can accumulate a substantial retirement nest egg if they start saving now.

Heather and Jason figure they can be comfortable in retirement on the equivalent of $40,000 a year in today's dollars. For planning purposes, they both expect to work until age sixty-seven, and they assume neither will live past age ninety-five. Currently, they have $5,000 between them saved in their IRAs. What does that make their retirement savings requirement? Based on the rate-of-return assumptions used above, they need between the two of them to save $3,899 a year for retirement.

Of course, for most twenty-five-year-olds this is not easily done,

WHAT YOU SHOULD DO

what with student loans to pay off, first homes to save for, and the rest. But trying to make that goal is well worth the effort because the cost of delay is so high. Suppose, for example, that Heather and Jason were to wait until they are thirty-five to begin saving for their retirement. They would have to save $8,596 a year to meet their retirement goals. True, by the time they reach age thirty-five, their salaries may be substantially higher than they are today, but not so much higher that saving $8,596 a year for retirement will come easy.

The high price of putting off saving for retirement is illustrated further in Table 1.

TABLE 1

Annual Savings Requirement to Finance a Twenty-Five-Year Retirement
with Inflation-Adjusted Purchasing Power of $30,000 a Year

Amount Already Saved for Retirement	*Years Remaining until Retirement*				
	50	40	30	20	10
($0)	$1,712	$3,354	$6,860	$15,484	$46,877
$10,000	$1,031	$2,643	$6,086	$14,553	$45,375
$20,000	$349	$1,932	$5,311	$13,621	$43,872
$30,000	(0)	$1,221	$4,536	$12,690	$42,370
$40,000	(0)	$510	$3,761	$11,758	$40,868
$50,000	(0)	(0)	$2,987	$10,827	$39,365
$60,000	(0)	(0)	$2,212	$9,895	$37,863
$70,000	(0)	(0)	$1,437	$8,964	$36,361
$80,000	(0)	(0)	$662	$8,032	$34,858
$90,000	(0)	(0)	(0)	$7,100	$33,356
$100,000	(0)	(0)	(0)	$6,169	$31,853

Assumptions: 6.5 percent real return on savings accumulated prior to retirement; 2.0 percent real return on savings held after retirement. All savings exhausted after twenty-five years in retirement.

SOLUTIONS

For someone still young enough to be fifty years away from retirement, little more than $20,000 in IRAs is required, under these assumptions, to finance a twenty-five-year retirement. Such a person would have no further need to save for retirement, unless he or she wanted to retire earlier or with more purchasing power. Few teenagers have that kind of money squirreled away for retirement, to be sure, but the point is still relevant to many people's lives. Let's say you've just had a child. By opening up an IRA account in his or her name and

TABLE 2

Total Nest Egg Needed, and Annual Savings Required, to Finance a
Twenty-Five-Year Retirement with Various Amounts of Annual Purchasing Power

Desired Annual Purchasing Power in Retirement (in today's dollars)	Total Nest Egg Needed on Date of Retirement (in today's dollars)	Annual Savings Required Assuming No Current Savings			
		Years Remaining until Retirement			
		40	30	20	10
$10,000	$195,235	$1,118	$2,287	$5,161	$15,626
$20,000	$390,469	$2,236	$4,574	$10,323	$31,251
$30,000	$585,704	$3,354	$6,860	$15,484	$46,877
$40,000	$780,938	$4,472	$9,147	$20,646	$62,503
$50,000	$976,173	$5,590	$11,434	$25,807	$78,129
$60,000	$1,171,407	$6,708	$13,721	$30,969	$93,754
$70,000	$1,366,642	$7,826	$16,008	$36,130	$109,380
$80,000	$1,561,877	$8,944	$18,294	$41,292	$125,006
$90,000	$1,757,111	$10,062	$20,581	$46,453	$140,632
$100,000	$1,952,346	$11,180	$22,868	$51,615	$156,257

Assumptions: 6.5 percent real return on savings accumulated prior to retirement; 2.0 percent real return on savings held after retirement. No current retirement savings. All savings exhausted after twenty-five years in retirement.

WHAT YOU SHOULD DO

contributing little more than $900 a year for the next fifteen years, you can give your child everything he or she will need to retire at age sixty-five on a comfortable income. (And then just maybe the kid will have the resources in midlife to take care of you as you age.)

Of course, not only is time a huge influence on one's retirement savings needs; so is the amount one plans to live on in retirement. Does $30,000 in today's dollars sound like more than you'll need, or too little to be comfortable? Table 2 illustrates the effect of lowering or raising your consumption goals in retirement.

Another major determinant of how much you need to save for retirement is the length of time you'll be retired. This, of course, is difficult to predict. Not only must you reckon at what age you'll retire but also guess how long you'll live. Table 3 illustrates the effect of lengthening or shortening one's years in retirement.

TABLE 3

Annual Savings Requirement to Finance a Retirement of Various Lengths
with Inflation-Adjusted Annual Purchasing Power of $30,000

Length of Retirement (Years)	*Years Remaining until Retirement*				
	50	40	30	20	10
1	$86	$168	$345	$778	$2,345
5	$413	$810	$1,656	$3,738	$11,317
10	$788	$1,543	$3,156	$7,124	$21,568
15	$1,127	$2,207	$4,515	$10,191	$30,852
20	$1,434	$2,809	$5,746	$12,969	$39,261
25	$1,712	$3,354	$6,860	$15,484	$46,877
30	$1,964	$3,847	$7,870	$17,763	$53,775
35	$2,192	$4,295	$8,784	$19,827	$60,023
40	2,398	$4,699	$9,612	$21,696	$65,682

Assumptions: 6.5 percent real return on savings accumulated prior to retirement; 2.0 percent real return on savings held after retirement. No current retirement savings.

It is possible to hedge the risk of living longer than expected by purchasing annuities: financial instruments that will pay you a fixed amount per year regardless of how long you live. But one still must bear the risk of inflation.

There is one last variable that dramatically affects one's required savings for retirement: the actual rate of return earned on savings. An annual investment of $1,000 will grow to $149,000 over twenty-five years if it earns a 12 percent annual return, but will grow to only $43,000 if it earns a 4 percent return. So choosing a realistic interest rate assumption is critical to intelligent retirement planning.

PROJECTING YOUR OWN RETIREMENT SAVINGS NEEDS

How do you go about figuring what you should be saving for retirement? Let's start by scrutinizing the rate-of-return assumption you should use for planning purposes. In the tables in this chapter, I used the average real return for common stocks between 1871 and 1992 in calculating the return on investment made during the preretirement years. That may seem like a conservative assumption, but actually it isn't. There is nothing to say you'll be so lucky as to earn the average rate of return that prevailed over that entire period. Markets go up and down, and often stay down for years at a time.

Suppose you had begun your retirement saving in 1953 by investing in a portfolio of all common stocks and had made equal investments each year through 1973. In that event, your average annual real return on your portfolio, as of December 1973, would have been −.65 percent—and that is *before* adjusting for the taxes you'd have to pay on your dividends and nominal capital gains.[1]

If you'd been trying to get by as retiree during that period with a conservative portfolio of blue chip bonds, you wouldn't have done much better. For example, if you had purchased equal amounts of intermediate-term U.S. Treasury bonds each year between 1953 and 1973, the real return on your portfolio would have been just 0.2075 percent as of December 1973.[2] And again, this meager return would be before taxes.

WHAT YOU SHOULD DO

Of course, your own portfolio may do much better than this over your remaining lifetime, but the point is that it could do as bad or worse, and so you must plan accordingly. Moreover, it certainly is not difficult to imagine that as the huge baby boom generation passes through its retirement years and begins consuming its savings, stocks and bonds will be under enormous selling pressure. A study by John Shoven, an economist at Stanford University, and Sylvester Schieber, an employee-benefits specialist at the Wyatt Co., projects that the employer pension system will shift from a net buyer of assets to a net seller by 2006. With pension funds distributing more in benefits than they invest in stocks and bonds, and with individual boomers also disinvesting, the real rate of return on financial assets is bound to plummet.[3] The flip side of the prediction is that the boomers are bound to inflate the prices of stocks and bonds between now and about 2006. That's all the more reason to start your retirement savings now, so as to take advantage of the boom while it lasts.

So what assumption should you use? There is no single right answer. I can only say that for planning purposes, I use a 4 percent real return on assets held before retirement and a 2 percent real return for assets held afterward. Such an assumption is consistent with a portfolio that becomes increasingly weighted with more conservative investments as retirement age draws near. Using a 3 percent real interest rate assumption for the preretirement years might be more prudent, but for most readers this assumption will generate savings requirements beyond the realm of the possible. Rather than getting discouraged and giving up, assume 4 percent and hope for the best.

But don't cheat yourself by being too optimistic about the other assumptions you'll have to make. For example, don't just presume that you'll be able to work well past age sixty-five. There has been a lot of happy talk recently about how there really is no entitlements crisis because boomers will just go on working into their eighties and beyond. In a cover story on the economics of aging, *Business Week*, for example, enthuses: "People can be productive far longer in an information-and-services economy than one dominated by factories and heavy industry."[4] Yet where is the evidence of this? When

America was dominated by factories and heavy industry, retirement was virtually unknown. But as the American economy has become more sophisticated and knowledge intensive, it has gotten by with less and less work from those in their sixties and beyond. Frankly, many, if not most, baby boomers are already finding that their job skills are becoming rapidly obsolete while they are still in their thirties and forties. Indeed, those who trained for a high-tech industry are often in the worst shape. Ask just about any aerospace engineer who came through school in the 1970s, or the legions of technicians trained to maintain mainframe computers.

Sure, many workers will surmount these challenges through retraining. And many will find themselves healthy and mentally alert enough to be productive into their eighties and beyond. But chances are that most workers won't, if for no other reason than because they will find the pace of new technology too fast to keep up with in their sixties and seventies, and often too expensive to learn as well. So if you think you have what it takes to postpone retirement into your eighties, go ahead and plug that assumption into your financial spreadsheet, but realize the risks you are taking.

Another assumption to scrutinize is the amount of purchasing power you think you'll need in retirement. Many retirement planning guides counsel that you will be comfortable in retirement earning only around two-thirds of what you made while working. It's true that by retiring, you will be able to save on commuting expenses and, if you move to another part of the country, perhaps on housing costs as well. Let's hope that any children you may have are through with college by that point, too. But against these potential savings you have to consider two enormous potential claims on your savings: health care cost and taxes.

Even without Medicare's having yet been means tested or otherwise substantially cut, senior citizens today are spending a greater percentage of their income on health care today than retirees did *before* Medicare was enacted in 1965. Retirees in the next century will spend more yet—come what may. This requirement may be enforced through higher deductibles and premiums for Medicare, taxation of benefits, or outright repeal of the programs, but it will happen. For high-income seniors, Medicare may not be available at all.

At the same time, you can bet that health care inflation will become a huge problem as boomers age into their sixties and seventies. Just as boomers caused huge housing inflation when they started buying houses, they will cause huge inflation in the cost of drugs, physician services, hospital nursing home care, and most other components of the health care system as they age.

How should you account for this in your retirement planning? Recall that couples retiring in 1994 are expected to consume more than $185,000 in Medicare expenses over their lifetimes.[5] If you wind up ineligible for Medicare, or if Medicare winds up being eliminated, you're probably going to need at least that much in real terms to purchase private health insurance during your retirement years. Similarly, you may well find it prudent to set aside a substantial sum for private nursing home insurance as well, since the government is bound to become less generous with its subsidies in this area.

Don't forget to account for taxes you'll pay in retirement. Of course, there is no way of knowing what tax rates will be at that time, but clearly they are bound to be much higher than they are today, given the magnitude of the government's indebtedness. Remember that all the self-congratulatory talk in Washington these days about reducing the deficits has nothing to do with actually reducing the national debt, only with reducing how fast it continues to grow.

Don't expect to cash in, either, on the many tax exemptions and credits today's seniors enjoy. As the population ages, these tax subsidies for seniors will become prohibitively expensive and are bound to be trimmed or eliminated.

Another reason to expect higher taxes in the next century: as the economy becomes more knowledge intensive, the United States will probably have to spend substantially more on education in order to stay competitive in world markets. And as the size of the American underclass continues to grow and millions of middle-class baby boomers approach old age without adequate savings, the cost of social programs targeted toward the poor no doubt will escalate dramatically in the next century. All of this means that when you go to withdraw your savings from your IRA or 401(k) twenty years from now, you can fairly well count on those savings' being taxed at a very high rate—through higher income taxes, consumption taxes, or both.

Finally, you are going to have to make some sort of realistic decision about how long you are likely to live. On this point, bear in mind that if you go by how long your parents or grandparents lived, you're quite likely to underestimate your remaining life span. Life expectancy continues to improve dramatically from generation to generation. Today men reaching age sixty-five have an average life expectancy of over fifteen years, and women can expect another nineteen years *on average.* Twenty years from now, people turning age sixty-five will probably have substantially higher average life expectancies, and of course substantial numbers will live into their nineties and even one hundreds.

Here's another reason to assume a long life span. If you plan to have just enough money to get by until, say, age eighty-five, how are you going to feel when you're age eighty-three? You might be blessed with wonderful health and an active retirement, but you'll go to bed each night knowing that if you don't die within two years, you'll become a pauper. Even if you do in fact wind up dying at age eighty-five, the years preceding your death will be marred by growing anxiety over a dwindling portfolio. Much better to have enough money on hand so that you don't have to worry about living well into your nineties if that is what fate has in store for you.

So what's the bottom line? That obviously depends on your individual circumstances, but Table 4 projects savings requirements based on some of the considerations we've just been making. It assumes you'll require the equivalent of $30,000 a year in today's dollars to run your household and an additional $10,000 a year on average to pay for health insurance and unreimbursed health expenses, making your total consumption needs $40,000 a year.

THE POSTCONSUMER SOCIETY

Do those numbers scare you? They should. Obviously few Americans can afford to save at these rates. A raging bull market might bail

WHAT YOU SHOULD DO

TABLE 4

Annual Savings Requirements to Finance a Twenty-Five-Year Retirement
with Inflation-Adjusted Purchasing Power of $40,000

(Based on Conservative Rate of Return Assumptions)

Current Retirement Savings	Years Remaining until Retirement				
	50	40	30	20	10
(0)	$5,149	$8,306	$14,177	$27,137	$70,955
$10,000	$4,680	$7,795	$13,588	$26,375	$69,610
$20,000	$4,212	$7,284	$12,999	$25,614	$68,265
$30,000	$3,743	$6,774	$12,411	$24,852	$66,920
$40,000	$3,275	$6,263	$11,822	$24,091	$65,575
$50,000	$2,806	$5,753	$11,233	$23,330	$64,230
$60,000	$2,338	$5,242	$10,644	$22,568	$62,885
$70,000	$1,869	$4,731	$10,055	$21,807	$61,540
$80,000	$1,400	$4,221	$9,467	$21,045	$60,196
$90,000	$932	$3,710	$8,878	$20,284	$58,851
$100,000	$463	$3,200	$8,289	$19,523	$57,506
$150,000	(0)	$646	$5,345	$15,716	$50,781

Assumptions: 4 percent real return on savings accumulated prior to retirement; 2.0 percent real return on savings held after retirement. No current retirement savings. All savings exhausted afer twenty-five years in retirement.

out some of us. But most Americans are going to have to work much longer than their parents did and to accept a dramatically altered standard of living both before and after retirement. Given this reality, it is high time our culture began to adjust its values.

Want to avoid becoming a prole in the next century? Then you must adapt to many of the values of the nineteenth-century bourgeoisie, who achieved middle-class status without the beneficence of a welfare state.

SOLUTIONS

The economic rules of middle-class life have changed fundamentally since the 1960s and 1970s, yet middle-class values and expectations have hardly begun to adjust to the new reality. In a world in which Social Security and other old age subsidy programs are clearly headed toward insolvency, *half* of all Americans have yet to put aside any savings for retirement. Even among white households approaching retirement age, median savings amounts to just $17,300.[6] Visit any national park in high summer and you'll see hundreds upon hundreds of these solid middle-class, middle-aged Americans in their quintessential element—people who haven't saved so much as six months of salary for their retirement but who have borrowed $40,000 or more to equip themselves with an RV, several dirt bikes, and a new sedan in tow. Do they really expect that their children are going to do their retirement saving for them?

Middle-class culture still celebrates play and time off, when a renewed commitment to work is required to pay off our personal and national debts. Middle-class culture still glorifies "self-actualization" and self-absorption, when economic necessity requires greater reliance on extended families to provide for the very young, the very old, the sick, and the unemployed. Middle-class culture, in short, is becoming less and less distinguishable from proletarian culture in its shortsightedness and self-indulgence at a time when, due to changing economic reality, it should be becoming more assertively entrepreneurial, family centered, and bourgeois.

Those who don't wake up to the new reality will soon enough become proles.

By the early 1990s, there was some cultural recoil from the trendy high-debt, high-consumption yuppie lifestyles celebrated in the previous decade but not enough to stem the long-term downward trend of the personal savings rate. At the same time, an explosion in casino and riverboat gambling throughout the American heartland seemed to symbolize America's final repudiation of thrift as a cultural value.

Perversely, legalized gambling has become in the 1990s one of the fastest-growing industries in the United States. By 1992, gross revenues from legal operations were running at nearly $30 billion a year—an average of more than $100 for every person in the country. Between 1982 and 1990, legal gambling by Americans grew at almost twice the rate of their personal incomes and climbed nearly two and a half times faster than that of the nation's manufacturing industries.[7]

Yet as Vicki Abt, James Smith, and Eugene Christiansen note in their book, *The Business of Risk: Commercial Gambling in Mainstream America*, the legitimization of gambling strikes at the core of capitalist culture:

> The self-made man, the archetypal embodiment of the American dream, owed his success to habits of industry, sobriety, moderation, self-discipline, and prudent investment. These qualities may still be seen in the successful recreational gambler, but they are caricatured in that he invests in the present—a chance for immediate reward in a culture characterized by self-indulgence.[8]

So pervasive has our debt-driven consumer culture become that it is next to impossible for any individual to step outside it and see it for the dangerous addiction it is. But that is what you must do if you want to belong to the shrinking middle class of the next century. Your parents, your neighbors, and your coworkers may all be carrying huge credit card debts while counting on Social Security and Medicare to finance their golden years. Movies, ads, and magazines may depict a world in which "normal" middle-class people drive brand-new $25,000 minivans (financed by tax-subsidized home equity loans), keep appearances up with face-lifts, tummy tucks, and breast enhancements (financed by tax-subsidized health insurance), and live in spacious suburban houses (financed by tax-subsidized mortgages). But if you act like such "normal" Americans, you will likely wind up like most such "normal" Americans: deep in debt, downwardly mobile, and headed for financial disaster as you age.

CAN GOVERNMENT HELP US HELP OURSELVES?

Why is the current culture unable to rediscover or reinvent the thrift ethos it so desperately needs to restore long-term prosperity? One reason is that thrift still has no champions. If the federal government were to undertake a public education program about the importance of saving, similar in scope to the campaigns it has launched against smoking, this would at least provide some counterbalance to the relentless pro-spending messages received from advertisers.[9] Similarly, schools, which until the early 1960s routinely taught lessons about the importance of savings, need to restore thrift to the curriculum. The success of Japan and other countries with such measures (including the United States of yesteryear) shows that they can be far from trivial in their influence over savings behavior.

Postwar Japan provides a prime example of how social pressure can drive savings behavior. Prior to World War II, the United States invested roughly 50 percent more than Japan as a percentage of gross national product. What turned Japan into the high-savings society it is today? After the war, the Japanese government launched a national campaign to promote thrift. To orchestrate this campaign, it established several new agencies, including the Central Council for Saving Promotion, the Savings Promotion Department of the Bank of Japan, and the Savings Promotion Center of the Ministry of Finance. To extol the virtues of saving and to provide workers with financial guidance, these agencies sponsored children's banks and appointed private citizens as savings promotion leaders. They disseminated magazines, booklets, leaflets, posters, advertisements, films, and the like, all of which were designed to build and reinforce the value of frugality.[10]

The strategy worked. Favorable tax treatment of savings undoubtedly played some role in elevating the Japanese savings rate. The tax code alone, however, cannot explain the extent of Japan's postwar conversion to thrift and its continued extraordinarily high rate of savings. During the 1980s, net national savings in Japan averaged 18.2 percent, as compared to just 3.6 percent in the United States.

But what if moral suasion isn't enough to prevent most Americans from consuming their futures? If we can mandate an increase in the minimum wage, we can mandate an increase in the savings rate as well, and we should.

WHAT YOU SHOULD DO

The idea is straightforward: require by federal law that individuals save a set amount toward their retirement, with wealthier citizens compelled to save a greater share of their income than the poor. Certainly that would be no more coercive or regressive than using ever higher Social Security payroll taxes to finance the federal budget deficit, nor would it leave the current working generation's retirement nest egg in the hands of a spendthrift Congress. Finally, unlike Individual Retirement Accounts and private pension plans that cost the Treasury tens of billions in forgone revenue each year, a mandated savings program would not contribute to the deficits.[11]

I originally proposed this idea in an address to the National Academy of Social Insurance in 1988.[12] Since then, the idea has gained respectability. In a paper published by the *Brookings Review* in 1993, for example, William G. Gale and Robert E. Litan worked out how the details of such a mandated savings plan might work.[13]

The simplest scheme would require working-aged Americans to set aside a certain percentage of their income each year in a mandatory savings account (MSA). As with income tax rates, the contribution rates for MSAs would rise with income. Individuals would be free to invest the assets in their MSAs as they saw fit. And after meeting all their required MSA contributions, individuals could still obtain tax breaks by further investing in IRAs, 401(k)s, and other qualified retirement plans.

For many people, the availability of MSAs would not necessarily cause them to save any more than they already do; it would just cause them to transfer some of their existing savings into their MSAs. For this reason, Gale and Litan sensibly suggest a requirement that all MSAs be funded with new savings.

How might such a requirement work? First, a taxpayer would have to calculate each year all purchases of financial assets and other qualified assets (such as residential real estate, automobiles, and other depreciable physical assets, including computers). Then, a taxpayer would have to subtract all sales of such assets. To this figure, increases in bank balances would be added, as well as reductions in debt. The result would be a taxpayer's net new savings.

Taxpayers with incomes below $20,000 might be exempted from

SOLUTIONS

any net new savings requirements. Other taxpayers could be required to have net savings of 4 percent income between $20,000 and $40,000, plus 6 percent of any income between $40,000 and $60,000 and so on, up to 10 percent of income above $80,000. If your net savings fell below those requirements, you would be obligated to pay a portion, perhaps all, of the shortfall to government.

What would such a plan do for the nation's savings rate? Gale and Litan estimate it would boost private savings by about 2.3 percent of gross domestic product (counting only financial assets) and by 4.1 percent if home equity is included as part of the net new savings calculations. That much new savings would more than make up for all the depletion of capital caused by the federal budget deficits and would make dramatic amounts of new capital available for productive investment.

Many other countries have adopted far more stringent mandatory savings requirements. Chile, for example, requires employees to contribute 13 percent of their wages; Sri Lanka 20 percent; Malaysia 22 percent; and 35 percent in Singapore.[14] In a recent study of retirement systems around the globe, the World Bank enthusiastically endorsed the adoption of mandatory savings plans, particularly for middle- and high-income countries such as the United States. Such plans, the World Bank notes, are an important source of capital formation, provide workers with what are in effect fully portable pensions, and are much less prone to political manipulation and abuse than traditional social insurance schemes.[15]

The fact that Social Security, Medicare, and other old age entitlements are likely to be effectively means tested by the early decades of the next century raises another virtue of the mandated savings idea: it avoids a potential free-rider problem created by means testing. Some improvident Americans might decide that since Social Security and Medicare will be means tested by the time they reach retirement age, there is no point in saving up for retirement on their own. The mandatory savings plan prevents such people from living beyond their means in their middle years and eventually becoming a burden to other taxpayers.

WHAT YOU SHOULD DO

Some people will no doubt object that the government has no business telling them how much to save and when. But consider the alternative. Without coercion, tens of millions of Americans will fail to save adequately to finance their old age or to prepare for other life contingencies. And as the ranks of the poor and the dependent grow as a result, rest assured the government will raise *your* taxes to pay for means-tested programs flowing to this population.

Some people no doubt would prefer that the government offer them more generous tax breaks for their savings, such as those available through IRAs. And it would indeed be a good idea if the United States derived more of its revenues from taxes on consumption and less from taxes on savings. But so far, there is no evidence that the tax subsidies the United States currently provides to savers have had any effect in raising the savings rate. And meanwhile, the $60-plus billion the United States spends in tax subsidies for IRAs, 401(k)s, and private defined-benefit pension plans winds up being financed largely through deficits that deplete the nation's store of capital.[16]

Another possible objection is that a mandatory savings plan of this size will seriously reduce consumer spending and thereby hurt the economy. It's true that increased savings will reduce consumer spending, especially for luxury items, in the short term. The yacht building industry is likely to take a big hit. Jobs will also be lost in tourism, the fashion industry, maybe even the casino industry, as Americans cut back on some of their discretionary spending in order to put more aside for a rainy day. But these job losses won't be permanent.

With an increased pool of savings available for investment, the Federal Reserve can let interest rates fall permanently without causing inflation. Lower-priced capital will spur more investment in new technology and increased productivity—just the sort of investment the United States must make in the next century as fewer workers remain available to support each retiree. There can be no question that in the not-so-long run, any measure that increases the U.S. savings rate will make the United States richer than it otherwise would be.

SOLUTIONS

TOWARD A NEW BOURGEOISIE

In 1967, *Time* magazine named the baby boom generation "Man of the Year." And who was this New Man? "Cushioned by unprecedented affluence and the welfare state, he has a sense of economic security unmatched in history," *Time* recounted. "Untold adventure awaits him. He is the man who will land on the moon, cure cancer and the common cold, lay out blight-proof, smog-free cities, enrich the underdeveloped world, and no doubt, write finis to poverty and war."[17]

For a generation weaned on such great expectations, the hard, practical truths described in this book often provoke a crying sense of unfairness. But though boomers, as well as younger Americans, have cause to be angry about the manner in which our future continues to be mortgaged by shortsighted government policies (and a right to demand that older Americans contribute to the solution) there is no cause for self-pity.

We have much to be grateful for: a standard of living that is still the envy of the rest of the world, access to health technologies that have dramatically prolonged our life expectancy and reduced our liability to debilitating pain, a much diminished threat of nuclear war, and a culture that, for all its faults, is still more humane and tolerant of self-expression and diversity than any that has come before.

Moreover, the regime of thrift that baby boomers will have to embrace is in many ways consistent with the values most celebrated by this generation. Thrift, properly understood, means wise use and abhorrence of waste—values at the heart of the modern environmental movement. A generation whose leading members denounced materialism in the 1960s and proclaimed themselves committed to spiritual exploration cannot feel entirely victimized when forced by practical necessity to cut back on trips to the mall, Club Med vacations, new Acuras, and nouvelle cuisine.

The demise of the middle-class welfare state will also foster another cultural change many Americans today say they yearn for: stronger families. In a world without Social Security and other middle-class subsidy programs, more and more stigma will attach to divorce, just as in Victorian times, because of the huge financial risks it will pose to all involved. Similarly, middle-class parents will once again have an extra and all-important incentive to invest their time, money, and energy in the well-being of their children: they will need their children's gratitude and support in old age. For many Americans, saving up enough to be protected against all potential financial threats will be impossible. Thus, Americans will have more reason than ever to build strong family relationships and other mutual aid networks, just as pioneers on the prairie did. And like those pioneers, we will all be able to take pride in our independence from distant governments.

In short, we have no particular reason to feel sorry for ourselves. As a nation, we unexpectedly became addicted to entitlements. As with those who contract the disease of alcoholism, there is no shame in our condition, so long as we recognize it and deal with it.

True, the pain of withdrawal will be excruciating, but every generation has its challenges. Measured by historical standards, the financial sacrifice required of today's younger Americans will not be all that great or unusual. (Would you prefer to have been a senior citizen in the 1930s?) Moreover, with the high rates of capital formation that will result from a renewal of middle-class thrift, we can expect the economy to grow much faster than it otherwise would and to raise the overall standard of living—perhaps dramatically so, as new technologies are exploited using the baby boomers' retirement savings.

For at least the past 250 years, thrift, capitalism, and population aging have been linked in ways that may have been largely forgotten in recent decades but cannot be ignored over time. Charles Moraze, in his classic study, *The Triumph of the Middle Classes*, notes that as human life spans began to increase dramatically in the late eighteenth century and as the cost of raising and educating children also began to rise, young families responded by acquiring the savings habit. "They counted their pence, planned their budget and calculated," Moraze writes. "Since each man felt master of his own destiny and responsible for his own children, young couples had to calculate their resources very carefully." And since such couples were also deciding to have fewer children during this period (in part to save money), they also had a correspondingly greater need to save in order to be supported in old age.

Thus lie the origins of the frugal bourgeois family and of the technology-driven, capitalistic system its thrift and industry made possible. Today we are all the beneficiaries of that discipline practiced by previous generations; our only burden is now to take up the same torch and to carry it into the twenty-first century.

Notes

Chapter 1: Introduction

1. Congressional Budget Office, *Reducing Entitlement Spending* (Washington, D.C.: U.S. Government Printing Office, September 1994), p. xi.
2. Congressional Budget Office, *Reducing the Deficit: Spending and Revenue Options* (Washington, D.C.: U.S. Government Printing Office, March 1994), p. 290.
3. General Accounting Office, *Tax Expenditures Deserve More Scrutiny* (Washington, D.C.: U.S. Government Printing Office, June 1994), p. 50.
4. Howard E. Shuman, *Politics and the Budget: The Struggle between the President and Congress* (Englewood Cliffs, N.J.: Prentice-Hall, 1984), p. 105.
5. Timothy M. Smeeding, "Why the U.S. Antipoverty System Doesn't Work Very Well," *Challenge* (January–February 1992): 30–35.
6. CBO, *Reducing Entitlement Spending*, p. 28.
7. Ibid., p. 13.
8. Ibid., p. 12.
9. Ibid., p. 16.
10. Neil Howe and Phillip Longman, "Next New Deal," *Atlantic* (April 1992): 94.
11. "Taxpayers Are Angry. They're Expensive, Too," *New York Times*, November 20, 1994, p. 5.

12. Howe and Longman, "Next New Deal," p. 93.

13. C. Eugene Steuerle and Jon M. Bakija, *Retooling Social Security for the Twenty-first Century: Right and Wrong Approaches to Reform* (Washington, D.C.: Urban Institute Press, 1994), tables 5.3, 5.7. Figures are for one-earner couples with average lifetime wages. All amounts are discounted to present value at age sixty-five using a 2 percent real interest rate. Calculations include actuarial value of all Old Age and Survivors Insurance (OASI) benefits payable over a lifetime. Includes both employer and employee portions of OASI payroll tax.

14. Florida Legislature, Joint Legislative Management Committee, unpublished data.

15. Sylvia Nasar, "Older Americans Cited in Studies of National Savings Rate Slump," *New York Times*, February 21, 1995, p. 1.

16. Board of Trustees of the Federal Hospital Insurance Trust Fund, *Annual Report* (Washington, D.C.: U.S. Government Printing Office, April 1995), p. 2 (hereafter cited as *HI Report*).

17. Neil Howe and Richard Jackson, *What We Need to Save to "Save" Medicare* (Washington, D.C.: Concord Coalition, 1995).

18. Board of Trustees of the Federal Supplementary Medical Insurance Trust Fund, *Annual Report* (Washington, D.C.: U.S. Government Printing Office, April 1995), p. 3.

19. Board of Trustees of the Federal Old-Age and Survivors Insurance and Disability Insurance Trust Funds, *Annual Report* (Washington, D.C.: U.S. Government Printing Office, April 1995), p. 16 (hereafter cited as *OASDI Report*).

20. Office of Personnel Management, *Civil Service Retirement and Disability Fund: An Annual Report to Comply with the Requirements of Public Law 95-595* (Washington, D.C.: U.S. Government Printing Office, March 1993), p. 29.

21. Office of the Actuary, Department of Defense, "Valuation of the Military Retirement System: September 30, 1994," p. 13. Flow of future benefits is calculated by the author using an assumed 5 percent average annual inflation rate.

22. Neil Howe and Richard Jackson, *The Facts about Federal Pensions* (Washington, D.C.: Concord Coalition, 1995), p. vi.

23. Financial Management Service, Department of the Treasury, *Statement of Liabilities and Other Financial Commitments of the United States Government as of September 30, 1992* (Washington, D.C.: U.S. Government Printing Office, 1993), schedule 5.

24. General Accounting Office, *Characteristics of Borrowers of FHA-Insured Mortgages* (Washington, D.C.: U.S. Government Printing Office, 1994), p. 1;

NOTES

Charles A. Bowsher, letter to Congress, January 27, 1994 (available for the General Accounting Office, publication GAO/AIMD-94-72R).

25. Grace Milgram, *HUD Housing Assistance Programs: Their Current Status* (Washington, D.C.: Congressional Research Service, August 31, 1993), p. 3.

26. *OASDI Report*, p. 110.

27. *HI Report*, p. 171. Based on intermediate-range assumptions; forecast includes Part A but not Part B of Medicare.

28. *OASDI Report*, p. 127.

29. *HI Report*, p. 171. Based on intermediate and high-cost assumptions.

30. Ibid.

31. Bipartisan Commission on Entitlement and Tax Reform, *Final Report to the President* (Washington, D.C.: U.S. Government Printing Office, 1995), p. 8.

32. Congressional Budget Office, *Who Pays and When? An Assessment of Generational Accounting* (Washington, D.C.: U.S. Government Printing Office, November 1995), p. 22.

33. Alice M. Rivlin, "Big Choices," White House memo, October 3, 1994, p. 10.

34. Historical stock and bond returns from John C. Bogle, *Bogle on Mutual Funds* (New York: Irwin, 1994), p. 25.

35. Steuerle and Bakija, *Retooling Social Security,* tables 5.3, 5.7. Figures are for one-earner couples with average lifetime wages. All amounts are discounted to present value at age sixty-five using a 2 percent real interest rate. Calculations include actuarial value of all Old Age and Survivors Insurance (OASI) benefits payable over a lifetime. Includes both employer and employee portions of OASI payroll tax.

36. Douglas B. Bernheim, *Is the Baby Boom Generation Preparing Adequately for Retirement? Summary Report,* (New York: Merrill Lynch, Pierce, Fenner & Smith, January 1993).

37. Congressional Budget Office, *Baby Boomers in Retirement: An Early Perspective* (Washington, D.C.: U.S. Government Printing Office, September 1993), p. 29.

38. N. Gregory Mankiw and David N. Weil, "The Baby Boom, the Baby Bust and the Housing Market," *Regional Science and Urban Economics* (May 1989).

39. Tax expenditures for private defined-benefit plans came to $8.2 billion in 1993 and are expected to total $44.5 billion between 1993 and 1997. See *Pension Tax Expenditures: Are They Worth the Cost?* (Washington, D.C.: Employee Benefit Research Institute, February 1993), p. 8. The value of pension insurance subsidies provided by the Pension Benefit Guaranty Corporation is estimated by Jim Smalhout, *Savings and Loan Redux: The Gathering Crisis Facing*

America's Pension Insurance Program, Policy Paper 7 (Washington, D.C.: National Taxpayers Union Foundation, April 12, 1993), p. 1.

40. Thomas G. Donlan, *Don't Count on It: Why Your Pension May Be in Jeopardy—and How to Protect Yourself* (New York: Simon & Schuster, 1995), p. 16.

41. Pension Benefit Guaranty Corporation, *Annual Report* (Washington, D.C.: U.S. Government Printing Office, 1993), p. 7. "Pension Gap Increases to $71 billion," *New York Times,* December 6, 1994.

42. House Subcommittee on Oversight, Committee on Ways and Means press release 1, January 14, 1993.

43. "Jobless at 50?" *Business Week,* December 20, 1993, p. 82.

44. Eileen M. Crimmins and Dominique G. Ingegneri, "Trends in Health among the American Population," in Anna M. Rappaport and Sylvester J. Schieber, *Demography and Retirement: The Twenty-first Century* (Westport, Conn.: Praeger, 1993), pp. 225–242.

45. Neil Howe, *Why the Graying of the Welfare State Threatens to Flatten the American Dream—or Worse,* Policy Paper 10 (Washington, D.C.: National Taxpayers Union Foundation, December 30, 1994), p. 10. This projection is based on the Social Security Administration's "scenario III," whose assumptions are closer than those of any other SSA scenario to recent experience.

46. B. Douglas Bernheim, "Adequacy of Saving for Retirement and the Role of Economic Literacy," in Dallas L. Salisbury and Nora Super Jones (eds.), *Retirement in the Twenty-first Century: Ready or Not* (Washington, D.C.: Employee Benefit Research Institute, 1994), p. 79.

47. *A Survey of Americans' Attitude Toward Entitlement Programs,* poll conducted by Matthew Greenwald & Associates, Washington, D.C., September 1994.

48. Lunt Research Companies and Mark Siegel & Associates.

49. "The Universal Fallacy," *New Republic,* March 14, 1994.

50. David Thomson, "The Welfare State and Generational Conflict: Winners and Losers," in Paul Johnson, Christoph Conrad, and David Thomson (eds.), *Workers Versus Pensioners: Intergenerational Justice in an Ageing World* (Manchester: Manchester University Press, 1989), p. 35.

51. *Averting the Old Age Crisis: A World Bank Policy Research Report* (New York: Oxford University Press, 1995), p. 1

52. Bipartisan Commission on Entitlement and Tax Reform, *Interim Report to the President* (Washington, D.C.: U.S. Government Printing Office, 1995), p. 8.

53. Poll conducted by Mathew Greenwald and Associates, Washington, D.C.

54. Laurence Kotlikoff and Alan J. Auerbach, "U.S. Fiscal and Savings Crises

and Their Impact for Baby Boomers," in Salisbury and Jones, *Retirement in the 21st Century*, p. 95.

55. James P. Smith, *Unequal Wealth and Incentives to Save* (Santa Monica, Calif.: RAND, July 1995), p. 10.

56. Calculation assumes 2.3 percent real return on assets held during retirement and that all savings will be exhausted after twenty years.

Chapter 2: Origins

1. Quoted by V. O. Key, Jr., *Politics, Parties and Pressure Groups*, 5th ed. (New York: Thomas Y. Crowell Company, 1967), p. 106.

2. Quoted by Richard Severo and Lewis Milford, *The Wages of War: When America's Soldiers Came Home—From Valley Forge to Vietnam* (New York: Simon & Schuster, 1989), pp. 32–33.

3. Quoted by Theda Skocpol, *Protecting Soldiers and Mothers* (Cambridge, Mass.: Belknap Press, 1992), p. xx.

4. Patterson, *America's Struggle Against Poverty 1900–1980* (Cambridge, Mass.: Harvard University Press, 1981), p. 56.

5. Eveline M. Burns, *Toward Social Security: An Explanation of the Social Security Act and a Survey of the Larger Issues* (New York: McGraw-Hill, 1936), p. 231.

6. David H. Bennett, *Demagogues in the Depression* (New Brunswick, N.J.: Rutgers University Press, 1969).

7. Jerry R. Cates, *Insuring Inequality: Administrative Leadership in Social Security, 1935–54* (Ann Arbor: University of Michigan Press, 1983), p. 52.

8. Ibid, p. 52.

9. Witte to Raymond Moley, May 10, 1935, box 15, Committee on Economic Security Files, SSA, quoted in Patterson, *America's Struggle*, p. 73.

10. Carolyn L. Weaver, *The Crisis in Social Security* (Durham, N.C.: Duke University Press, 1982), p. 126.

11. Quoted by Jerry R. Cates, *Insuring Inequality: Administrative Leadership in Social Security, 1935–54* (Ann Arbor: University of Michigan Press, 1983), p. 52.

12. Arthur Meier Schlesinger, *The Coming of the New Deal* (Boston: Houghton Mifflin, 1965), pp. 308–9.

13. *Social Security after 18 Years*, A Staff Report to the Hon. Carl T. Curtis, Chairman of the Subcommittee on Ways and Means, 83d Cong., 2d session (Washington, D.C.: Government Printing Office, 1964), appendix.

14. Congressional Record (September 16, 1957), p. 28874.

15. *Social Security After 18 Years,* appendix.

16. Ibid., p. 53.

17. Ibid., p. xx.

18. Ibid., p. 3.

19. Arthur J. Altmeyer, *The Formative Years of Social Security* (Madison: University of Wisconsin Press, 1968), p. 226.

20. Ibid., p. 228.

21. Carl T. Curtis and Regis Courtemanche, *Forty Years against the Tide: Congress and the Welfare State* (Lake Bluff, Ill.: Regnery Books, 1986), p. 338.

22. Quoted by Altmeyer, *Formative Years,* p. 221.

23. Martha Derthick, *Policymaking for Social Security* (Washington, D.C.: The Brookings Institution, 1979), p. 154.

Chapter 3: Hubris

1. Margaret Mead, "The Pattern of Leisure in Contemporary American Culture," *Annals of the American Academy of Political and Social Science* 313 (September 1957): p. 13.

2. David Riesman, *Abundance for What? And Other Essays* (Garden City, N.Y.: Doubleday, 1964), p. 306.

3. Joseph J. Spengler, "Wage-Price Movements and Old-Age Security," in Irving L. Webber, ed., *Aging: A Current Appraisal* (Gainesville: University of Florida Press, 1956), pp. 110–119.

4. Carolyn L. Weaver, *The Crisis in Social Security* (Durham, N.C.: Duke University Press, 1982), p. 160.

5. Michael Harrington, *The New American Poverty* (New York: Holt, Rinehart and Winston, 1984), p. 21.

6. John J. Broesamle, *Reform and Reaction in Twentieth Century American Politics* (Westport, Conn.: Greenwood Press, 1990), p. 312.

7. Jonathan Rauch, *Demosclerosis: The Silent Killer of American Government* (New York: Times Books, 1994), p. 35.

8. Robert Theobald, "The Guaranteed Income in Perspective," in Thomas A. Naylor (ed.), *The Impact of the Computer on Society* (Atlanta: Southern Regional Education Board, 1966), p. 71.

9. Allen Schick, *The Capacity to Budget* (Washington, D.C.: Urban Institute, 1990), p. 23.

10. Robert M. Ball, "Is Poverty Necessary?" *Social Security Bulletin* (August 1965): p. 18.

11. Robert M. Ball, "Policy Issues in Social Security," *Social Security Bulletin* 29 (June 1966).

12. Interview with Wilbur J. Cohen, December 29, 1977, quoted by Martha Derthick, *Policy Making for Social Security* (Washington, D.C.: Brookings Institution, 1979), p. 342.

13. "Paul A. Samuelson on Social Security," *Newsweek*, February 13, 1967, p. 88. For an earlier, and more scholarly, exposition of the same idea, see Samuelson, "An Exact Consumption Model of Interest with or without the Social Contrivance of Money," *Journal of Political Economy* 66 (1958): pp. 467–482.

14. Senate, Special Committee on Aging, *Economics of Aging: Toward a Full Share in Abundance*, December 31, 1970, p. 64.

15. Derthick, *Policy Making for Social Security*, p. 352.

16. Ibid, p. 382.

17. Juanita Kreps, *The Lifetime Allocation of Work and Income: Essays in the Economics of Aging* (Durham, N.C.: Duke University Press, 1971), p. 77.

Chapter 4: Denial

1. Robert Linsey, "Elderly in Arizona Town Fight to Keep Children Out," *New York Times*, January 29, 1976, p. 35.

2. *Youngtown News-Sun*, March, 5, 1976, quoted by William A. Anderson and Norma D. Anderson, "The Politics of Age Exclusion: The Adults Only Movement in Arizona," *Gerontologist* 18, no. 1 (February 1978): pp. 6–12.

3. K. D. Shafer, letter to the editor, *New York Times*, February 13, 1976, p. 32.

4. David Hackett Fischer, "Putting Our Heads to the Problem of Old Age," in Ronald Gross, Beatrice Gross, and Sylvia Seidman, *The New Old: Struggling for Decent Aging* (Garden City, N.Y.: Anchor Books, 1978), p. 60. Fischer's history of old age is entitled *Growing Old in America* (New York: Oxford University Press, 1978).

5. Laurence J. Kotlikoff, *Generational Accounting* (New York: Free Press, 1992), p. 178.

6. See, for example, Stanley S. Surrey, *Pathways to Tax Reform: The Concept of Tax Expenditures* (Cambridge: Harvard University Press, 1973).

7. Office of Management and Budget, *Special Analyses, The Budget of the United*

States Government for Fiscal Year 1980 (Washington, D.C.: U.S. Government Printing Office, 1979), special analysis G.

8. General Accounting Office, *Tax Expenditures Deserve More Scrutiny* (Washington, D.C.: U.S. Government Printing Office, 1994).

9. Theresa Funiciello, *The Tyranny of Kindness: Dismantling the Welfare System to End Poverty in America* (Boston: Atlantic Monthly Press, 1995), p. 78.

10. Charles Reich, "The New Property," *Yale Law Review* 73 (1964): 733–787. See also Reich's "Individual Rights and Social Welfare," *Yale Law Review* 74 (1965): 1245.

11. For a description of the legal significance of *Goldberg* v. *Kelley* and *Board of Regents of State Colleges* v. *Roth*, see Robert J. Jonosik (ed.), *Encyclopedia of the American Judicial System* (New York: Charles Scribner's Sons, 1987), p. 220.

12. Ibid.

13. Michael B. Katz, *In the Shadow of the Poorhouse: A Social History of Welfare in America* (New York: Basic Books, 1986), pp. 266–267.

14. Special Committee on Aging, *Economics of Aging*.

15. Robert Kuttner, *Revolt of the Haves: Tax Rebellions and Hard Times* (New York: Simon & Schuster, 1980), p. 66.

Chapter 5: The Big Crack-Up

1. Allen Schick, *The Capacity to Budget* (Washington, D.C.: Urban Institute, 1990), p. 86.

2. From Martha Derthick, *Uncontrollable Spending for Social Services Grants* (Washington, D.C.: Brookings Institution, 1975), p. 3.

3. Language on entitlements is contained in section 401(a) of the bill.

4. Allen Schick, *Congress and Money: Budgeting, Spending and Taxing* (Washington, D.C.: Urban Institute, 1980), p. 400.

5. *New York Times*, August 24, 1974, p. 1.

6. Ibid., September 22, 1974 3:2.

7. Eileen M. Crimmins, "Recent and Prospective Trends in Old Age Mortality" (paper presented at the annual meetings of the American Association for the Advancement of Science, Detroit, May 26–31, 1983).

8. Robert L. Clark and J. J. Spengler, "Changing Demography and Dependency Costs: The Implications of Future Dependency Ratios," in Barbara R. Herzog (ed.), *Aging and Income: Essays on Policy Prospects* (New York: Human Sciences Press, 1977), pp. 55–89.

9. House, Committee on Ways and Means, *Social Security and Welfare Proposals:*

Hearing, 91st Cong. 1st sess., quoted by Martha Derthick, *Policy Making for Social Security* (Washington, D.C.: Brookings Institution, 1979), p. 393.

10. Peter G. Peterson and Neil Howe, *On Borrowed Time* (San Francisco: Institute for Contemporary Studies, 1988), p. 241. The measure of real inflation used in this comparison is the personal consumption expenditure deflator.

11. Derthick, *Policy Making for Social Security*, p. 393.

12. Quoted by Norman Ornstein, "Roots of 'Entitlements,' and Budget Woes," *Wall Street Journal*, December 14, 1993.

13. James Fallows, "Entitlements," *Atlantic Monthly* (November, 1982).

14. "A Conversation with Robert Nozick," *U.S. News & World Report*, March 21, 1983, p. 69.

15. William Safire, "Cop the Entitlement," *New York Times Magazine*, January 1983, p. 9 (2).

16. David A. Stockman, *The Triumph of Politics: The Inside Story of the Reagan Revolution* (New York: Avon, 1987), p. 409.

17. Quoted in ibid., p. 405.

18. Ibid.

19. Ibid., p. 381.

20. William Greider, *Who Will Tell the People: The Betrayal of American Democracy* (New York: Simon & Schuster, 1992), p. 92.

21. Stockman, *The Triumph of Politics*, pp. 409–410.

Chapter 6: Manufacturing Social Security

1. Neil Howe, *How to Control the Cost of Federal Benefits: The Argument for Comprehensive Means-testing*, Policy Paper 3 (Washington, D.C.: National Taxpayers Union, November 4, 1991). Income distribution is for calendar year 1991 using unpublished Congressional Budget Office data. Table A-2, p. 31.

2. Quoted by Arnold Bornstein, "When Half the Population Is Elderly," *New York Times*, May 2, 1993, p. 1.

3. Michael D. Hurd, "Research on the Elderly: Economic Status, Retirement and Consumption and Saving," *Journal of Economic Literature* (June 1990): 567–637, and Bureau of Labor Statistics, *Employment and Earnings* (Washington, D.C.: U.S. Government Printing Office, 1993).

4. Martha Derthick, *Policy Making for Social Security* (Washington, D.C.: Brookings Institution, 1979), p. 199.

5. I am indebted to Neil Howe for this description and for much of the reporting on Social Security operations.

6. Testimony before the Entitlements and Tax Reform Commission, September 23, 1994, unpublished transcript.
7. C. Eugene Steuerle and Jon M. Bakija, *Retooling Social Security for the 21st Century* (Washington, D.C.: Urban Institute Press, 1994), Table 5.3, p. 107.
8. Ibid., Table 5.3.
9. Ibid.
10. Mortality data underlying the 1992 Social Security Board of Trustee reports, from U.S. Social Security Administration, Office of the Actuary, cited by ibid., p. 41.
11. In a 1950 study of steel workers aged fifty-five and over, for example, the majority felt that retirement was only for the physically impaired; by 1960, less than 25 percent of older workers in the same company agreed with that assessment. Philip Ash, "Pre-Retirement Counseling," *Gerontologist* (June 1967): 97–99, quoted in Anne Foner and Karen Schwab, "Work and Retirement in a Changing Society," in Matilda White Riley et al. (eds.), *Aging in Society* (Hillsdale, N.J.: Lawrence Erlbaum Associates, 1983), p. 71.
12. Mortality data underlying the 1992 Social Security Board of Trustee reports, from Social Security Administration, Office of the Actuary, cited by Steuerle and Bakija, *Retooling Social Security*, p. 41.
13. K. Manton, "New Biotechnologies and the Limits to Life Expectancy," in W. Lutz (ed.), *Future Demographic Trends in Europe and North America* (New York: Academic Press, 1991), pp. 97–115.
14. Samuel H. Preston, "Demographic Change in the United States, 1970–2050," in Anna M. Rappaport and Sylvester J. Schieber (eds.), *Demography and Retirement: The Twenty-First Century* (Westport, Conn.: Praeger, 1993), p. 35.
15. Ibid., p. 40.
16. Bureau of the Census, *Marital Status and Living Arrangement* (Washington, D.C.: U.S. Government Printing Office, 1991), p. 43.
17. Richard Jackson, "The Inevitability of Entitlement Reform: An Analysis of the Social Security and Medicare Long-term Cost Projections," in Bipartisan Commission on Entitlement and Tax Reform, *Final Report to the President* (Washington, D.C.: U.S. Government Printing Office, 1995), p. 135.
18. Board of Trustees of the Federal Old-Age and Survivors Insurance and Disability Insurance Funds, *Annual Report* (Washington, D.C.: April 1995), pp. 82–83 (hereafter cited as *OASDI Report*).
19. Ibid., pp. 179–180.

20. Ibid., pp. 171–172.
21. Ibid., p. 61.
22. Ibid., pp. 62–63.
23. Richard Jackson, "The Inevitability of Entitlement Reform: An Analysis of the Social Security and Medicare Long-term Cost Projections," in Bipartisan Commission, *Final Report*, p. 129.
24. *OASDI Report*, p. 57.
25. Ibid.
26. Ibid., pp. 62–63.
27. Ibid., pp. 171–172.

Chapter 7: Hair of the Dog

1. Ronald Kessler, study published in the *Archives of General Psychiatry*, reported by Spencer Rich, *Washington Post*, January 14, 1993.
2. Bert Hansen, "American Physicians' 'Discovery' of Homosexuals, 1880–1900: A New Diagnosis in a Changing Society," in Charles E. Rosenberg and Janet Golden (eds.), *Framing Disease: Studies in Cultural History* (New Brunswick, N.J.: Rutgers University Press, 1992), pp. 104–133.
3. "Cost of Heart Revival Found to Be $150,000 a Survivor," *New York Times*, March 21, 1993, p. 15.
4. Carolyn L. Weaver, "Reassessing Federal Disability Insurance," *Public Interest* (Winter 1992): 114.
5. "Ex–Drug Use Sabotages Dream of a Police Career," *New York Times*, January 17, 1994.
6. *Averting the Old Age Crisis: A World Bank Policy Research Report* (New York: Oxford University Press, 1995), p. 47.
7. Roger Cohen, "Europe's Recession Prompts New Look at Welfare Costs," *New York Times*, August 9, 1993, p. A6.
8. Uwe E. Reinhardt, "A Billion Here, a Billion There," *New York Times*, October 18, 1993.
9. Eileen M. Crimmins and Dominique G. Ingegneri, "Trends in Health among the American Population," in Anna Rappaport and Sylvester Schieber (eds.), *Demography and Retirement: The Twenty-first Century* (Westport, Conn.: Praeger, 1993), p. 229.
10. J. D. Kleinke, "The Health Care Inflation Fantasy," *Wall Street Journal*, October 18, 1993.

NOTES

11. Willard Gaylin, "Faulty Diagnosis," *Harper's* (October 1993): 62.
12. *The Nation's Health Care Bill: Who Bears the Burden* (Waltham, Mass.: Center for Health Economics Research, July 1994).
13. Robert Pear, "Clinton's Budget Falls Well Short of G.O.P. Demands," *New York Times,* February 5, 1995, p. 12.
14. Eugene Feingold, *Medicare: Policy and Politics* (San Francisco: Chandler Publishing Co., 1966), p. 213.
15. *Nation's Health Care Bill,* p. 20.
16. Richard Jackson, "The Inevitability of Entitlement Reform: An Analysis of the Social Security and Medicare Long-term Cost Projections," in Bipartisan Commission on Entitlement and Tax Reform, *Final Report to the President* (Washington, D.C.: U.S. Government Printing Office, 1995), p. 143.
17. Quoted by Paul Cotton, "Must Older Americans Save Up to Spend Down?" *Journal of the American Medical Association,* May 12, 1993, p. 2344.
18. Stephen A. Moses, *The Magic Bullet: How to Pay for Universal Long-Term Care, A Case Study in Illinois* (Seattle, Wash.: LTC Incorporated, November 1994).
19. Harley Gordon, *How to Protect Your Life Savings from Catastrophic Illness and Nursing Homes* (Boston, Mass.: Financial Strategies Press, 1994), p. 6.
20. General Accounting Office, *Long Term Care: Projected Needs of the Aging Baby Boom Generation,* Report to the Honorable William S. Cohen, Special Committee on Aging, U.S. Senate, GAO/HRD-91-86 (Washington, D.C.: U.S. Government Printing Office, June 1991), p. 14.
21. Patricia M. Danzon, remarks on Sylvester J. Schieber, "Can Our Social Insurance Systems Survive the Demographic Shifts of the Twenty-First Century," in Rappaport and Schieber, *Demography and Retirement* (Westport, Conn.: Praeger, 1993), p. 157.
22. *Nation's Health Care Bill,* p. 22.
23. General Accounting Office, *Tax Expenditures Deserve More Scrutiny,* Report to the Honorable William J. Coyne, U.S. House of Representatives, GAO/GGD/AIMD-94-122 (Washington, D.C.: U.S. Government Printing Office, June 1994), p. 50.
24. Paul Jesilow, Henry N. Pontell, and Gilbert Geis, *Prescription for Profit* (Berkeley: University of California Press, 1993), p. 2.
25. General Accounting Office, *Health Insurance, Vulnerable Payers Lose Billions to Fraud and Abuse* (Washington, D.C.: U.S. Government Printing Office, May 1992).
26. General Accounting Office, *Canadian Health Insurance: Lessons for the United States* (Washington, D.C.: U.S. Government Printing Office, June 1991).

Chapter 8: The Private Pension Bailout

1. Richard S. Belous, cited by Mary H. Cooper, "Jobs in the '90s," *CQ Researcher*, February 2, 1992.
2. Congressional Budget Office, *Displaced Workers: Trends in the 1980s and Implications for the Future* (Washington, D.C.: U.S. Government Printing Office, 1993).
3. Thomas G. Donalan, *Don't Count On It* (New York: Simon & Schuster, 1995), p. 29.
4. Tax expenditures for private defined-benefit plans came to $8.2 billion in 1993 and are expected to total $44.5 billion between 1993 and 1997. See *Pension Tax Expenditures: Are They Worth the Cost?* (Washington, D.C.: Employee Benefit Research Institute, February 1993), p. 8.
5. The value of pension insurance subsidies provided by the Pension Benefit Guaranty Corporation is estimated by Jim Smalhout, *Savings and Loan Redux: The Gathering Crisis Facing America's Pension Insurance Program*, policy paper 7 (Washington, D.C.: National Taxpayers Union Foundation, April 12, 1993).
6. *New York Times*, November 31, 1995, p. 1.
7. The standard source for the history of U.S. pensions is Murray W. Latimer, *Industrial Pension Systems* (New York: Industrial Relations Counselors, 1932).
8. For an account of the Railroad Retirement Program and its fiscal difficulties, see Phillip Longman, "The Great Train Robbery," *Washington Monthly* (December 1987): 12.
9. Congressional Budget Office, "The Origin and Evolution of Tax Advantages for Retirement Savings," in *Tax Policy for Pensions and Other Retirement Saving* (Washington, D.C.: U.S. Government Printing Office, April 1987), p. 134.
10. Steven Sass, "The Heyday of US Collectively Bargained Pension Arrangements," in Paul Johnson, Christoph Conrad, and David Thomson (eds.), *Workers Versus Pensioners: Inter-generational Justice in an Ageing World* (Manchester: Manchester University Press, 1989), p. 98.
11. Ibid., p. 108.
12. I am indebted to pension expert James H. Smalhout for this account and for much of the analysis of this chapter.
13. Smalhout, *Savings and Loan Redux*, p. 3.
14. Paine Webber, Inc., *Steel's Retirement Cost Time Bomb* (June 1987), p. 20H.
15. Christopher M. Lewis and Richard L. Cooperstein, "Estimating the Cur-

rent Exposure of the Pension Benefit Guaranty Corporation to Single Employer Pension Plan Terminations" (Washington, D.C.: Office of Management and Budget, April 9, 1992).

16. Cited by Donalan, *Don't Count On It*, p. 130.

17. Patricia B. Limbacher, "GATT Reworks Pensions," *Pensions and Investments*, December 12, 1994, p. 3.

18. Zvi Bodie and Robert C. Merton, "Pension Benefit Guarantees in the United States: A Functional Analysis," in R. Schmitt (ed.), *The Future of Pensions in the United States* (Philadelphia: University of Pennsylvania Press, 1993), p. 208.

19. Department of Labor, *Private Pension Plan Bulletin: Abstract of 1990 Form 5500 Annual Reports*, no. 2 (Summer 1993): table A2.

20. James H. Smalhout, *Securing Pension Promises* (forthcoming).

21. Ibid., p. 15.

22. Ibid.

23. Leslie Wayne, "Pension Arithmetic with Low Rates," *New York Times*, November 29, 1993, p. C1.

24. Ray Schmitt and Gene Falk, "Are Pension Guarantees Another Savings and Loan Collapse in the Making?" Congressional Research Service, Report to Congress, February 1, 1993, p. 5.

Chapter 9: Subsidizing Suburbia

1. Based on unpublished Congressional Budget Office data.

2. Department of Housing and Urban Development, *Housing in the Seventies: A Report of the National Housing Policy Review*, quoted in J. Paul Mitchell, "Historical Overview of Federal Policy: Encouraging Homeownership," in J. Paul Mitchell (ed.), *Federal Housing Policy and Programs: Past and Present* (New Brunswick, N.J.: Center for Urban Policy Research/Rutgers University, 1985), p. 45.

3. John F. Witte, *The Politics and Development of the Federal Income Tax* (Madison: University of Wisconsin Press, 1985), p. 78.

4. Grace Milgram, *Trends in Funding and Numbers of Households in HUD-Assisted Housing, Fiscal Years 1975–1991*, Congressional Research Service, April 23, 1991, p. 17.

5. Grace Milgram, *HUD Housing Assistance Programs: Their Current Status*, Congressional Research Service, August 31, 1993, p. 3.

6. U.S. Department of Housing and Urban Development, *Housing in the Sev-*

enties, quoted by J. Paul Mitchell, "Historical Overview of Federal Policy," p. 46.

7. Grace Milgram, *HUD Housing Assistance Programs: Their Current Status,* Congressional Research Service, August 31, 1993, p. 3.

8. Based on unpublished Congressional Budget Office data.

9. General Accounting Office, *Characteristics of Borrowers of FHA-Insured Mortgages* (Washington, D.C.: U.S. Government Printing Office, 1994), p. 1.

10. Charles A. Bowsher, letter to Congress, January 27, 1994 (available from the General Accounting Office, GAO/AIMD-94-72R).

11. For a description of the competition between housing and industrial competitiveness in the 1970s, see Amitai Etzioni, "Housing: An Early Reagan Reindustrialization Test," *National Journal,* December 20, 1980, p. 2195.

12. Alan Carlson, "Housing Policy's Threat to Families," *Chicago Tribune,* February 4, 1992, p. 15.

13. George Sternlieb and James W. Hughes, "The Evolution of Housing and Its Social Compact," *Urban Land* 41, no. 12 (December 1982): 17–20.

14. Alan Carlson, "Housing Policy's Threat to Families," *Chicago Tribune,* February 4, 1992, p. 15.

Chapter 10: Everyman a Hero

1. Financial Management Service, Department of the Treasury, *Statement of Liabilities and Other Financial Commitments of the United States Government as of September 30, 1992* (Washington, D.C.: U.S. Government Printing Office, 1993), schedule 5.

2. Sharon R. Cohany, "The Vietnam-era Cohort: Employment and Earnings," *Monthly Labor Review* (June 1992): 3.

3. Congressional Budget Office, *Reducing the Deficit: Spending and Revenue Options,* CBO electronic bulletin board, file ENT-73, February 1993.

4. Herbert B. Tasker, National Association of Realtors, statement to the House Committee on Veterans Affairs, Subcommittee on Housing and Memorial Affairs, *Hearing,* 103 Cong., 1st sess., March 13, 1994, p. 16.

5. Ibid.

6. Department of Veterans Affairs, *Federal Benefits for Veterans and Dependents* (Washington, D.C.: U.S. Government Printing Office, 1993), p. 63.

7. Franklin P. Kilpatrick, Milton C. Cummings, Jr., and M. Kent Jennings, *The Image of the Federal Service* (Washington, D.C.: Brookings Institution, 1964), p. 43.

8. Congressional Budget Office, *Reducing the Deficit.*

9. Al Gore, *Creating a Government That Works Better and Costs Less: Report of the National Performance Review* (Washington, D.C.: U.S. Government Printing Office, September 7, 1993), p. 100.

10. Anne C. Stewart and William Krouse, "Major Veterans' Legislation in the 103rd Congress," in Congressional Research Service, Library of Congress, *CRS Report for Congress* (Washington, D.C.: U.S. Government Printing Office, August 26, 1993), p. 1.

11. V. O. Key, *Politics, Parties and Pressure Groups*, 5th ed. (New York: Thomas Y. Crowell, 1967), p. 108.

12. Anne C. Stewart, "Veterans Health Care Program: A Fact Sheet," in Congressional Research Service, Library of Congress, *CRS Report for Congress* (Washington, D.C.: U.S. Government Printing Office, April 1, 1993), p. 2.

13. General Accounting Office, *VA Health Care: Verifying Veterans' Reported Income Could Generate Millions in Copayment Revenues*, GAO/HRD 92-159 (Washington, D.C.: U.S. Government Printing Office, 1992).

14. Eric Konigsberg, "S*M*A*S*H: Don't Fix Those Deadly Veterans Hospitals; Abolish Them," *Washington Monthly* (May 1992): 33. Eric Schmitt, "Angry Veterans Groups Say They Made Bush Oust Agency's Head," *New York Times*, September 29, 1992.

15. Jack A. Underhill, "The Veterans Administration and the American Legion (1945–1947)" (master's thesis, Columbia University, 1959), quoted by Richard Severo and Lewis Milford, *The Wages of War: When America's Soldiers Came Home—From Valley Forge to Vietnam* (New York: Simon & Schuster, 1989), p. 307.

16. Davis R. B. Ross, *Preparing for Ulysses: Politics and Veterans during World War II* (New York: Columbia University Press, 1969), p. 27.

17. For the value of GI Bill education benefits, see Mary F. Smith, "Veterans Educational Assistance Programs," in Congressional Research Service, Library of Congress, *CRS Report for Congress* (Washington, D.C.: U.S. Government Printing Office, April 2, 1992), p. 13. For FDR's address to Congress, see *New York Times*, November 24, 1943; quoted by Severo and Milford, *The Wages of War,* p. 288.

18. Timothy F. Greene and William L. Walsh, "Demography—1990–2010," in Veterans Administration, *Proceedings of the Commission on the Future Structure of Veterans Health Care* (Washington, D.C.: U.S. Government Printing Office, 1991), p. C-1.

19. Geoffrey Perrett, *Days of Sadness, Years of Triumph* (New York: Coward, Mc-Cann & Geoghegan, 1973), pp. 399, 400, 401.
20. Veterans of Foreign Wars of the United States, *1994 Member Benefit Handbook* (Kansas City, Mo.: VFW, 1993).
21. James A. Thurber, "Dynamics of Policy Subsystems in American Politics," in Allan J. Cigler and Burdett A. Loomis (eds.), *Interest Group Politics* (Washington, D.C.: Congressional Quarterly Press, 1991), p. 338.
22. Phil Duncan (ed.), *Politics in America: 1994* (Washington, D.C.: CQ Press, 1993), p. 851.
23. Greene and Walsh, "Demography," p. C-1.
24. Ibid., p. C-12.
25. Alan L. Otten, "Veterans Shed the Uniform Look," *Wall Street Journal*, November 11, 1993, p. B1.
26. Sharon R. Cohany, "The Vietnam-era Cohort: Employment and Earnings," *Monthly Labor Review* (June 1992): 3–15.
27. Greene and Walsh, "Demography" pp. C5–C6.

Chapter 11: Yesterday's Generals

1. Telephone interview, November 18, 1993.
2. Susan Kraft, "The Few, the Proud, and the Well to Do," *American Demographics* (April 1991).
3. U.S. Senate, Special Committee on Aging, *Developments in Aging: 1992* (April 20, 1993), 1: 57.
4. Office of the Actuary, Department of Defense, *Valuation of the Military Retirement System: September 30, 1994* (Washington, D.C.: U.S. Government Printing Office, 1992), p. 11.
5. Office of the Actuary, Department of Defense, *FY 1992, DOD Statistical Report on the Military Retirement System*, RCS No. DD-FM&P (Q) 1375 (Washington, D.C.: U.S. Government Printing Office, 1993), p. 267.
6. Ibid., p. 59.
7. Worksheet. Average officer's basic pay at age forty-two with twenty years' experience is $4,285 a month. Office of the Actuary. *Valuation of the Military Retirement System*, p. C-2. Replacement ratio = 2.5 × years of service = 50 percent. This formula yields a retirement benefit of $2,125.50 a month, or $25,710 a year. Assumed inflation rate (5 percent, per trustee report). Yields cumulative benefits of $1,144,146 on the twenty-fourth year of retirement, or at age sixty-five. Cumulative benefits by year 34: $2,187,072.

8. Robert L. Goldrich, "Military Retirement and Separation Benefits: Major Legislative Issues," *CRS Issue Brief,* September 8, 1993.
9. Edward Ericson, "How the Geezers Cashed In on the Gulf War," *Washington Monthly* (November 1991): 29.
10. Office of the Actuary, *DOD Statistical Report,* pp. 12–13.
11. Office of the Actuary, *Valuation of the Military Retirement System,* table 1, p. 2.
12. Ibid., table 7, p. 14.
13. Henry D. Gilpin, *The Papers of James Madison* (Mobile, 1842), 1: 572, quoted in William H. Glasson, *History of Military Pension Legislation in the United States* (New York: AMS Press, 1968), p. 20.
14. See, for example, C. Robert Kemble, *The Image of the Army Officer in America* (Westport, Conn.: Greenwood Press, 1973), p. 4.
15. Truman Seymour, *Military Education* (Williamstown, Mass., 1864), p. 6, quoted in ibid., p. 33.
16. Total military expenditures in 1945: $57,443,000. Total retirees: 64,456. Office of the Actuary, *DOD Statistical Report,* pp. 9, 11.
17. Ibid., p. 268.
18. U.S. Senate, *Hearings before the Subcommittee on Manpower and Personnel, of the Committee on Armed Services,* 99th Cong., 1st sess., December 4, 5, 1985, p. 36.
19. Quoted by Tim Noah, "How to End the Federal Pension Scandal," *Washington Monthly* (May 1984): 22.
20. Senate, *Hearings before the Subcommittee on Manpower and Personnel,* p. 527.
21. Office of the Actuary, *DOD Statistical Report,* p. 117.
22. Advertisement, *Retired Officer Magazine* (January 1994): 38–39.
23. Frederick Day and Charles Jackson, "How to Reach Military Retirees," *American Demographics* (April 1991).
24. Kraft, "The Few, the Proud."
25. David F. Burrelli, "Military Retiree Health Care: Base Closures and Realignments," in Library of Congress, Congressional Research Service, *CRS Report to Congress* (Washington, D.C.: U.S. Government Printing Office, September 21, 1992), p. 22.
26. Congressional Budget Office, *Reducing the Deficit, Spending and Revenue Options,* CBO electronic bulletin board, file DEF-50.
27. Department of the Treasury, Financial Management Service, *Consolidated Financial Statements of the United States Government: Prototype 1991* (Washington, D.C.: U.S. Government Printing Office, 1991), p. 26.
28. David F. Burrelli, "Military Health Care/CHAMPUS Management Initiatives," in Library of Congress, Congressional Research Service, *CRS Report*

for Congress (Washington, D.C.: U.S. Government Printing Office, May 14, 1991), p. 11.

29. Jack O. Lanier, "Restructuring Military Health Care: The Winds of Change Blow Stronger," *Hospital and Health Services Administration* (Spring 1993): 121.

30. Congressional Budget Office, *Reducing the Deficit.*

31. Elizabeth A. Palmer, "Base Closings May Add Weight to Health-Care Burden," *Congressional Quarterly,* February 27, 1993, p. 473.

32. "An Open Letter to President Bush, Other Administrative Leaders, Each Member of Congress and the Leadership of the Republican and Democratic Parties," February 21, 1992, reprinted in Senate, *Hearings before the Committee on Armed Services, Part 6, Manpower and Personnel,* 102 Cong., 2nd sess., March 25, April 8, 30, May 13, June 2, 1992, p. 151.

33. Chares D. Cooper, "Reflections on TROA 1993—A Very Good Year," *Retired Officer Magazine* (January 1994): 6.

34. Paul W. Arcan, "Washington Scene: COLA Challenges Are Unrelenting," *Retired Officer Magazine* (January 1994): 16.

35. Advertisement, *Retired Officer* (January 1993): 21.

Chapter 12: Yesterday's Bureaucrats

1. William Dudley Foulke, *Fighting the Spoilsmen* (New York: G. P. Putnam's Sons, 1919, republished by Arno Press, 1974), p. 106.

2. Paul P. Van Riper, *History of the United States Civil Service* (Evanston, Ill.: Row, Peterson and Company, 1958), pp. 197, 246.

3. Carolyn L. Merck, "Financing the Federal Civil Service Retirement System," in Congressional Research Service, *CRS Report to Congress* (U.S. Government Printing Office, June 25, 1993), p. 3.

4. Office of Personnel Management, *Civil Service Retirement and Disability Fund: An Annual Report to Comply with the Requirements of Public Law 95-595, September 30, 1992* (Washington, D.C.: U.S. Government Printing Office, March 1993). Total liability figure is the actuarial present value of future benefits and administrative expenses for the combined Civil Service and Federal Employees Retirement system, as shown in Table 1. (Federal public debt and agency securities outstanding in fiscal year 1992: $4.082871 trillion.)

5. Jane D. Pacelli, *Report of the Coast Guard Military Retirement System as of September 30, 1992, As Required by Public Law 95-595* (Washington, D.C.: Milliman & Robertson, 1993), tables 1, 2.

6. U.S. Department of State, Retirement Division, *Foreign Service Retirement and Disability Fund: Annual Report Required by P.L. 95-595*, unpublished, September 30, 1991, attachment 2.

7. Financial Management Service, Department of the Treasury, *Statement of Liabilities and Other Financial Commitments of the United States Government as of September 30, 1992* (Washington, D.C.: U.S. Government Printing Office, 1993), Schedule #5.

8. Kenneth R. Cahill, "Entitlements and Other Mandatory Spending," in Congressional Research Service, *CRS Report to Congress* (Washington, D.C.: U.S. Government Printing Office, April 6, 1993), p. 13.

9. This estimate assumes the ratio of current cost to unfunded liabilities is roughly the same for the CIA as for the foreign service. Worksheet: Total federal contributions to the foreign service fund in 1991 were $395 million; total unfunded liabilities were $8210.7 million. CIA federal contributions are $169 million (8210.7 × 169)/395) = $3,510).

10. A. Foster Higgins & Co., *United States Tax Court Retirement Plan, Actuarial Report for Year Ending December 31, 1990* (Washington, D.C.: June 1991).

11. Committee on Employee Benefits, Board of Governors of the Federal Reserve System, *1992 Annual Reports: Retirement Plan, Thrift Plan* (Washington, D.C.: U.S. Government Printing Office, 1993), p. 5. The ratio of assets at market value to the Financial Accounting Standards Board accrued liabilities was 2.49 as of January 1, 1992.

12. U.S. Treasury, schedule 5. Estimate includes actuarial liabilities of the following federal employee pension plans: Comptrollers General, U.S. Tax Court, Federal Judiciary, National Oceanic and Atmospheric Administration, Foreign Service, Coast Guard, Panama Canal Commission, Tennessee Valley Authority, Federal Reserve System, Federal Home Loan Management Corporation, and the Farm Credit System.

13. Congressional Budget Office, *Reducing the Deficit: Spending and Revenue Options*, CBO electronic bulletin board, file ENT-37, February 1993; Office of Personnel Management, quoted by *Retirement Life* (December 1993): 7.

14. General Accounting Office, *Financial Reporting: Accounting for the Postal Service's Post-retirement Health Care Costs*, AFMD-32 (Washington, D.C.: U.S. Government Printing Office, May 20, 1992). The study found that if the Postal Service's postretirement health care liabilities were accrued and fully funded, first-class rates would have to jump by three cents by 1994 and increase again by a cent before 2011.

15. Department of Treasury, Financial Management Service, *Consolidated Financial Statement of the U.S. Government, Prototype 1991* (Washington, D.C.: U.S. Government Printing Office, 1992), p. 27.

16. Kenneth Cahill, "The Largest Entitlement Programs," Congressional Research Service Issue Brief, April 15, 1993, p. C-5.

17. Foulke, *Fighting the Spoilsmen*, p. 109.

18. Paul P. Van Riper, "The American Administrative State: Wilson and the Founders," in Ralph Clark Chandler (ed.), *A Centennial History of the American Administrative State* (New York: Free Press, 1987), p. 21.

19. Congressional Research Service, *Background on the Civil Service Retirement System: A Report for the Committee on Post Office and Civil Service, U.S. House of Representatives* (Washington, D.C.: U.S. Government Printing Office, April 20, 1983), p. 2.

20. Dan M. McGill (ed.), *Financing the Civil Service Retirement System: A Threat to Fiscal Integrity* (Homewood, Ill.: Richard D. Irwin, 1979), p. 16.

21. Robert W. Hartman, *Pay and Pensions for Federal Workers* (Washington, D.C.: Brookings Institution, 1983), p. 2.

22. Carolyn L. Merck, "Federal Retirees: FY 1994 Budget Proposals," Congressional Research Service Issue Brief, August 12, 1993, p. 3.

23. Hartman, *Pay and Pensions*, p. 17.

24. Peter G. Peterson and Neil Howe, *On Borrowed Time* (San Francisco: Institute for Contemporary Studies Press, 1988), p. 308.

25. Neil Howe and Richard Jackson, *The Facts about Federal Pensions* (Washington, D.C.: Concord Coalition, 1995), p. ii.

26. Ibid.

27. Peterson and Howe, *On Borrowed Time*, p. 312.

28. Ibid., p. 308.

29. Hays Gorey, "The Golden Rocking Chair," *Time*, June 10, 1991.

30. Mathew Cooper, "A Pension for Trouble," *Washington Monthly* (July–August 1989):28.

31. Howe and Jackson, "Facts," p. 5.

32. Office of Personnel Management, *Civil Service Retirement and Disability Fund: An Annual Report to Comply with the Requirements of Public Law 95-595* (Washington, D.C.: U.S. Government Printing Office, March 1993), tables 1, 5a.

33. Matt Cooper, "A Pension for Trouble," *Washington Monthly* (July–August 1989).

34. "NARFE Perks," *Retirement Life* (December 1993): 46.

35. Congressional Budget Office, *Reducing Entitlement Spending* (Washington, D.C.: U. S. Government Printing Office), p. 16.
36. "It's Already Time for Lobby Week 1994," *Federal Employee* (February 1994): 1.
37. PAC Funds Affect Us All," *Federal Employee* (February 1994): 6.

Chapter 13: *What the Country Must Do*

1. Aristotle, *A Treatise on Government*, trans. William Ellis (London: T. Payne, B. White, T. Caddell, 1776), pp. 212, 213–214.
2. Karl Marx, *The Communist Manifesto* (New York: W. W. Norton, 1988, [1848], p. 59.
3. Quoted by Paul Gigot, "The Suburban New Deal," *Wall Street Journal*, December 19, 1993, op-ed page.
4. Max Weber, *The Protestant Ethic and the Spirit of Capitalism*, trans. Talcott Parsons (London: G. Allen & Unwin, 1930).
5. Peter G. Peterson, "What I Really Believe about Balancing the Budget," *American Prospect* (Fall 1994).
6. Peter G. Peterson, memorandum to Members of the Bipartisan Commission on Entitlement and Tax Reform, September 23, 1994.
7. Neil Howe, *Why the Graying of the Welfare State Threatens to Flatten the American Dream—or Worse*, Policy Paper 10 (Washington, D.C.: National Taxpayers Union Foundation, December 30, 1994), p. 10. These projections are based on demographic assumptions used by the Social Security Administration.
8. Neil Howe and Phillip Longman, "The Next New Deal," *Atlantic*, April 1992, pp. 88–99.
9. Congressional Budget Office, *Reducing Entitlement Spending* (Washington, D.C.: U.S. Government Printing Office, September 1994), p. 36.
10. "Reform Proposal of Commissioner Peter G. Peterson," in Bipartisan Commission on Entitlement and Tax Reform, *Final Report to the President* (Washington, D.C.: U.S. Government Printing Office, January 1995), p. 51.
11. Matthew Greenwald & Associates, "Survey of Public Attitudes toward Entitlements" (August 1994). Poll sponsored by the Congressional Institute for the Future and the National Taxpayers Union Foundation.
12. Peter G. Peterson, "Reform Proposal of Commissioner Peter G. Peterson," p. 50.
13. *The Nation's Health Care Bill: Who Bears the Burden* (Waltham, Mass.: Center for Health Economics Research, July 1994), p. 20.
14. Congressional Budget Office, *Reducing the Deficit* (Washington, D.C.: U.S. Government Printing Office, March 1994), p. 272.

Chapter 14: What You Should Do

1. Lawrence Fisher and James H. Lorie, *A Half Century of Returns on Stocks and Bonds* (Chicago: University of Chicago Graduate School of Business, 1977), p. 27.
2. Ibid., p. 125
3. "Will Retiring Boomers Sink the Stock Market?" *Business Week*, October 25, 1993, p. 24.
4. Christopher Farrell, "The Economics of Aging," *Business Week*, September 12, 1994, p. 60.
5. *The Nation's Health Care Bill: Who Bears the Burden* (Waltham, Mass.: Center for Health Economics Research, July 1994), p. 20.
6. James P. Smith, *Unequal Wealth and Incentives to Save* (Santa Monica, Calif.: RAND Corporation, July 1995), p. 10.
7. John Goodman, *Legalized Gambling as a Strategy for Economic Development* (Amherst, Mass.: Center for Economic Development, University of Massachusetts, 1994), p. 6.
8. Vicki Abt, James F. Smith, and Eugene Martin Christiansen, *The Business of Risk* (Lawrence, Kans.: University Press of Kansas, 1985), p. 208.
9. For a cultural history of attacks on the thrift ethos by mass merchandisers and liberal policymakers since the 1920s, see "Consuming Visions: Thrift and Productivity in an Aging Society," in Phillip Longman, *Born to Pay: The New Politics of Aging in America* (Boston: Houghton Mifflin, 1987), pp. 152–181.
10. B. Douglas Bernheim, *The Vanishing Nest Egg: Reflections on Saving in America* (New York: Priority Press, 1991), p. 89.
11. Ibid., p. 69.
12. The address is reprinted in Henry J. Aaron (ed.), *Social Security and the Budget: Proceedings of the First Conference of the National Academy of Social Insurance* (Lanham, Md.: University Press of America, 1990), pp. 63–70.
13. William G. Gale and Robert E. Litan, "Saving Our Way Out of the Deficit Dilemma," *Brookings Review* (Fall 1993). For a discussion of other policy intellectuals now advocating mandated savings, see Paul Starobin, "Thrift Begins at Home," *National Journal*, October 30, 1993, p. 2592.
14. *Averting the Old Age Crisis: A World Bank Policy Research Report* (New York: Oxford University Press, 1995), p. 205.
15. Ibid., p. 229.
16. For a rigorous study of the effectiveness of tax subsidies on savings behav-

ior, see Eric M. Engen, William G. Gale, and John Karl Scholz, "Do Saving Incentives Work," *Brookings Papers on Economic Activity* 1 (1994): 85.

17. *Time* magazine, 1967, reprinted in Alexander Klein (ed.), *Natural Enemies: Youth and the Clash of Generations* (Philadelphia: J. B. Lippincott, 1969), p. 63.

Index

Abscam scandal, 113
Abt, Vicki, 199
ADA. *See* Americans with
  Disabilities Act (ADA)
Addiction, 1–2, 89, 205
Adults Only, 53
AFDC. *See* Aid to Families with
  Dependent Children (AFDC)
Affluence: of baby boom
  generation, 204; challenge of, in
  1950s, 41–43; connection
  between welfare state, contract
  between the generations and,
  43–44; politics of, during
  Kennedy-Johnson
  administrations, 44–47
AFL-CIO, 34
Aging. *See* Elderly; Retirement
Aid to Families with Dependent
  Children (AFDC), 45, 56, 75,
  177. *See also* Welfare

AIDS, 82, 91, 106
Alcoholism, 1–2, 89, 205
Altmeyer, Arthur J., 37–38
Alzheimer's disease, 89, 91
American Association of Retired
  Persons, 10, 33, 52
American Express Company, 110
American Legion, 135, 136, 155
American Medical Association, 167
American Society for Public
  Administration, 47
Americans with Disabilities Act
  (ADA), 89–90
AMVETs, 136–37
Antichildren's movement, 52–53
Araneo, Joseph L., 140
Aristotle, 171
Arizona, 6, 51–53, 75
Army and Air Force Vitalization
  Act, 146
Ash, Roy, 62

Ball, Robert, 46–47, 49
Ballentine's, 113
Baltimore and Ohio Railroad, 110
Base Closure Commission, 153
Belous, Richard, 107–08
Bernheim, B. Douglas, 14
Bethlehem Steel, 117
Birthrate, 82–83, 176
Board of Regents of State Colleges v. *Roth*, 57
Bodie, Zvi, 116
Bodo, Erwin, 96–97
Bourgeois values, 23–25, 173, 183, 197–206. *See also* Middle class
Brennan, William, 57
Broesamle, John J., 45
Budget. *See* Federal budget and budget deficit
Budget and Impoundment Act of 1974, 61–62
Burns, Eveline, 31, 42
Bush, George, 69, 134, 137, 153

California, 32, 34, 58–59, 84, 89–90, 150
Cancer, 91, 106
Capital expenditures, public, 46
Carlson, Alan, 124–25
Carter, Jimmy, 49, 66, 69
Cates, Jerry, 33
CBO. *See* Congressional Budget Office (CBO)
Central Intelligence Agency (CIA) retirement system, 159–60, 161
CHAMPUS, 152–53
Child care credit, 6
Children: antichildren's movement, 52–53; illegitimacy rate, 83; poverty of, 5, 83
Chile, 202

Christiansen, Eugene, 199
CIA. *See* Central Intelligence Agency (CIA)
Citizenship, 24–25
Civil Service Retirement Act, 158, 163
Civil service retirement system: amount of benefits, 164–66; Central Intelligence Agency, 159–60, 161; and civil service lobby, 164, 167–68; Coast Guard, 159; compared with private pension systems, 164–65; and federal employee unions, 162–64; Federal Employees Retirement System (FERS), 166–67; Federal Reserve, 160; foreign service, 159; global means test for, 178; health care benefits, 161–62; history of, 157–58, 162–64; long-term liabilities of, 158–62, 167; members of Congress, 165–66; middle-class recipients of, 6; postal workers, 161; Public Health Service, 160; statistics on, 7, 8, 158, 162, 164–66; Tennessee Valley Authority, 160; U.S. Tax Court Retirement Plan, 160; warnings about collapse of, 8
Civil War, 29–30, 121, 146, 157
Civilian Health and Medical Program of the Uniformed Services (CHAMPUS), 152–53
Clinton, Hillary, 172
Clinton administration: Entitlements Commission, 10; health care plan of, 18, 172; and Medicare, 8; military during, 147; and PPGC premiums, 115; veterans affairs secretary, 136

Coast Guard retirement system, 159
Cohen, Wilbur, 35, 47
COLAs (cost-of-living adjustments), 64–66, 68, 154, 164
Colorado, 33, 34
Commerce Department, 161
Communist Manifesto, 171
Concord Coalition, 176
Congressional Budget Office (CBO), 3, 5–6, 131, 142, 152, 177, 181
Congressional Institute on the Future, 20
Congressional Research Service, 158
Consumer price index (CPI), 64–65
Contract between the generations, 43–44, 174–75
Costa Rica, 90
Cost-of-living adjustments (COLAs), 64–66, 68, 154, 164
Council of State Planning Agencies, 46
Courter, James A., 153
CPI (consumer price index), 64–65
Crimmins, Eileen M., 91
Cruikshank, Nelson H., 48
Cummins, Ann, 51
Curtis, Carl T., 36–40

Danzon, Patricia M., 104
Defense Department, 129, 142, 174
Democratic party, 37, 49
Depression. *See* Great Depression
Derthick, Martha, 39, 76
Derwinski, Edward, 134
Disability: concept of, 89–90; rates of, 16
Disability benefits for veterans, 128, 132

Disability Insurance: for addicts, 1; and changing concept of disability, 89–90; creation of, 68; warnings about collapse of, 8, 84
Disabled American Veterans, 136
Doobie Brothers, 89
Drug dependency, 1–2, 89–90

Early, Mary Ellen, 99
Education benefits for veterans, 131, 132, 135, 173
Eisenhower, Dwight D., 39–40
Elder-law attorneys, 97–99
Elderly: and cult of seniority, 51–54; desire for higher quality of health care, 91–92; life expectancy of, 16, 63, 196; middle-class elderly, 58–59; morbidity rates of, 16; poverty of, 44; and rising health care costs, 195–96; taxes paid by, 195–96. *See also* Medicare; Retirement; Retirement benefits; Social Security
Eliot, Charles, 30
EM. *See* Entitlement Management, LLC (EM)
Embourgeoisement, 175, 183, 197–206
Employee Retirement Income Security Act (ERISA), 113–14, 118
Engels, Friedrich, 171, 172
Entitlement Management, LLC (EM), 95
Entitlements: addiction to, 205; and budget deficits, 61–62, 67, 175; compared with tax expenditures, 3–4; and contract between the generations, 43–44, 174–75; definition of, 2–3, 67;

Entitlements *(cont.)*
  first uses of word, 60, 61, 62;
  flaws in system of, 173–75;
  global means test for, 176–179;
  impact of, on economy, 19–21;
  media interest in, 66–67; middle-
  class recipients of, 5–7, 21,
  172–75; origins of, 25, 29–40;
  projections for, 11–17, 184;
  public support for reform of,
  17–19; and Reagan, 66–69; social
  trends affecting, 62–64; statistics
  on, 3, 4, 5, 8–11, 30, 175;
  warnings on collapse of, 8–11;
  and welfare rights, 56–58. *See also*
  specific entitlement programs
Entitlements Commission, 10
ERISA, 113–14, 118

Fallows, James, 67
Families, 23–24, 204–06
Farmers Home Loan
  Administration loans, 132
FBI. *See* Federal Bureau of
  Investigation (FBI)
Federal budget and budget deficit,
  11, 60–62, 67, 92, 137, 175–76
Federal Bureau of Investigation
  (FBI), 73
Federal employees: health care for,
  161–62; number of retirees, 163;
  organizations, 164, 167–68;
  retirement age for, 166; unions
  for, 162–64. *See also* Civil service
  retirement system
Federal Employees Health Benefits
  Program, 161–62
Federal Employees Retirement
  System (FERS), 166–67
Federal Housing Administration
  (FHA), 9, 123–24

Federal Reserve, 160, 203
Federal Reserve Bank of Boston, 112
Federal tax expenditures. *See* Tax
  expenditures
FERS, 166–67
Fertility rates, 62–63, 82–83
FHA. *See* Federal Housing
  Administration (FHA)
Financial Accounting Standards
  Board, 161
Finland, 119
Fischer, David Hackett, 53
Florida, 6, 7, 75, 90, 96, 97, 99–102,
  150, 153, 165
Ford, Gerald, 40, 62
Foreign service retirement and
  disability fund, 159
Foulke, William Dudley, 157
Franklin, Ben, 173
Funiciello, Theresa, 56

Gale, William G., 201–02
Gambling, legalized, 198–99
Gaylin, Willard, 92
General Accounting Office, 3, 56,
  100, 104, 105, 123–24, 132, 134,
  161
Germany, 119, 146
Gerontocracy, 53
GI Bill of Rights, 135–36, 173
Gingrich, Newt, 7
Glenn, John, 148
Global means test for entitlement
  programs, 176–179
Goldberg v. *Kelley*, 57
Gordon, Harley, 98
Gore, Al, Jr., 165
Gore, Albert, Sr., 165
Gray Panthers, 33
Great Britain, 155
Great Depression, 110

Greenberg, Stanley, 172
Greenspan, Alan, 160
Group health insurance tax
subsidy, 102–04, 108

Hartman, John, 89–90
Health, definition of, 88–91
Health care: Clinton's plan for, 18,
172; and concept of disability,
89; and concept of life, 89;
conservative approach to, 87;
cost of, 90, 91–93, 104–06, 179,
194–95; and definition of health,
88–91; federal spending on, 92;
and inflation, 195; liberal
approach to, 87; market-based
solution for, 105; for military
retirees, 151–53; nationalizing,
105–106; recommendations for
reform of, 179–83; for retired
federal employees, 161–62; as
right or entitlement, 87–91;
social trends affecting, 91–93;
for veterans, 131, 133–34, 137;
waste, fraud and abuse in,
104–05. See also Medicaid;
Medicare
Health insurance: for federal
employees, 161; and politics of
risk, 181–82; tax subsidy for
employer-provided health
insurance, 102–04, 108, 177, 180
Health maintenance organizations,
181
Heart disease, 91
Hewitt, Paul, 78
Home loan guarantee for veterans,
131, 135–36
Home mortgage deduction, 3, 6, 9,
120–26, 177
Homosexuality, 88

Housing and Urban Development
Department (HUD), 121
Housing subsidies: benefits of,
124–25; compared with HUD
programs, 121; cost of, 121;
home loan guarantee for
veterans, 131, 135–36; home
mortgage deduction, 3, 6, 9,
120–26, 177; mortgage guarantee
programs, 123–24; types of, 121;
and values, 125–26; warnings on
collapse of, 9
Howe, Neil, 16, 176
HUD. See Housing and Urban
Development Department
(HUD)
Hudson, James, 107
Hughes, James, 125

IBM, 16, 114–15
Illegitimacy rate, 83
Illinois, 96
Immigration, 83–84, 85
Income: projections on real after-
tax income, 16; from Social
Security, 75; of veterans, 138
Income tax, 121, 195–96. See also
headings beginning with Tax
Individual Retirement Accounts
(IRAs), 108–09, 116, 118, 122,
190–91, 196, 201, 203
Infertility, 88–89
Inflation, 64–66, 85
Inheritances, 16–17
Interior Department, 60
Internal Revenue Service, 55, 77,
109, 178
Intravartolo, Santo, 75
IRAs. See Individual Retirement
Accounts (IRAs)
Iroff, Ronald, 77

Japan, 200
Johnson, Lyndon, 44–47, 55

Kane, Robert, 95
Kasich, John, 154
Keith, Hastings, 142–43
Kennedy, John F., 44, 55
Keynes, Lord, 42
Korean War, 123, 147
Kotlikoff, Lawrence J., 20, 55
Kreps, Juanita, 49
Kristol, Irving, 68
Kuttner, Robert, 59

Labor Department, 109, 118, 133
Langdon, Robert L., 74
Levitt, William, 126, 172
Lewis, John L., 111–12
Life, concept of, 89
Life expectancy, 16, 63, 81, 82, 85, 196
Lincoln Memorial, 107
Lipscomb, Bentley, 96
Litan, Robert E., 201–02

Madison, James, 144
Malaysia, 202
Mandatory savings accounts (MSAs), 201–03
Marx, Karl, 171, 172, 173
McMillan, Colin, 153
McMullin, Eileen, 95
Mead, Margaret, 41
Means-tested entitlements, 56–58
Medicaid, 56, 94–102, 104, 177, 178, 179, 181
Medical deduction, 56
Medicare: benefits versus payroll tax contributions for, 93–94, 180; costs of, 90, 94, 179, 195; enactment of, 44, 68, 194; flaws in, 174; fraud and abuse in, 104; global means test for, 177; increases in, during 1970s, 54; middle-class recipients of, 6–7; for military retirees, 142; per capita cost variations, 90; public support for reform of, 17; recommendations for reform of, 179–81; trust funds, 101; warnings about collapse of, 8
Mental health and mental illness, 88
Merton, Robert C., 116
Mica, Dan, 165–66
Michigan, 90, 124
Middle class: baby boom generation as *Time* "Man of the Year," 204; bourgeois values needed by, 23–25, 173, 183, 197–206; case studies on savings for retirement, 185–92; definition of, 172–73; desirability of strong middle class, 171–72; embourgeoisement of, 175, 183, 197–206; financial crisis of, 21–23; Marx on bourgeoisie, 171, 172, 173; Medicaid used by, 94–102; and postconsumer society, 196–99; as recipients of entitlements, 5–7, 21, 172–75; scapegoating of the poor by, 4–5, 45, 50, 58–59; and self-actualization, 198; subsidizing middle-class consumption, 172–73; unemployment of, 16; values of baby boom generation, 125–26, 198–99, 204; victimology of, 24–25, 58–59; Weber on bourgeoisie, 173. *See also* Entitlements; and specific entitlement programs
MILI-BUCK$, 140

Military Reform Act of 1986, 143
Military retirement system:
    amount of benefits, 141–43, 147;
    average retirement age of
    military retirees, 140; compared
    with private pensions, 141–42;
    defense of, 147–51; in Great
    Britain, 155; and health care for
    military retirees, 151–53; history
    of, 144–47; long-term liabilities
    of, 143–44, 151, 155–56; middle-
    class recipients of, 6; and perks
    for military retirees, 150–51;
    reform of, 143; and retired
    military groups, 153–55;
    Revolutionary War veterans, 25,
    29; statistics on, 7, 8–9, 141–43,
    146, 147; trust fund, 144; types
    of benefits, 141; warnings on
    collapse of, 8–9. *See also* Veterans'
    benefits
Military Retirement Trust Fund, 144
Minnesota, 90
Montgomery, G. V. "Sonny," 137
Moraze, Charles, 205
Morbidity rates, 16
Mortgage guarantee programs,
    123–24
Mortgage interest deduction, 3, 6,
    9, 120–26, 177
Moynihan, Daniel Patrick, 10
MSAs. *See* Mandatory savings
    accounts (MSAs)

NARFE. *See* National Association
    of Retired Federal Employees
    (NARFE)
National Academy of Elder Law
    Attorneys, 98
National Academy of Social
    Insurance, 201

National Association of Realtors,
    131, 167
National Association of Retired
    Federal Employees (NARFE),
    164, 167–68
National Association of Uniformed
    Services, 153–54
National Civil Service Reform
    League, 157
National Conference of Social
    Work, 39
National Council of Senior
    Citizens, 48
National Family Association, 155
National Federation of Federal
    Employees, 162
National Oceanic and Atmospheric
    Administration, 161
National Park Service, 107
National Planning Association, 107
National Taxpayers Union, 78
National Taxpayers Union
    Foundation, 20
National Treasury Employees
    Union, 164
Netherlands, 90
Nevada, 75
New Jersey, 58, 75, 113
New York, 90
New Zealand, 18
Nixon, Richard, 40, 49, 61
Noncommissioned Officers
    Association, 155
North Carolina, 75
Nozick, Robert, 67
Nursing homes, 94–97, 99–102,
    178, 181

OASDI. *See* Old Age, Survivors
    and Disability Insurance
    (OASDI)

Office of Economic Opportunity, 45
Office of Management and Budget, 2–3, 11, 56, 115
Old age. *See* Elderly; Retirement
Old Age, Survivors and Disability Insurance (OASDI), 77–78, 84
Oregon, 102
Osterhout, Julie, 97, 98

PACs, 168
Pan American World Airlines, 109
Panetta, Leon, 137
Paralyzed Veterans of America, 136
PBGC. *See* Pension Benefit Guaranty Corp. (PBGC)
Pellegrino, D. Victor, 95
Pennington, J. C., 153–54
Pennsylvania Railroad, 110
Penny, Tim, 154
Pension Benefit Guaranty Corp. (PBGC), 113–18
Pensions. *See* Civil service retirement system; Military retirement system; Private pension systems
Persian Gulf War, 137, 149
Pickle, J. J., 15
Postal Letter Carriers union, 164
Postal workers, 161, 164
Postconsumer society, 196–99
Poverty: and abolition of want, 46–47; of children, 5, 83; of elderly, 44; and housing assistance programs, 121; and illegitimacy rate, 83; Johnson's war on poverty, 44–45; scapegoating of poor by middle class, 4–5, 45, 50, 58–59; Social Security to poor, 75
Preston, Samuel, 82

Private pension systems: compared with civil service retirement benefits, 164–65; compared with military retirement benefits, 141–42; and ERISA, 113–14, 118; in European welfare states, 119; historical development of, 110–12; moral hazard of pension insurance, 114–16; in 1970s and 1980s, 112–16; and PBGC, 113–18; problems with PPGC subsidies, 116–18; recommendations on, 118–19; as replacement for entitlement programs, 14–15; tax subsidies for defined-benefits plans, 109; underfunding of, 109, 110
Proposition 13, 58–59
Public capital expenditures, 46
Public Health Service retirement system, 160
Public Welfare Association, 34

Railroad Retirement Program, 110, 177
Rainwater, Lee, 83
Rausch, Jonathan, 45
Raybestos-Manhattan Co., 113
Reagan, Ronald, 66–69, 137, 147
Reed, Thomas Brackett, 29
Reich, Charles, 57
Republican party, 37, 40, 67–69, 144–45
Retired Enlisted Association, 155
Retired military groups, 143, 149, 153–55
The Retired Officers Association (TROA), 143, 149, 154–55
Retirement: age for collecting Social Security, 6; average age of, 63, 75, 81; of federal employees,

166; later age needed for, 15–16; military retirees, 140–41, 150–51; taxes paid during, 195–96. *See also* Civil service retirement system; Individual Retirement Accounts (IRAs); Military retirement system; Private pension systems
Retirement savings. *See* Savings
Revenue Acts of 1864 and 1865, 121
Revolutionary War veterans, 25, 29, 144–45
Riesman, David, 41–42
Robinson, Charles F., 99, 100
Robinson, Eric, 52
Rockford Institute, 124–25
Roosevelt, Franklin, 34–35, 41–42, 135–36, 174

Safire, William, 67
Samuelson, Paul A., 47–48, 63
Sass, Steven, 112
Save Youngstown for Retirees (SYR), 52, 53
Savings: by divorced woman, 187–88; by single man, 185–87; case studies on retirement savings, 185–92; impact of Social Security on, 20; in Japan, 200; mandatory savings account (MSA), 201–03; projecting personal retirement savings needs, 192–97; as replacement of entitlement programs, 11–14; statistics on, 19, 22, 198; for young married couple, 188–92
Scapegoating: of health care costs, 104–05; of poor, 4–5, 45, 50, 58–59
Schick, Allen, 46, 60–61

Schott, Mrs. Fred, 51
Schumpeter, Joseph P., 108
Schwarzkopf, H. Norman, 142
Secret Service, 73
Self-actualization, 198
Seniority, cult of, 51–54
Sepsis, 91
Seymour, Truman, 145–46
Sir Lanka, 202
Smalhout, James H., 114, 115
Smiles, Samuel, 23
Smith, James, 199
Social Security: benefits versus amount paid in, for different ages of workers, 79–80; change in calculating long-term debts, 48; COLAs for, 64–66; Congressional hearings on, 37–38; delivery of Social Security checks, 73–75; for federal employees, 166; flaws in, 173–74; global means test for, 177, 179; history of, 31–40; and household income, 75; impact of, on savings, 20; increases in, during 1960s, 44–45, 47, 66; increases in, during 1970s, 49, 54–55, 66, 68; as insurance, 35–36, 76; long-term solvency of, 80–86; middle-class recipients of, 6–7; opposition to, 36–40; privatizing of, 179; projections concerning, 84–85; public support for reform of, 17–18; societal trends affecting, 80–81; sources of money for, 76–78; statistics on, 9–10, 33–34, 75; as transfer program, 78–80; "trust funds," 76–78, 101; warnings on collapse of, 9–10, 84–86. *See also* Disability Insurance

Social Security Act, 31, 33, 35, 37
Social Security Administration
    (SSA), 1–2, 8, 35, 74, 77, 83–85,
    115, 159
Soviet Union, collapse of, 176
Spanish-American War, 128, 134
Special Committee on Aging, 48
Spengler, Joseph J., 43–44, 49
SSA. *See* Social Security
    Administration (SSA)
SSI. *See* Supplemental Security
    Income (SSI)
State Department retirement
    system, 159
Steel industry, 114–15, 117
Sternlieb, George, 125
Stewart, Potter, 57
Stockman, David, 69
Supplemental Security Income
    (SSI), 1–2, 177
Supreme Court, 35, 57–58, 161
Surrey, Stanley S., 55–56
Sweden, 119
SYR. *See* Save Youngstown for
    Retirees (SYR)

Taft, William Howard, 162
Tax cuts, by Reagan, 68–69
Tax rate increases, 195–96
Tax subsidies, credits and
    exemptions: child care credit, 6;
    compared with direct
    entitlements, 3–4; complaints
    against, 4; for elderly, 58, 195;
    employer-provided health
    insurance, 102–104, 108, 177,
    180; global means test for, 177;
    home mortgage deduction, 3, 6,
    9, 120–26, 177; housing
    subsidies, 9; IRAs, 116, 122, 203;

medical deduction, 56; in 1970s,
    55–56; statistics on, 3, 56
Taylor, John T., 135
Temporary workers, 107–108
Tennessee Valley Authority
    retirement system, 160
Theobald, Robert, 46
Thomson, David, 18–19
Thrift ethos, 23, 42, 199–206
Townsend, Francis, 32–33, 34, 42
Treasury Department, 73–74, 77,
    151, 162
TROA. *See* Retired Officers
    Association (TROA)
TWA, 114

UMW. *See* United Mine Workers
    (UMW)
Unemployment, 16, 108
Unemployment benefits, 6, 177
United Mine Workers (UMW),
    111–12
U.S. Tax Court Retirement Plan,
    160
University of Michigan Institute
    for Social Research, 88
University of Minnesota School of
    Public Health, 95
University of Pennsylvania
    Wharton School, 104

VA. *See* Veterans Administration
    (VA)
VA hospitals, 133–34
Values: of baby boom generation,
    125–26, 198–99, 204; bourgeois
    values needed by contemporary
    middle class, 23–25, 173, 183,
    197–206; and housing subsidies,
    125–26

Veterans: aging of veterans' population, 138–39; definition of, 127, 128, 130–31; median income of, 138. *See also* Military retirement system; Veterans' benefits
Veterans Administration (VA), 123, 131–34, 137, 139, 145
Veterans Affairs Department, 9, 30, 127, 131–34
Veterans' benefits: and aging of veterans' population, 138–39; and definition of veteran, 127, 128, 130–31; disability benefits, 128, 132; education benefits, 131, 132, 135, 173; GI Bill of Rights, 135–36, 173; health benefits, 131, 133–34, 137; history of, 25, 29–30, 55, 128, 135, 144–45; home loan guarantee, 131, 135–36; median income for veterans, 138; middle-class recipients of, 6; as reward for valor, 127–30; statistics on, 30, 127, 128; types of, 131–34; VA hospitals, 133–34; and veterans' groups, 134–37, 139; and veterans with combat or war zone experience, 127–29, 137–38; warnings on collapse of, 9. *See also* Military retirement system
Veterans' Employment and Training Service program (VETS), 133
Veterans' groups, 134–37, 139, 155
Veterans of Foreign Wars (VFW), 136, 137, 155

VETS. *See* Veterans' Employment and Training Service program (VETS)
VFW. *See* Veterans of Foreign Wars (VFW)
Victimology of middle class, 24–25, 58–59
Vietnam War, 49, 60, 130, 132, 134, 141
Virginia, 150

War on poverty, 44–45
Washington, George, 25, 29, 144, 149
Wealth. *See* Affluence
Webb, Beatrice, 47
Webb, Sidney, 47
Weber, Max, 173
Welfare: middle-class resentment of, 4–5, 45, 50, 58–59; middle-class welfare, 5–7; as right, 56–58; statistics on, 58
Welfare states, 18–19, 43–44, 119
Wharton School, University of Pennsylvania, 104
Wichert, Bill, 155
Williams, Harrison A., 113
Wilson, Woodrow, 163
Witte, Edwin E., 33
Work as value, 24
Works Progress Administration, 41–42
World Bank, 19, 202
World War I veterans, 55, 128, 135
World War II, 110–11, 134, 136, 137, 146, 163
World Wide Web, 95